MONEY
ADVISER
1999

◆ STEVE GELMAN
AND THE EDITORS OF MONEY

MONEY BOOKS
Time Inc. Home Entertainment
1271 Avenue of the Americas
New York, NY 10020

Manufactured in the United States of America
First Printing 1999

MONEY STAFF
managing editor Robert Safian

TIME INC. HOME ENTERTAINMENT
president David Gitow

MONEY BOOK SERIES
designer Laura Ierardi, LCI Design

HARDCOVER ISBN: 1-883013-59-3
ISSN: 1522-7618

We welcome your comments and suggestions about MONEY Books. Please write to us at:

MONEY Books
Attention: Book Editors
PO Box 11016
Des Moines, IA 50336-1016

If you would like to order any of our Hard Cover Edition books, please call us at 1-800-327-6388
(Monday through Friday, 7:00 a.m.–8:00 p.m. or Saturday, 7:00 a.m.–6:00 p.m. Central Time).

◆ CONTENTS

CHAPTER 1

WHERE TO INVEST MONEY NOW

Last year we advised you to put yourself in a position to ride out expected high volatility. We suggested that you take advantage of market upswings to unload some of your winners—particularly any stocks with price/earnings ratios above 25—and not to feel that you had to reinvest that money in stocks right away. Instead, we said, you should begin writing down a buy list of at least two or three dozen stocks you would like to own for the next 10 years and the prices at which you would be willing to buy each of them if the stock market were to break.

Well, we did go through a short, nasty bear market, and investor anxiety ran high. There's no reason, however, to be rattled by stories about collapsing hedge funds, submerging foreign markets and an approaching recession. There are risks—but their likely effects are greatly exaggerated. With inflation down to a minimal 1.5% and earnings headed up, albeit more slowly than in the early '90s, stocks look likely to continue rising. Of course, the market's behavior over the next 12 to 18 months depends on two other factors as well—Federal Reserve policy and current stock valuations (shares that are overpriced enough can go down even in good times, while cheap stocks can rise in mediocre markets).

You won't find this market in the textbooks. Many time-honored indicators say stocks should have stalled long ago. We see the current stock market as what statisticians call an outlier—an exceptional case that doesn't fit with normal patterns. Precisely because the current market isn't behaving normally, you can't rely on historical benchmarks to guide you. For example, there's no question that most popular stocks are overpriced by every standard measure—yet that doesn't mean they won't climb still higher. Even as they speed by traditional stop signs, however, share values still respond to the same things they always have: the trends in inflation and interest rates and the outlook for economic growth. And while it would certainly be foolish to ignore the risks of today's stock market, where many shares are overpriced and volatility is increasing (up more than 50% since 1994), a careful analysis suggests that the Dow could gain another 10% in 1999 and continue climbing for another two or three years.

THE OUTLOOK FOR 1999

Before you can decide whether the current bull market is over, you have to figure out which bull market you're talking about. Generally, people focus on the boom that began after the 1990–91 recession. This powerful uptrend has continued for more than eight years, with a slight correction in 1994 (down 9.7%) and a more severe correction this past summer (down almost 20%). However, to understand why stocks are so astonishingly resilient today, it's more enlightening to consider the past 16 years as a single extended bull market.

Here's why. The past 50 years of stock market history break clearly into three periods, each lasting a little over 16 years and characterized by a distinct inflation trend. From 1949 to 1966, inflation was low and the Dow rose sixfold. From 1966 to 1982, inflation soared and stock prices didn't move up at all. And from 1982 through 1998, inflation dropped again, fueling a tenfold gain in share prices. As long as inflation is tame, you can be fairly sure the major bull market hasn't ended and any corrections will likely be short-lived.

The other important force propelling stock prices is corporate profit growth. And since 1982, the average profits of the Dow stocks have more than tripled, thanks mainly to a robust economy and relentless cost cutting.

The economy. If there's any nearly foolproof rule of investing, it's this: Don't fight the Fed. Chairman Alan Greenspan cut rates three times from late September to mid-November. Similar periods of Fed easing have occurred 19 times in this century; on average the market has gained 28% within a year of those rate cuts. That includes times when stock prices were high to begin with (even if not quite as lofty as they are today).

Whatever P/Es stocks sport today, the key to their moving higher is a continuation of favorable interest rates. And Greenspan's actions reflect a consistent strategy. He believes in stomping inflation with high rates when the economy is strong enough to take it. But when he sees a slowdown brewing, Greenspan starts lowering rates—fairly quickly, if necessary. That's why he cut rates in the fall and why he may keep trimming them over the next 12 months.

Many economists think a downturn in the U.S. this year is entirely possible. But even if the economy turns down for a couple of quarters, which would technically count as a recession, we wouldn't be surprised if it were over within six months—without the market taking much of a hit.

Economic growth, running above 3.5% in '98, is likely to slow to 2.5% or less in '99. In that environment, earnings for the S&P 500 will be hard-pressed to grow more than 6%. That's way below the double-digit earnings gains the S&P 500 posted in the early '90s. So you'll have to look for exceptional stocks to beat the market in 1999. They could be tech companies that are growing much faster than the overall economy; they could be firms that are restructuring to wring more profits out of their existing revenues; or they could be prime beneficiaries of current business conditions. But they've got to have something extra.

The hot stocks are expensive. No matter how you analyze stocks, there's no question that the most popular ones are expensive. And we're referring not only to nutty Internet issues but also to the large-caps that are the cornerstone of most investors' portfolios and most growth mutual funds.

Since 1979, the average P/E of the S&P 500 has climbed from less than 10 to 25. Given that the historical average is 15, the current level of big-cap stocks looks high enough to induce nosebleeds. In fact, though, the market's current P/E isn't quite as dizzying as it appears. The fair P/E for stocks increases as inflation declines. And while 10 was the fair P/E back in 1979, when inflation was running in double digits, today's 1.5% inflation rate justifies a P/E of 18 to 19. That doesn't make today's 25 market multiple cheap, but it's not as bad as it looks.

Many other stocks are cheap. It's a mistake, however, to consider only the S&P 500 or the 30 stocks in the Dow Jones industrial average in assessing today's stock market prices. Thousands of stocks are actually undervalued, including small-cap and midcap issues, as well as the shares of companies in depressed industries like oil and mining. If you look at the market as a bundle of different sectors, you'll see that there are an enormous number of bargains.

During the early 1980s, the P/Es of both big and small-to-mid-size stocks moved more or less in sync. Then, in the year and a half before the

1987 crash, big-caps rocketed to a huge premium. The two groups came back together after the 1990-91 recession but then moved apart again during the past five years.

Because the sharp market correction this past summer hit small and mid-size stocks even harder than blue chips, the gap between the high-flying titans and their smaller siblings grew wider than at any time since before the 1987 crash. To some extent, the higher valuations for blue chips reflected the faster earnings growth that multinationals have enjoyed. But that explains only part of the gap. The rest reflects the fact that thousands of stocks have been neglected—and many of those are fairly priced or downright cheap.

Stick with stocks, but think defensive. Any number of possible but unexpected jolts—from renewed troubles in Asia to an unanticipated jump in inflation—could hurt the market. So there's good reason to remain cautious. Also, given the already high level of stock prices and the likelihood of only modest earnings growth, the Dow's current upside looks limited enough that you shouldn't be swinging for the fences.

If events follow this forecast, you will get the highest return with the least risk over the coming year by sticking mostly with stocks. Also, diversify as broadly as possible, making sure to include sectors in your investing mix that have the potential to outpace the overall market in 1999. If you've become overweighted in blue-chip stocks, consider dipping into the relatively undervalued choices among midcaps and small-caps. And be sure to include some stocks (or funds) in industries that would benefit from a rise in inflation, such as energy, mining, paper or other natural resources.

If you're a typical fund investor, you can assemble a well-balanced portfolio by putting at least 60% of your money in stock funds, with 30% in bond funds. The remaining 10% can go into a money-market fund, so that you have buying power next time the stock market corrects, as it surely will. For those who buy individual issues, try to focus on stocks or other investments that have the best chance of adding incremental returns to your portfolio in 1999.

WALL STREET'S PICKS AND PREDICTIONS

To help point the way to a profitable year, MONEY asked six of the best minds on Wall Street for their broad views—and specific suggestions. We got plenty of both. Whether you are looking to buy a sector stock, are scouting for defensive choices or are thinking of dipping into battered emerging markets, our seers can help you out. They don't always agree with our views, or with one another, but their expertise is respected throughout the financial world. Here's the lineup. The Optimist: Lehman Bros.' Jeffrey Applegate. The Small-Cap Sage: Prudential Securities' Claudia Mott. The Boomer: PaineWebber's Edward Kerschner. The Globalist: Salomon Smith Barney's Leila Heckman. The Bond Guru: PIMCo's William Gross. The Skeptic: Warburg Dillon Read's Gail Dudack.

The optimist. Envision this: You're at a cocktail party, swapping stock stories and—talk about luck!—right next to you is the stock market guru you just saw on television. Being mobbed at cocktail parties isn't even the worst of it, says Lehman Bros. chief investment strategist Jeffrey Applegate: "Airport lounges are the worst." The telegenic bull, who started 1998 expecting the Dow to close the year at 9200 and now calls for a Dow of 9800 at year-end 1999, can't even exercise without being prodded for stock picks. "I was in the gym on the StairMaster, and I was reading something, and the guy who wipes off the machines says, 'Well, should I buy American Express here?'" Okay, so we asked Applegate for some stock picks too. But, hey, we did it during business hours.

Q. You've been one of the more bullish voices on Wall Street. What keeps you bullish when signs seem to say stocks are too high?
A. There are a lot of very smart people who have had very cogent bearish arguments for years. I'm not saying I'm smarter than the average bear, or the average bull. I just think we're in an environment that requires you to think out of the box, and that a lot of traditional relationships aren't going to work. I think about how we've done some very interesting things in the '90s. We ended the cold war; we created a globalization of capital and labor in a way that has never existed. So, gee, if we've done some things we've never done before, then the chances are that traditional measures of valuation might fall apart. And they have.

Q. How bullish are you for 1999?
A. We think we're heading into slower U.S. growth and slower global growth, but not a recession domestically or globally. We've been operating with a view that the trough in stock market prices was back on Aug. 31, and we're beginning a sometimes fairly tortuous climb out. We think the Federal Reserve will reduce interest rates fairly significantly in 1999.

Q. And that will be enough to spur stocks on?

A. Yes. If you look at the forward 12-month price return for Standard & Poor's 500 from the date after the Federal Reserve first began to cut rates, the average is 18%. So we'd say we've got more to go, and we'd expect to see low double-digit returns in 1999.

Q. What else will make a difference?

A. The biggest event that will help equity prices at some point in 1999— and the timing is uncertain—is that the developed nations and emerging market countries will come up with some kind of global debt-swap package, which is crucial to reviving global growth.

Q. So what sector makes sense?

A. One should be financials. We're forecasting that the Federal funds rate will be at 3% by the middle of 1999, down from 5% now. We think the Fed is addressing an anomaly in the bond market, where the gap between Treasury yields and yields on other bonds has been far wider than normal. We think one of the Fed's goals is to bring those spreads back into a more customary relationship. If that's right, by definition it should be good for the stock market and even better for financials.

Q. Where in the financial sector would you look?

A. I'd look at some of the stocks that have really been crushed. If you look at financials, some stocks had declines of 25% to 70% from midsummer to early fall, when the market was off only 20%.

Q. But haven't they come back?

A. A lot are up 25% to 30% but are still far off their peaks. Look at the 1999 price/earnings ratios for **Chase Manhattan** or **Citigroup**. Chase's P/E on our forecast 1999 earnings is 10.4; Citigroup's is 12.2. Those are very modest P/Es, compared with our projected P/E for the market, which is 23.2. Has the market more than discounted the worst-case scenario for a lot of these companies, especially money center banks that are globally exposed? I think so. We'd also use more purely domestic names like **USBancorp** and **BankBoston**, broker-dealers like **Morgan Stanley Dean Witter** and asset managers like **Alliance Capital Management**, **Franklin Resources** and **State Street Corp**.

Q. What other sectors look good?

A. The other big sector we like a lot is technology. Even though we have a forecast that capital spending will slow by a lot, and half of the capital spending in the U.S. these days is on technology, our bet is that most of the slowdown will occur in the bricks and mortar spending. Companies don't need to add a lot to capacity, but they do need to upgrade their technology, so we're not looking for capital spending to fall apart.

Q. What sectors should investors avoid?
A. The basic materials—chemicals, paper, steel and energy. Some growth is going to come back from Asia, but it won't be as robust as it was, so I have a tough time seeing how these companies will have much pricing power.

Q. How long can the good times last?
A. The last time we had such favorable conditions—low interest rates, good labor production, moderate economic growth, consistent profit growth, little or no inflation, a good mix of monetary and fiscal policies—was the early '60s. And now we have things we didn't have then—globalization and a more peaceful environment. Even though we've had this great cycle already, I don't see the thing coming unstuck.

Q. May we have a sampler of your 1999 plays?
A. Cisco Systems (recent price: $64.75). Uniquely positioned to benefit from growth in the Internet. **EMC Corp.** ($67.00). Leader in burgeoning enterprise data storage market. **State Street Corp.** ($64.25). Increased global stock trading fuels demand for its sophisticated back-office services. **Walgreen** ($52.25). Strong presence in major markets; size gives it clout with suppliers.

The small-cap sage. The bumper sticker taped outside Claudia Mott's office says it all: "Have you hugged your small-cap manager today?" Last year was a trying one for Prudential Securities' director of small-cap research. While she had predicted that small companies would lag the overall market, she was dismayed to see the Russell 2000 small-stock index plummet by nearly 40% at one point during the year. Now, with small-caps seemingly on the rebound, Mott is decidedly upbeat about the prospects for her battered group.

According to Mott, the outlook for small stocks is rosier than it has been in four years. "This is a rally that has a six- to 12-month time horizon," she says. Last summer's meltdown in the large-cap market is one reason Mott thinks small-caps will take center stage in 1999. "You needed the lust for large-caps to dissipate, and I think that's happening." Foreign demand for the big blue chips has abated, and so have the "amazing" inflows into large-cap mutual funds, she notes. "My thesis for why the small-cap market is ripe to rally hinges on that," she says. "You're going to go to a market that cares about fundamentals and valuation again, and not one that is driven by ancillary factors. As long as the U.S. economic picture continues to look good, and especially if we see any improvement, you've just got a lot of compelling reasons why the small- and midcap sectors of the stock market should look better."

Investors' diminished ardor for large-caps, however, wouldn't by itself be enough of a catalyst for a small-cap rally. The Fed gave small-caps the push they needed with its Oct. 15 rate cut, says Mott. "Following a rate cut, small-caps have tended to be the best performers and to give you the best absolute returns," she says. Mott looked at 10 time periods when the Fed was lowering the discount rate. In eight of the 10, small-caps outperformed large-caps by an average of 8% in the year after the initial cut. One reason: Rate cuts spur U.S. economic growth, and that gives more of a boost to small-caps than to large-caps because "they are much more domestically based than the large caps," says Mott.

Valuation is also working in favor of small-caps now. How cheap are they? "Screamingly cheap," says Mott. "Statistics show that any time you had this magnitude of a decline in the broad market, the next three to 12 months were always better for small-caps than for large-caps." It's possible, says Mott, that we could see a reprise of what happened to small-caps after the brutal 1973-74 period in the stock market. In December 1974, the Federal Reserve cut rates, she recalls, "and large-caps did zero, and small-caps went ballistic." Her definition of ballistic? During the rate-cut period of December 1974 to December 1976, small-caps soared 127.6%. "The only thing that might limit the scale of a rally now is if the market as a whole hasn't corrected by as wide a margin as it did then," says Mott.

Judging from the past, the first sectors to lead small-caps up would be technology, health care and, to some extent, the consumer names. Then, if U.S. economic growth improves, you could see the more commodity-oriented companies pick up, says Mott. For now, however, Mott is parking herself on the growth bandwagon, although she anticipates a possible shift in the market toward cyclical stocks in the spring.

Mott is optimistic, but she sees some potential problems. As foreign economies recover and as big multinationals stop losing so much money when they convert foreign profits into dollars, Mott fears that small-caps could lose some of their profit edge over their big-cap brethren. Another risk is simply that small-caps move too far, too fast, and then pull back.

One of the most common questions Mott is asked: "Is now the time to get into small-caps?" It is not a welcome query. She gets frustrated by attempts at market timing. "All the data we have about the small-cap effect and the risk premium isn't based on market timing," she says. "It's based on more than 70 years of owning a particular asset class. It seems people have two investing time horizons. Large-cap time horizons are forever. Small-cap time horizons are for the moment."

A sampler of Prudential's small- and midcap picks and comments: **Consolidated Graphics** (recent price: $54.00). Strong earnings momentum from recent acquisitions. **Gilead Sciences** ($28.75). Biotech firm has promising products in pipeline. **Linens 'n' Things** ($30.00). Favorable demographic trends; great expansion opportunities. **Orthodontic Centers of America** ($19.75). Leader in managing orthodontic practices. **Select Appointments** ($21.00). Well-run temporary-staffing firm; very strong balance sheet.

The boomer. "Boomers are probably the most stressed generation in history," says Edward Kerschner. As a boomer himself, the 45-year-old chairman of PaineWebber's investment policy committee exemplifies many of the themes and attitudes that he predicts will drive the stock market in the next millennium. Case in point: His theory about how boomers are experiencing a "time drought"—that even though Americans are working fewer hours, they feel short of time because they're always racing to do several things at once. As we spoke with Kerschner, who was fresh from a business trip that included a day when he breakfasted in Frankfurt, lunched in Amsterdam, raised a glass in London and fell asleep in New York, we noticed we had competition: the four computer screens in his office that his eyes would flick to every 15 seconds or so. To help relieve some of our stress about where to invest in 1999, and to help Kerschner multitask successfully, we asked him to share his 1999 forecast.

Q. What will drive the stock market in 1999?

A. You're going to see earnings strength in technology, simply because of the recovery there. Also, the domestic consumer sector is going to stay strong. Income growth is the driver of consumer spending, not the level of the stock market. With record-low unemployment, even if it picks up a few decimal points, you'll have good income growth in 1999. With continued low energy prices, low interest rates and people refinancing their mortgages, you'll have more discretionary spending. It's hard to make a case that the consumer, who has been the engine of growth in this economy for the past few years, will not continue to drive the economy.

Q. What is your earnings forecast?

A. If I use some very conservative assumptions, I still would see earnings up 5% to 7% in 1999. There are lots of positives. The tech rebound is one. Even if the energy sector doesn't do as well as expected, it will be less of a drag on overall earnings growth than it was in 1998. The decline in the dollar will boost profits at companies with foreign operations. And it's pretty safe to say we're not going to have another General Motors strike.

Q. Where does 5% to 7% earnings growth put the Dow?

A. At roughly 10,000 by year-end.

Q. Recently, you wrote about how changing attitudes of boomers will drive consumer behavior. Would you give us your five favorite stocks that will benefit from that trend?

A. Do I have to? I have 24 favorite stocks. Well, one of our key themes that we first wrote about in 1991 is the big shift into equities. Households are not buying stocks because the market is going up. People are investing in stocks because they are at the age in which you invest and plan for retirement. There is a pretty good correlation between the percentage of people ages 45 to 54 and the household allocation to equities. That doesn't peak until 2007 and doesn't start going down until 2012. You've got another 15 years when the business of providing investments to households should be a very good business. That's good for brokerage stocks.

Q. What else looks good?

A. Investors certainly want exposure to technology, and **Compaq** (recent price, $33.50) is very well situated. The idea with Compaq is the continued proliferation of the personal computer as the delivery device of the information age. Compaq is the premier brand, and new buyers are probably going to be more apt to buy a branded than an unbranded product.

You also want exposure to health care. Basically, the aging baby–boomer generation is a pill-popping generation. We take pills not to cure ourselves but to change our lifestyle—we take Dexatrim for weight loss, Propecia for hair loss, Viagra for sexual problems. I like **Warner–Lambert** ($73.00). We have a 15% growth rate on it for 1999. I also want heavy exposure to the consumer. At one end, consumers want really efficient, low-cost service. At the other end they want high-quality service at a cost. The middle will die—you can't become the low-cost, full-service provider. **Wal-Mart** ($69.75) is the low-cost, low-service provider. I want to be there. And while we talk about aging baby boomers a lot, the second-largest-growing group is Generation Y, teenagers. **Gap** ($68.75) has captured the hearts, minds and pocketbooks of Generation Y.

Q. What could derail the market?

A. For the past decade, I've argued that the risk is too little growth. With the appropriate monetary and fiscal policy, you can stop inflation. The problem with monetary and fiscal policy is that unless it is executed very well, it might not stop deflation.

The globalist. From her sunny, scrupulously tidy office overlooking the Hudson River, Leila Heckman imposes order on the unruly foreign markets. By analyzing the world's bourses as if they were stocks, Salomon Smith Barney's head of global asset allocation provides the firm's clients with a monthly ranking of 44 stock markets.

You won't find Heckman ensconced as a regular on CNBC, making bold predictions about the direction of world markets. Heckman doesn't make interest-rate calls or forecast the dollar or pick specific stocks. Her disciplined approach to global asset allocation involves feeding a computer the vital statistics on foreign markets and economies—Portugal's price-to-book, France's forecast earnings, Mexico's price momentum, Japan's GDP—to help large institutional investors divvy up their global dollars. "I try to provide a framework for investing, because it's important to define and measure things," says Heckman. "But the investment business is ultimately one of judgment."

Heckman's judgment on how much the typical American individual investor should keep in the U.S. markets: 60% to 80%. For investors who want to maintain a stake overseas with the remainder, she suggests focusing first on Continental Europe, which she also favored a year ago. Earnings growth in Europe, though probably slowing in 1999 and hardly robust at 2.5%, looks strong relative to other countries, she says. Low interest rates help countries such as Austria, Belgium, France, Germany and Italy achieve high scores in Heckman's interest-rate ranking. Heckman also goes country by country, measuring the number of companies with upward earnings forecast revisions over one month, then divides that by the total number of companies with revisions. On that score, Continental Europe as a whole again ranks high. Heckman is not particularly upbeat, however, on the United Kingdom, which she says is further along in its economic cycle than its Continental European counterparts.

What about hunting for value in Japan? Has the Nikkei seen its lowest levels? Japan makes up about 16% of Heckman's recommended portfolio, which represents a slight underweighting compared with her benchmark for developed markets, the Salomon Smith Barney primary market index. On a price-to-book basis, Japan looks cheap at 1.7, says Heckman. It is close to its historic low price-to-book of 1.5, a level reached 23 years ago. But Japan's P/E of 106 (based on recent four quarters' earnings) makes it pricey. "Earnings are still very weak, gross domestic product is falling, and momentum is working against Japan," she says. "I'm not sure you can even bottom fish in Japan at this point."

Well, then, what about bargain hunting in emerging markets? At the start of 1998, Heckman expected some of the smaller emerging markets to do well. But then came the Asian crisis. In its wake, some emerging markets certainly look cheap. But a lot of the very cheap markets are also very illiquid. "It's almost like a patient wheeled into the emergency room, and he's stabilized, but his condition is still somewhat tenuous," says Heckman. She cautions investors hoping to get big returns in the region to be prepared to wait five years. "I hope the worst is over," she says, "but these markets are very dependent on export growth, and that growth is dependent on what happens in the U.S. and, to some extent, Japan."

Within the emerging markets, Heckman is shying away from Latin America. "In 1998, Latin America was suffering from Asian contagion," she notes. "Now there are more concrete issues—interest rates have been going up to defend currencies, and growth is slowing. Brazil is probably in recession in 1999." Heckman has a "guardedly favorable" rating on parts of emerging Asia, such as South Korea, India, Philippines and China, where currencies are stabilizing, interest rates are on the decline and current account balances are improving. She notes, however, that the corporate sector still faces significant earnings problems and that such countries' banking systems are weak. "If these countries stabilize, they should do very well, but it's still touch and go."

Given all the turmoil overseas and the relative strength of the U.S. economy, should investors bother sending any money abroad? The basic argument for going global has been to earn higher returns while reducing risk through diversification. But world stock markets have increasingly been moving in unison, says Heckman, and she suspects that this trend will continue. "The diversification argument holds a little less today than it used to, if you're hoping to reduce overall risk by investing abroad," she says. "But the return part holds—there are a lot of opportunities outside the U.S. where investors can get some incremental return."

The bond guru. The foundation for William Gross' successful Wall Street career: the gaming tables of Las Vegas. Twenty-two years after he learned some seminal investment lessons about odds as one of that town's first card-counting blackjack players, Gross has raised his bet. As a founder and the chief investment officer of Pacific Investment Management Co., or PIMCo, he manages the top-performing $22.7 billion PIMCo Total Return fund. Gross' 1998 call for the 30-year Treasury bond to bottom at about 5% was close to the mark. By spring 1999, Gross expects a series of cuts to bring short-term rates down to 4%.

Q. In your 1997 book, *Everything You've Heard About Investing Is Wrong!*, you wrote about the coming end of the bull market, or what you termed the end of the Era of Money and the beginning of the Era of 6%, or a period of muted returns. Where do we stand now?
A. In this type of global environment, in which disinflation—and in some cases deflation—dominates, it's almost impossible to manufacture 20% to 30% returns from the stock market. That doesn't suggest you should stuff your money in the mattress. It simply means you should lower your expectations. After all, in a world of 1% inflation, you're doing pretty well if you're getting returns of 6% to 8% from stocks and bonds.

Q. What's behind the drop in inflation—and returns?
A. It's primarily due to globalization. As economic societies globalize, the world becomes more and more competitive, and that basically lowers profit margins and keeps inflation down. The introduction of new players into the marketplace keeps a lid not only on prices but on wage demands. If corporate profit margins are limited, that means profits in general can't rise on double-digit rates.

Q. Where does the 6% to 8% figure come from?
A. The typical growth rate of corporate bonds for the past 50 years has been 6%. If you tack on 1% or 2% in dividend growth for stocks, you have your 8%.

For bonds, we've achieved much of the decline in yields that I've been looking for. It's not that we can't go lower, but I think we are close to the bottom of a 17-year bull market in bonds. I don't think yields are headed back up. I'd say investors shouldn't expect much in the way of capital gains but should be content earning relatively high inflation-adjusted returns.

Q. What bond sectors look promising now?

A. In terms of confidence in economic growth in the U.S. over the next six to 12 months, I'm more pessimistic than the market. I expect a substantial slowdown in the U.S. economy based upon the global contagion that has taken over in the past year. The U.S. economy can inch down close to zero to 1% growth rates next year. If that's the case, then the best choice in bonds rests with higher-quality bonds, whether they be Treasury or government-guaranteed mortgages, as opposed to high-yield corporate bonds and emerging market bonds. I think it pays to stick with high quality for the moment and wait two to five months before going after higher-yielding bonds.

Q. What maturity would you suggest?

A. Intermediate—so anywhere from two to 10 years. The **intermediate U.S. Treasury bond** will do best if the economy slows and the Fed lowers interest rates. As the Fed cuts short-term interest rates, intermediate maturities get more of a boost than long-term maturities do. Probably, if you're an investor working through a 401(k), a good intermediate bond fund with an average maturity of around seven years would be appropriate.

Q. What about investing outside a 401(k)?

A. For individuals investing outside a 401(k), **municipal bonds** are the most attractive bonds. Munis have been the forgotten stepchildren of the past six months or so, while Treasuries roared ahead. Today you can buy a long-term muni at the same yield as a long-term Treasury, and while the muni bond doesn't carry the same quality—well, in my case, I live in the state of California, and it's not the same as the U.S. Government, but it's not that far away either. California is 12% of the U.S. economy and is not going to default anytime soon, so if I can get California at a 5.25% yield vs. a Treasury, the tax advantages are enormous.

To put this in perspective, six to 12 months ago, long-term munis were trading at 85% of long-term Treasury yields. In other words, in the example I just gave, they'd be trading at a yield of 4.25% instead of 5.25% today.

We're at historical highs in terms of muni yields relative to Treasuries. They represent an unprecedented bargain and opportunity.

Q. If an investor wants to reach for yield and is prepared to take some risk, where should he or she look?

A. The mortgage market is not a bad place to reach for moderate yield. You could recently get 6.5% on **seven-year mortgage bonds**, as opposed to 4.5% for the same maturity Treasury, so a good mortgage fund is not a bad start. That's a triple-A type of alternative. If you really want to move out on the yield spread and take additional risk, an investor can buy some **Brady bonds** in countries such as Mexico and Argentina and get 10% to 11% yields.

Q. Do the yields compensate for the risk?

A. I think yes. It all depends on whether the rescue efforts of Federal Reserve chairman Alan Greenspan and Treasury Secretary Robert Rubin are successful. My sense is that there's an increasing probability that will be the case, so markets like Mexico and Argentina are less subject to contagion than they were a while ago.

Q. In your book, you talk about distinguishing between the "small stuff" and the "big stuff" when investing. What is the big stuff now?

A. The very big stuff now has to do with the global economic environment and what Rubin has called the most serious financial environment in the past 50 years. The big picture these days is whether global capitalism as we've come to know it continues to expand or begins to contract, sort of like a quasar or a star that ultimately implodes. If capitalism all of a sudden starts to reverse its trend—not to suggest it'll implode, but if trade stops growing—then corporations are obviously at risk in terms of their profits and economies are at risks in terms of their growth rate.

Q. You're a fan of Jesse Livermore, the 1920s trader immortalized as Larry Livingstone in Edwin Lefevre's *Reminiscences of a Stock Market Operator*. Is there a thought of his that is apt today?

A. I have his picture up on my wall here at the office, top hat and all, along with pictures of Bernard Baruch and J.P. Morgan, and under each one I have a quote I felt was appropriate to the business of investing. Jesse's quote is, "In actual practice, an investor has to guard against many things. And most of all, against himself."

That to me says that one of the most important things in the business of investing is this swing in human emotion from greed to fear and back again. If you can guard against yourself in terms of being not too greedy at the top or too afraid at the bottom, if you can become a little like Spock in *Star Trek*—not a lot, or we'd all turn into computers—then you can improve your investment results.

Q. This isn't a question, but a summary of your bond outlook.

Emerging markets: For risk-takers only; Mexican Brady bonds yielding 10% to 11% are among the safer bets. High-yield corporate: Attractive yields, but their prices fluctuate with the stock market, so prepare for a roller-coaster ride. Mortgage: High-quality investments with 6%-plus yields, but income investors should watch out for prepayments. Municipal: An unprecedented bargain and opportunity to duck taxes outside of retirement accounts. Treasury: Lowest yields, at about 5%, but absolute safety—they let you sleep at night.

The skeptic. It's tough being a bear today. Just ask Gail Dudack, Warburg Dillon Read's chief equity strategist. "It's not good for your career, and it's not good for making friends," she says. "But someone has to talk about the fact that stocks are not cheap today and that therefore there is risk." Dudack's longtime call for a 20% market correction panned out during 1998. But once the market recovered, she again found herself out of step with the Wall Street crowd.

Q. What is your outlook for this year?

A. My view now is that we'll be in a trading range. On the Dow, I think 7000 is the bottom of the range and that the top of the range will be 8500. That translates into a range of 900 to 1100 on the S&P 500. At 1100, we're trading at 25 times S&P 500 earnings, which was the historical high recorded in June of 1998. I think that's a very rich multiple if you don't have any earnings growth in 1998 and none in 1999.

Q. Why will earnings be so weak?

A. Investors missed a very important shift. Prior to 1996, earnings were growing better than GDP activity would have suggested. Companies were finding all kinds of productivity gains—they were laying off people, wage pressures were nonexistent, the health-care industry was restructuring. Interest rates were declining, so the cost of capital was going down and the dollar was strong, which was good for earnings abroad and earnings translation.

Q. What changed?

A. In 1997, you started to see S&P 500 earnings not keep up with economic activity. There was a true turning point with the United Parcel Service strike. For me, it suggested that we'd squeezed all the productivity out of labor that we were likely to get. The next profit squeeze will come from health-care costs. You're seeing HMOs and insurance companies getting real pricing increases—not huge, but high single digits. Corporations won't be able to pass all of that on. Third, we've seen a real increase in borrowing costs. It's easing a bit, but it suggests the cost of capital for corporations has increased. These are long, steady trends that are hard to reverse.

Q. How do investors react?

A. I'm trying to avoid negative earnings surprises. If the IBES consensus earnings number is for an 18% increase and I'm looking for a decrease of 4%, I see the equity market as filled with minefields. So I'm looking for areas with pretty reliable revenues. I've been asking our analysts which of their stocks or industries are recessionproof. Not because I think we're going to have a U.S. recession—I don't—but because what I see happening on the earnings front resembles an earnings recession.

Q. So which industries do you see having the most reliable earnings in 1999?

A. I'm interested in things like insurance, telecommunications, service companies, electric utilities, pharmaceuticals, managed-care hospitals and biotechnology. I'd avoid money center banks and consumer-finance companies.

Q. What are some attractive stocks in those sectors?

A. I like **Aetna**, **United Healthcare**, **HCR Manor Care**, **Guidant**, **American Home Products**, **Bell Atlantic**, **American Electric Power**, **First Union** and **Philip Morris**.

Q. Will we see much in the way of consolidation plays in 1999?

A. If you look at finance, telecommunication services, utilities and health care, you have the bulk of merger activity. That creates a different scenario with new productivity gains. When you boost productivity, you're able to get around the profit-margin squeeze we've been talking about.

Q. Are there historical parallels you find useful in analyzing today's market?

A. The most striking one is to the 1966 period. Two things happened then that are happening today. We saw corporate profit margins peak, and with that we had peak earnings and virtually no earnings growth for several years.

Q. That sounds a little ominous.

A. Doesn't it? Maybe this helps explain my trading range. In January 1966, the stock market peaked at 1000, and it was in a very wide trading range for quite a few years. I think in 1999 a lot of the stocks may rally and collapse, then rally again and collapse. After the stock market trained you for eight years to buy and hold, we may find ourselves unable to outperform the market unless we have more of a trading outlook and buy stocks when they are cheap and sell them when market has recognized that value.

Q. What do you think your stress level is going to be like in 1999?

A. High! It's been high for a long time. At 7500, people said, don't you feel vindicated? I said no. People looked at me as though I was responsible for the market's fall.

Q. Here's our sample of your picks for 1999, and your comments.

American Electric Power (recent price, $49.75): Large size and low electric rates give it an edge. American Home Products ($47.50): One of the best 1999 new-product pipelines. Bell Atlantic ($53.75): Strong growth in data and wireless revenues. **Fannie Mae** ($69.50): Solid performer in both good and bad markets. **IBM** ($157.50): Key beneficiary of the year 2000 problem.

A WAY TO PROSPER IN CHOPPY MARKETS

While investors devote most of their energy to guessing which way the overall market is going to hop next, they generally ignore much more important trends—the ups and downs of major stock groups. "The key to investment performance is not just being in the market at the right time but being in the right sector," says First Albany investment strategist Hugh Johnson.

Now we're not suggesting that you become a frantic market timer, switching sector funds every month in the hope of catching each market blip. That strategy is almost certain to hurt your performance. But we do believe that paying close attention to market sectors will help you be a better investor. In particular, it will enable you to spot great stock bargains because when a sector is lagging, the stocks of superb businesses often suffer along with the rickety ones. Think of this as the stock market version of guilt by association. Sooner or later, the problems pass and most stocks in a depressed sector recover.

Paying attention to sectors when you buy stocks is key today. When the Dow was rocketing up more than 20% annually, you could count on the bull market dragging pretty much any stock along. But for big gains these days, you can generally do best if you concentrate on underpriced stocks whenever you have additional money to invest. And as a general rule, you'll find the best bargains among stock groups that are lagging. Conversely, if you have successful investments you want to sell, you would be wisest to take your profits after their sectors have been riding high for six months or so.

Let's get down to the specific mechanics of sector analysis. There are plenty of ways to divide up the market. Perhaps the simplest is to begin by dividing the market into eight broad industry groups: utilities; financials; consumer nondurables; industrials; consumer cyclicals; energy; basic materials; technology. In case you're unfamiliar with the jargon, basic materials include stuff like steel; consumer cyclicals are big-ticket items like cars; and consumer nondurables are inexpensive products you use up, such as soap and toothpaste.

By watching the zigs and zags of these eight groups, you can improve your timing when you buy and sell. The one caveat is that trends don't always shift immediately. Sometimes poor performance lasts for several years. Depressed sectors offer the most bargains—but it's smartest to wait to buy until you see leading stocks in the group perking up.

Of course, if you're investing for retirement and have a time horizon of more than 10 years, you don't have to worry about catching upturns exactly. Identify depressed stocks groups, buy the strongest companies in those sectors and your bargain-rich portfolio will stand a good chance of beating the market by the time you start cashing out.

INVESTING'S NEW FRONTIER

There's a revolution going on. You may know it as cloned mice, or the Human Genome Project, or perhaps insect-resistant corn. It's a revolution with many fronts but one clear quest: unlocking the secrets of genes, the DNA strands that contain the code of life. The implications for humanity are staggering: the prevention of disease, the feeding of the world. The implications for you as an investor are less profound but still momentous: Biotechnology is America's most promising industry, and it's the stock market's next big thing.

Sure, you're thinking, I've heard that before. Well, think again. It's true that in the mid-1980s, biotech burst onto the scene with promises of miracle cures and big payoffs that rarely materialized. But today, the industry is broader and healthier than ever, thanks to four key developments: huge advances in the study of genes; abundant research capital; a more sympathetic Food and Drug Administration; and the burgeoning health-care demands of an aging U.S. population. The players are no longer just scientists and dreamers in university labs and small industrial parks; they include the CEOs of the biggest drug and chemical concerns in the world.

That said, we're not suggesting that you dump today's Microsoft in a quixotic pursuit of tomorrow's big winner. Biotech's main segments are genomics, health-care biotech, big drugmakers and agricultural biotech. Genomics and biotech drug stocks have serious short-term hurdles to overcome. They are mostly small-cap companies in a market where large-caps are king, and many of them have cost a lot of one-time believers a lot of money. Moreover, chasing the gene is a risky business. Remember EntreMed? The small biotech drug firm shot up 600% last May after a *New York Times* article suggested, prematurely, that the company might have a cancer cure, only to crash when investors came to their senses.

Nonetheless, it's foolhardy not to at least consider putting a small portion of your assets into biotech. "The biotechnology revolution is in Stage 1," says William Scouten, director of the biotech center at Utah State University. Ultimately, he contends, "it will have more of an impact than the computer revolution."

The force that's driving biotech's coming boom is the rapidly advancing science of genomics, the study of how genes work. Humans have an estimated 100,000 genes made up of DNA sequences that carry the encoded instructions that provide hereditary characteristics, normal and mutated. If DNA is the software that runs life processes, then scientists want to search for bugs in the program. Why? As defective software can crash a computer, defective DNA can make you sick. Understand the errors in the code, and you're on the way to a cure.

Knowledge of genes is doubling every 12 to 24 months. Indeed, scientists will soon finish mapping the complete sequence of DNA subunits in the human genome or genetic code. That data will allow health-care providers to develop better treatments. For example, by analyzing genes associated with osteoporosis, SmithKline Beecham scientists have isolated an enzyme that contributes to the disease. By finding a way to inhibit the enzyme, they may be able to stop or reverse bone degeneration.

The potential market for such treatment is enormous, and it's growing. The number of Americans between 45 and 64 will increase 40% by 2010. Baby boomers will soon become obsessed with later-life chronic diseases. The health insurance industry already is. Consider: Five maladies—cardio-vascular disease, cancer, Alzheimer's, diabetes and arthritis—account for nearly half the $1 trillion spent annually in the U.S. on health care, mainly to treat symptoms. Insurers, looking for ways to contain that tab, don't mind spending for drug treatments, which are cheaper than other therapies. And with biotech comes the possibility of not only controlling more diseases but curing more patients or preventing them from getting sick—and saving money for their insurers. A drug that cures, say, diabetes could be worth tens of billions of dollars to its owners.

The prospect of such riches has attracted a new biotech banker, the global pharmaceutical company. To sustain their remarkable growth rates, these giants need new drugs, fast. So they're spending billions on scores of partnerships with biotech and genomics firms and on their own biotech-related R&D, creating a pool of cash that all but guarantees more drugs to fill biotech's pipeline. And unlike the computer industry, biotech is not likely to be dominated by one or two Microsoft-like giants. With so many diseases to cure, the number of potential winners is large.

The revolution won't stop at drugs. Pharmaceutical and chemical giants are pouring money into the agricultural side of biotech, buying seed producers and distributors to form a chain that will run from farm to dining room to drugstore. Engineered DNA can now keep food from spoiling or make it more nutritious. Someday soon, it will turn crops into factories. A genetically altered plant might produce a substitute for plastic or perhaps a vaccine for malaria.

It's heady stuff, and not all the promises will come to pass. But in the decades ahead, many will. Our discussion of biotech's players and prospects will give you the tools to start assessing an investment opportunity that's probably more complicated—and more promising—than any you've known.

Genomics. The faster scientists decode genes, the faster drug and agricultural researchers can use the information to target genetic diseases or develop enhanced crops. Genomics companies provide those researchers with decoded data and the software and other tools needed to manipulate them. That means the companies aren't betting on one innovative seed or drug— they're betting on all of them. "This is the foundation upon which medicine and agriculture are going to rest in the next century," says Elizabeth Silverman, a molecular biologist and BancAmerica Robertson Stephens biotech analyst.

While scientists are close to deciphering the human genome, that's only a first step. Because genetic variation is the key to many diseases, genes need to be analyzed again and again, from patients both healthy and sick. Big drug companies have already made it clear that they recognize the value of genomics. SmithKline Beecham alone has made a $125 million commitment to genomics pioneer Human Genome Sciences for "special access" to that company's database.

So how does an investor tap into this bounty? Carefully. The market for genetic data and technology could grow into the tens of billions of dollars over the next decade, says Jeremy Rifkin, a social critic and author of *The Biotech Century*. But now there are just a dozen or so publicly traded genomics companies, and last year only one was making money. Still, there are ways to uncover tomorrow's successes. So here's our approach and the results it yielded.

We first looked for companies that have more than databases; we wanted patented technologies that make it easier for customers to analyze and manipulate genetic data. Then we made sure those patents had obvious commercial value, as evidenced by real paying customers, not just ones on a business plan. We also tried to find companies with product lines that weren't confined to big-ticket items that clients would buy only once. In addition, we wanted companies to have enough cash or committed revenues to fund research and other expenses for at least three years. Finally, we sought experienced management. If an outfit has yet to make money, you want to know that its executives have taken a business into the black before.

Our screen first led us to **Incyte Pharmaceuticals**, last year's lone profitable genomics firm. Like the federally sponsored Human Genome Project and other for-profit gene-sequencing companies, Incyte produces genetic databases. What sets it apart from the pack is the quality of the software it sells to mine the data. Pharmaceutical giant Rhone-Poulenc, for instance, is buying access to an Incyte microbial database that has the genome for *Streptococcus pneumoniae*, the major cause of pneumonia. Rhone-

Poulenc's researchers are using Incyte software to search for ways to treat and prevent the disease. Incyte counts among its customers 21 of the top 50 pharmaceutical companies, which pay it an average of $5 million a year each. Down the road, the company also stands to receive royalties from products developed from its database.

On the agricultural side, Monsanto and others use Incyte software as they look for ways to improve crop yields as well as pest and disease resistance. Analyst Mike King of Vector Securities thinks that Incyte should see earnings increases of nearly 60% annually over the next four years. With that growth rate, he thinks the stock ought to be trading at 58 times estimated 1999 earnings of $1 per share.

One of the most fascinating developments in genomics is the DNA biochip—the analysis of DNA on a glass wafer. The clear leader in the field is **Affymetrix**, which designs biochips and sells scanners that read them. By inducing a chemical reaction between synthetic DNA on the chip and a cell sample they want to test and then running the chip through the scanner, Affymetrix clients can spot genetic mutations in the sample. Affymetrix has 80 of its chip-scanners placed with major companies such as Hoffmann-La Roche and agricultural seed firm Pioneer Hi-Bred. Those customers will keep coming back because new projects require new chips. One vote of confidence from a knowledgeable source: Pharmaceutical giant Glaxo Wellcome owns a third of Affymetrix.

Research and development expenses have kept Affymetrix in the red, but its patent position and continuing advances in chips should make it profitable by 2000. Revenues, which have risen steadily from $1.4 million in 1993, should reach $80 million in 1999, says Robertson Stephens' Elizabeth Silverman.

Drug biotech. The stock market history of biotech drug companies goes back almost 20 years, but the seminal event was the 1989 run-up of market darling Amgen. Unfortunately, the tale gets fairly depressing from there. Optimists predicted an avalanche of billion-dollar drugs; instead, stocks went into a coma as Wall Street and the industry realized they had grossly underestimated the cost and difficulty of bringing drugs to market. Drug biotech has barely moved since 1993.

But it should awaken soon. Biotech's pipeline is bursting with more than 2,200 drugs in development, including more than 200 awaiting approval from the Food and Drug Administration, according to Ernst & Young. And those approvals are starting to come at a faster pace. The average time for

FDA review has fallen to 16 months, from 30 in 1991. About half the biotech drugs now on the market have been approved since 1996.

As for funding, biotech drug companies raised $11.7 billion in 1997, according to San Francisco merchant bank Burrill & Co. The pace has continued with $5.7 billion raised in the first half of 1998 alone—and that's in an industry with a total market capitalization of less than $100 billion. What's more, the big pharmaceutical companies providing much of that financing have such an insatiable need for new drugs that biotech firms are in a strong negotiating position when cutting marketing and distribution deals. A few years ago, the big drug firm typically grabbed 75% or more of a drug's profits. Today the biotech company might retain 50%. Better capital and a bigger share of revenues will mean more profitable biotech companies. In 1986, there was just one; by 2000, there could be 50.

Nevertheless, investors have largely ignored biotech drug stocks. One reason is the success of other industries. "If you can make 25% a year investing in Coke, why on earth would you buy a biotech stock?" asks SG Cowen Securities Corp. biotech analyst David Stone. The Internet, meanwhile, has captured the imagination of speculative investors. As a result, most biotech stocks, including those of profitable companies, have been languishing at low relative valuations. That presents an opportunity to buy promising stocks on the cheap. We found a couple of exceptional choices.

In coming up with them, we first looked for companies with drugs that weren't in a pitched battle for market share. We also wanted to see that there was a truly large market for those drugs. If a company is going to split profits with a distribution partner, even a $50-million-a-year market is a pittance, especially when it can cost $350 million to develop a drug. We also made sure that companies had the cash to sustain development—at least three times annual R&D costs. Collaboration with a pharmaceutical partner, which is a source of funds and an endorsement of efforts, was also important.

Finally, we sought out companies whose next big sellers were far enough along in the FDA approval process to make us confident about their getting to market. Hambrecht & Quist biotech analyst Richard van den Broek recommends waiting to invest until a drug has passed either Phase III testing, which is a placebo-controlled test in hospitals and clinics, or has won FDA approval. You'll miss a stock's speculative run, but you'll avoid many disasters—and still be positioned for significant gains. (Of course, these stocks are hardly risk-free.)

We're passing on the industry's big three: Amgen, Chiron and Genentech. The reason? We concluded that, given their pipelines, their stock prices fully reflect their earnings prospects. Our choices:

BioChem Pharma's 3TC drug is now the No. 1 treatment for HIV. Sales in 1997 topped $700 million, of which BioChem receives 12% to 13%, the rest going to its marketing partner, Glaxo Wellcome. In 1998 BioChem and Glaxo completed Phase III trials and applied for approval to use the same drug (under the name lamivudine) to treat chronic hepatitis B, which affects 300 million people. That use could push 3TC sales to $2.4 billion by 2001, according to SG Cowen's Stone. Jay Silverman, another BancAmerica Robertson Stephens analyst, thinks BioChem can sustain 30% to 40% earnings growth through 1999.

Aviron is an anomaly: It's been a money loser that nevertheless has had enough financial strength to have made it through Phase III trials without going to a pharmaceutical partner for help—and giving up a big chunk of future profits. Aviron completed trials of its FluMist flu vaccine and filed for FDA approval last June. Administered as a nasal spray—eliminating the unpleasantness of an injection—FluMist acts directly on the mucous lining in the nose and throat. Aviron hopes to make the drug available for the 1999-2000 flu season, with realistic expectations of pocketing a big piece of a potential $500 million market.

Big pharma.

Big pharma. The average drug company's stock has quadrupled during the past five years, but big pharma, as it's known, is in danger of becoming a victim of its own success. Many of its best-selling drugs, including Zoloft and Prozac, will lose patent protection over the next five years, meaning profit margins of those drugs will all but evaporate. Moreover, because drug companies have grown so big, a new drug must have near-Viagra sales to jazz earnings. And conventional methods aren't likely to produce the stream of blockbuster drugs the industry needs. Andersen Consulting estimates that a top-tier drug company would have to put out five new drugs a year with sales of $350 million each to maintain the 13% annual growth rate the industry has racked up in the 1990s. Yet from 1990 to 1994, the top makers launched an average of one new drug every two years.

Big drug companies are hoping biotech can pump up their pipelines quickly. In the 18 months through the first half of 1998, drug and biotech companies struck 330 alliances. In a typical deal, the pharmaceutical company makes a small, up-front investment for a biotech company to pursue promising research. It makes additional payments as a drug reaches various stages of development, then handles marketing and/or distribution. Drug companies are also beefing up their own biotech research. They buy access to the databases owned by genomics companies and use that information to develop drugs.

Should you buy a drug company solely, or even partly, because of its biotech investing? Not yet. Biotech will play an increasingly important role in the fortunes of nearly all big drug companies. But with the possible exception of Eli Lilly, big pharma won't see significant profits from biotech for several years. And it's impossible today to tell which companies will end up as the biggest biotech winners.

What we can tell you is that biotech is a reason to be bullish on drug stocks for the long term, and that drug stocks are a relatively safe way to play the coming biotech boom. That's because the failure of one drug won't sink a giant like Pfizer; it might doom Pfizer's tiny biotech partner.

Right now, pharmaceuticals are among the more expensive stocks, but there are still a few good buys. Two, at recent prices of about $80 and $145 respectively: **Merck** and **Eli Lilly**. Eli Lilly has already had biotech success, and over the next five years, analysts expect the company to increase earnings by 17% a year.

Ag-bio. Investors are paying attention to ag-biotech. Despite qualms among some consumers and regulators, especially in Europe, genetic manipulation of crops and vegetables is a fact of modern agriculture; 30 genetically manipulated seeds, including soybeans, squash and potatoes, have the U.S. Department of Agriculture's blessing. Fully a third of the nation's 155 million acres of corn, soy and cotton are planted with genetically altered seeds. Mark Wiltamuth, an analyst with ING Baring Furman Selz, figures that the gross margin on Bt corn, which is sold by several seed companies, is 71% vs. 59% on normal corn seed.

Making "smarter," higher-yielding seed is only the beginning for ag-biotech. Next, companies will alter "output traits." Corn, for example, may be modified to contain more oil or protein. That would cut the amount that livestock producers, who buy 80% of the U.S. corn crop, must spend on feed supplements. Ultimately, pharmaceutical and chemical concerns have greater ambitions. Altered seeds will also begin to take over manufacturing processes, says Robert Giaquinta, chief of biotechnology for Du Pont. Engineered seeds could, for example, extract unhealthy oils in soybeans. Companies will "do in the green plant," Gianquinta says, "what is normally done in the steel plant."

Investors who want to plow into ag-biotech have several big-cap stocks to pick from. Besides Du Pont, companies getting into life sciences include

Dow Chemical, Swiss food and drug giant Novartis, German chemical maker Hoechst and the United Kingdom's Zeneca. But the industry leader is **Monsanto**, and while it may not show earnings growth until 2002, over the long term it is an ag-biotech player you want to bet on. Another is **Pioneer Hi-Bred**, the last publicly traded stand-alone seed company. Pioneer's ace is a recent fifty-fifty venture with Du Pont, a leader in developing the next generation of seeds. The combination could bring $3.5 billion in revenues and 20%-plus margins within 10 years. Why buy Pioneer, not Du Pont? Earnings leverage. Splitting profits of, say, $700 million would more than double Pioneer's recent per-share earnings. Du Pont's cut would add a mere 9%.

TECH HARDWARE CAN TAKE OFF

Historically, the year before a presidential election year tends to have the biggest stock market gains (since World War II, increases for the S&P 500 in pre-election years have averaged more than 15%). The chief reason: The Federal Reserve generally tries to provide an easy monetary climate in the 18 months or so leading up to a presidential election. In addition, tax selling was intense last year—and with that selling ended, many depressed stocks are rebounding.

Computermakers should be among the major rebounders, since they were hard hit early last year, with declines of 30% or more in many cases. A couple of other trends may give computer stocks a lift as well. By November stock markets in Hong Kong, South Korea and Thailand had rallied more than 30% from their lows. Also, Congress passed legislation last year favorable to tech firms, including more visas for skilled foreign workers and stricter limits on certain lawsuits.

Which companies stand out? Dell's growth was breathtaking last year, but the stock is richly priced, and Dell's growth rate could slow this year as **Compaq**'s new sub-$1,000 machines nip into its market share. Hewlett-Packard seems to be stagnating, partly because of an uninspiring product mix and partly because it has resisted cutting prices as fast as the other firms have.

In our view Compaq, which Edward Kerschner recommended earlier in this chapter, boasts the best mix of price and prospects. It is rapidly improving its position in the industry. Computermakers' profits slumped last year because they produced too many machines and ended up having to slash prices to shed all that excess inventory. Compaq, for instance, had 10 to 12 weeks' worth of machines on hand at the start of the year but managed to work that down to just over three weeks' worth toward the end of the year.

Compaq's earnings, reported as 7¢ a share for the third quarter last year, are obscured by substantial costs stemming from the company's June takeover of Digital Equipment. The acquisition should be a contributor to earnings by early this year, however. And the deal brings promising opportunities in upper-end computer markets. For instance, Compaq acquired DEC's 64-bit Alpha chip, the fastest processor of its time. Compaq has incorporated that chip into Unix-language servers that could possibly double the speed of previous-generation machines.

Bear Stearns projects that earnings for technology hardware companies will increase at an 18.7% annual rate over the next five years. And, of course, PC makers wouldn't be the only beneficiaries of a general boom in hardware sales. The chief subcontractor for the industry is **SCI Systems**, which assembles components into subassemblies such as motherboards. SCI stock fell nearly 60% from its high late in 1997 to $21 in October, then quickly rebounded to $33. That's still quite reasonable, at 15 times estimated 1999 earnings, for a company with 19% annual sales growth over the past decade and projected earnings growth of better than 20% over the next five years.

Other likely beneficiaries include chipmakers such as **Intel**, whose strong advance orders reflect the coming pickup in computer sales. Also on the list are semiconductor equipment manufacturers, which make the machines that make the chips. The leader in the group is **Applied Materials**. And we wouldn't be surprised if **Microsoft** finds a way to profit too.

CARD STOCKS DESERVE SOME CREDIT

When investors ran away from all things financial last August and September, credit-card companies suffered just as banks and brokerages did. After all, if the domestic economy took a turn for the worse, more deadbeat cardholders could push the 6% default rate up dramatically. That said, the 20% to 40% pummeling that credit-card stocks took seems excessive. Third-quarter earnings were strong, and issuers hadn't racked up losses in Russia or in hedge funds.

In fact, they've been benefiting from the fallout of global anxiety—falling interest rates. The wave of mortgage refinancing has helped improve card companies' credit quality because consumers are a bit less strapped. And interest margins will likely rise because issuers traditionally take their time passing along lower rates to their customers.

For investors, card issuers aren't just a near-term play on interest rates. The business is getting better. First, issuers have made great strides in risk-reward analysis. They target consumers who will carry a balance but won't default on their debt, and they can spot a cardholder on the brink of bankruptcy, which gives them time to step up collection efforts. Second, the industry is in the midst of massive consolidation. By buying up smaller players, companies whose card operations are their main business can add to their portfolios quickly and for less money than they would spend rustling up new customers. Third, companies are beginning to get the hang of cross-selling—using card databases to sell other financial services. CIBC Oppenheimer analyst Steven Eisman, for one, predicts cross-selling will be a major growth factor in coming years.

We focused our search for card issuers on those that are showing low charge-off rates, solid growth through acquisition and, finally, better than average customer loyalty—which translates to lower marketing costs and more opportunity to cross-sell. That meant shying away from the fastest-growing issuers, which are using low rates to try to steal market share. Of course, we like 'em cheap, so companies not trading at low valuations were sidelined.

MBNA, the third largest credit-card issuer, has grown earnings more than 20% annually over its seven years as a public company. Its default rate (recently 4.3%) averages 30% better than its peers. Instead of just trying to drum up business among the general public, MBNA issues more than half its cards to members of 4,500 affinity groups—from Georgetown University alumni to Green Bay Packers fans. Those cardholders have income that's twice the national average. MBNA is expected to keep adding 20% a year to its $56 billion portfolio, largely by swallowing up smaller issuers, as it did Fidelity's $450 million business in 1997. Analysts expect 21% earnings improvement in 1999.

Household International's $18 billion credit-card portfolio hasn't grown at the same clip as MBNA's, but this company is admirably conservative, with reserves of more than 4% (many issuers have no reserves) and a charge-off rate of just over 5% for its cards. Additionally, Household, which is among the top 10 card issuers even though one-third of its business is home-equity lending, is expected to realize cost savings from its recent acquisition of Beneficial Corp., which has a similar business mix. Analysts expect earnings to improve 34% this year.

Our final pick isn't primarily a lender, but **American Express** is a big competitor in the card game. More than 60% of AmEx's card revenues come from merchants, who fork over 2.7% of charges (member fees make up much of the rest). In 1997 AmEx card charges reached $209 billion, a number that's been growing by more than 10% a year. Although a recession would push volume growth down, Christopher Davis and Ken Feinberg, whose Davis Financial fund has 5% in AmEx, aren't too concerned. "Credit is usually the problem in recessions," says Davis, "not decreased spending."

Credit-card companies could do worse than copying AmEx. Its rewards program is the class of the industry, and it has succeeded in feeding cardholders into its financial services division. In 1997, 30% of the services group's new customers were cardholders.

AmEx is also a model in another area—one that's the source of short-term pain. AmEx shares dropped 23% between mid-July and mid-November, in part because more than one-fourth of its card business is international (mostly Europe and Canada). But plastic is continuing to gain popularity worldwide. American Express, with a big international brand, is in good position to capture such growth, and the company has said that it intends eventually to pull 50% of its revenue from abroad. Although 1999 earnings are expected to grow a modest 14%, over the long term ownership should have its rewards.

TAKE STOCK OF A FUND COMPANY

Wise guys finish last. If you want to make money in the stock market over the long term, you can't be too much of a cynic. You've got to be an optimist, because share prices rise far more often than they fall. Since 1960, for instance, the Dow has posted losses in only nine years—or less than a quarter of the time. Most investors who want to cash in on this long-run uptrend in stock prices stash their savings in mutual funds and do just fine. But here's another smart move: Put your money in a fund company's common stock. Most likely, it will outperform the firm's mutual funds by a wide margin over a decade or so. Our favorite in this group is **T. Rowe Price**, which recently traded at $32 a share.

Most analysts are cautious on the stocks of brokerages and money managers because such issues would underperform the Dow during a market downturn. T. Rowe Price acknowledged as much when it reported third-quarter earnings last October, saying that results would be adversely affected if the market didn't rebound fairly quickly from the summer slump. The

Dow did bounce back rapidly, but we understand the reasons for caution. Nonetheless, this sort of thinking is a form of short–term market timing that investors are always told to avoid. Volatility shouldn't matter to long–term investors who are truly prepared to ride out temporary price swings.

The case for T. Rowe Price is so good that it looks like a compelling buy. Here's why:

Most of a no-load fund company's profits come from the annual fee charged as a percentage of the assets in the company's funds. And those assets—and the profits they generate—have risen dramatically in recent years, thanks to the sharp rise in stock prices and huge amounts of new cash added by investors seeking to get in on the market bonanza. Recently, T. Rowe had about $135 billion in assets under management, of which $87.5 billion was in the firm's mutual funds. That's more than a double in total assets since 1994—and over the same period, earnings have soared from 50 cents a share to an estimated $1.35 in 1998. Moreover, T. Rowe figures to show steady growth in assets even if the bull market falls. Retirement and pension accounts make up more than half the money the company manages. Most of those accounts enjoy inflows no matter what the overall market is doing.

The chief reason we single out T. Rowe Price, however, is that there aren't a whole lot of fund company stocks you can buy. Moreover, no-load fund companies are the purest play on asset growth. With its strong lineup of funds in all major categories, T. Rowe is the largest and best–quality no-load company with publicly traded stock. (Fidelity is privately held, and Vanguard is indirectly owned by the shareholders of its funds.)

T. Rowe's track record over the past eight years is absolutely phenomenal. From its low during the 1990-91 recession, the stock soared more than four-teenfold to nearly $43 at the peak last summer (after adjusting for three two-for-one splits). By contrast, the Dow climbed 3 1/2 times over the same period.

Some analysts think T. Rowe's shares have become a bit overvalued. Steven Eisman at CIBC Oppenheimer, for instance, downgraded T. Rowe to a hold on Oct. 21 because the stock was trading at 22.6 times estimated 1999 earnings, which he considered high, given the market uncertainty. In the short run, he may be right. But we think that if you take a longer–term view, T. Rowe actually looks kind of cheap.

Over the past five years, the company's earnings have increased at a 27.5% compound annual rate. That kind of growth certainly ought to justify a P/E in the low 20s.

Nonetheless, T. Rowe has traded at average multiples between 14 and 19 for seven of the past nine years. One reason: The stock has a high 1.55 beta, meaning that it's 55% more volatile than the overall market. Investors generally grant lower P/Es to volatile stocks, particularly when the economic outlook is uncertain. So it's entirely possible the stock could sell off sharply during a market dip. But remember, this one's for long-term investors, and the odd dip here or there isn't going to change T. Rowe's investment potential.

The company is also a natural takeover target and could command a takeover premium of 50% to 60%. Given the firm's great franchise and brand name—not to mention the likelihood that its stock will leave the Dow in the dust—T. Rowe looks like a pearl of great price.

UP FROM THE BASEMENT

Recessions may be hard on home builders, but recessionary panics are murder on their share prices. Consider that the S&P 500 lost 19% between mid-July and early October—but Standard & Poor's home-building index fell 38%.

Recently, home-builders' stocks were rallying with the broader market—but not as strongly as they should have been. The industry's P/E ratio was 12.3, a 51% discount to the S&P 500, more than double the traditional 24% discount. "Many home builders are still trading at recessionary prices," said Sam Lieber, manager of the Alpine U.S. Real Estate Equity Fund, who was loading up on Lennar, D.R. Horton, Toll Bros., U.S. Home and Standard Pacific. Also, market guru and money manager Elaine Garzarelli sees a rosy 1999 for the group. She's predicting 12% earnings growth (vs. zero growth for the S&P 500). "It's an industry that always comes out on top," she says, "after a fear market or a major correction."

But it's not just low prices that make home-building stocks attractive. First, news of a housing slowdown has been exaggerated. The National Association of Home Builders expects housing starts to decline slightly in 1999, but the absolute figure—1.47 million homes—would still be among the best totals ever.

Second, the economy continues to provide a near-ideal environment for home builders. Job and wage growth are up, consumer confidence is still close to an all-time high, while long-term interest rates wallow near 30-year lows. At the end of 1998, Barbara Allen, an analyst for Arnhold and S. Bleichroader, a New York City investment bank, reported that applications for new mortgages had been beating 1997 levels at least 30% a week since August.

Third, in case of an unexpected slowdown, bankers have taken steps to avoid yesterday's worst mistakes. More are reducing risk by holding land options rather than land. Likewise, companies now tend to build only after an order is placed. In December, inventories of unsold homes were down to a four-month supply (seven months is the historical level) while backlogs of new orders were at record levels. That "augurs well for the next six to nine months, no matter what happens to the economy," said Southeast Research Partners analyst Tim Jones in Boca Raton, Fla.

Last, a consolidation wave is creating a handful of large, professionally managed public companies among thousands of small, privately held builders. Major builders (with market caps near or above $1 billion) should be able to grow in any economic climate and in the event of recession will be able to pick competitors at bargain prices. Salomon Smith Barney analyst David Dwyer estimates that the top five builders now control 16% of the market but will hold almost 30% by 2002.

Of course, no home builder is recessionproof. "These companies will tell you they're better at managing the peaks and valleys," says Steve Friedman, a consultant for E&Y Kenneth Leventhal Real Estate Group. "But housing has always been a cyclical industry, and it probably always will be."

We focused our search for builders on industry leaders that have solid growth histories and prospects, increasing backlogs and a desirable geographic concentration. Industry giant **Centex** (recent price, $37.50) fits the bill, but its stock had largely rebounded by December. We found four other companies that were still trading at substantial discounts, each with P/Es of less than 10.

Lennar ($22.00) and **D.R. Horton** ($17.25) have been buying established local builders and pushing into the fast-growing West. Based in Miami, Lennar entered California only in 1996, but that state now accounts for 9% of the company's deliveries and 45% of its $1 billion order backlog. What's more, California's strong demand has allowed Lennar to raise its average home price by 15% (to $194,000) since 1997. Last April, D.R. Horton cemented its presence in Arizona by purchasing Continental Homes in Scottsdale, a move that nearly doubled the acquirer's size. Analysts expect backlog increases and cost savings from the merger to help boost D.R. Horton's earnings 17% in fiscal 1999. At $22 and $17.25 respectively, both Lennar and Horton were trading more than 28% below their 52-week highs.

Already California's No. 1 builder, Los Angeles-based **Kaufman & Broad** ($27.00) isn't resting on its lead there, but is expanding. It's also expanding in Texas and the Southwest. The company built 25% of its homes outside California in 1995; two years later that figure had risen to 54%. Analysts projections are for 41% growth in 1999, but at $27, the stock was trading 22% below its high.

Selling detached, single-family homes for the lofty average price of $385,000, **Toll Bros.** ($23.75) is the leading builder of manses for empty-nesters and second-home buyers. Toll has broad demographics on its side. The number of households with ages between 55 and 64 is projected to grow 70% by 2010, and 9.6 million households now earn more than $100,000, up 33% (in constant dollars) from a decade ago. The Pennsylvania-based builder continues to crank out impressive numbers. Toll increased revenues 25% to $1.2 billion and its backlog 30% to $815 million in its just-ended fiscal year. Thanks to strong demand in its expanding western and southwestern operations, the company is expected to increase earnings 19% in 1999. At $23.75, Toll was still 23.4% off its 52-week high.

FAVORITE BLUE CHIPS STILL ON COURSE

In last year's *MONEY Adviser*, with markets rattled by the beginnings of the Asian economic crisis, we picked eight blue-chip companies that seemed likely to withstand the turmoil and, more important, deliver solid returns over the next five years. We think you can comfortably continue to hold seven of the eight.

Six of our picks—AirTouch Communications, Carnival Corp., Home Depot, Kroger, Warner-Lambert and Xerox—have performed as well as or better than expected, gaining 22% to 62% in the year beginning Nov. 17, 1997 vs. 15% for the S&P 500. The laggards have been Traveler's Group and Compaq. But Traveler's Group has since merged with Citicorp to create the financial services supermarket called Citigroup. That stock is one of the picks of the Wall Street experts quoted earlier in the chapter—and is on our recommended list as well. The same is true of Compaq.

Carnival is a different story. Carnival is still poised to ride the wave of aging baby boomers demanding cruise travel, but many analysts expect the cruise industry to get slammed for the short haul. Because Carnival's outlook for the next year or so is uncertain, consider taking your profits.

CHECK OUT GOOD DRIP DEALS

Sick of paying commissions to a broker every time you buy a stock? There's a better way, and the Web can take you there.

Some 1,600 or so U.S. and foreign companies allow shareholders to buy stock through dividend-reinvestment plans, or DRIPs. Instead of taking your quarterly payout in cash, you plow it into more shares. Almost all DRIPs also allow you to purchase additional shares directly from the sponsoring company. To sign up for most plans, however, you must already own the stock. But almost 500 companies now offer "no load" DRIPs, meaning you can obtain even those first shares straight from the source—so you'll never have to pay a sales commission to a brokerage.

DRIPs appeal to investors who are willing to do their own research rather than consult a broker for recommendations. The Internet makes doing DRIP homework a breeze. There are at least seven Websites devoted exclusively to the plans. A few other investing sites, including the Motley Fool, carry sections on DRIPs. The sites' offerings generally fall into one of three categories: 1) basic information on how DRIPs work; 2) recommendations of specific DRIP stocks; and 3) help on enrolling in plans.

To get started, use DRIP Central (www.dripcentral.com) as your reference library. The site carries articles on the basics of DRIP investing, but DRIP Central's real value lies in its links to other sources of information. If you want to buy a book on DRIPs, for instance, DRIP Central lists several good ones and provides a link to Amazon.com so you can make your purchases online. If you want to grill other individual investors about their experiences with DRIPs, click on "DRIP Talk," and you'll find links to a handful of message boards on DRIPs, like the one hosted by Armchair Millionaire. To obtain lists of companies that offer DRIPs, click on "DRIP Resources."

Once you've found a DRIP you like, Netstock Direct (www.netstockdirect.com) makes enrolling easy. The Netstock database includes 1,600 DRIP-friendly companies. For about 50 of them you can download prospectuses and fill out enrollment forms electronically. All that's left is to write out a check and put it in the mail. Several companies—including Equitable, Fannie Mae, Ford and Wal-Mart—go a step further and will, at your electronic request, debit your checking account for a stock purchase. Another 350 or so companies allow you to order prospectuses and enrollment forms via computer. (They'll arrive in the mail.) Netstock Direct provides phone numbers and addresses for the remainder of the companies in its database.

Netstock Direct also alerts you to any fees charged by DRIPs. About 75% of all DRIPs charge such fees; they don't come close to broker commissions but can amount to a sizable percentage of your investment if you're buying small amounts of stock. Recently, for example, in Gillette's plan, you paid $10 to enroll and for each purchase you paid $5 plus 8 cents a share. Owens Corning, by contrast, charged nothing for those services.

DON'T OVERLOOK FOREIGN MARKETS

We know last year's numbers look bad. From January to November of 1998, the average emerging markets fund had lost 34.5%, Latin American funds were off 40% on average, and even diversified foreign portfolios like Oakmark International and Warburg Pincus International had lost 12.5% and 4.4%, respectively. Meanwhile, despite a wild ride, U.S. stocks were up. At first glance, the hostility many Americans have long felt toward investing in other parts of the world seems justified. Who wants to invest where currencies bounce around like jumping beans, tanks can be as common as taxis on city streets and countries switch governments in an instant? When our own market is so familiar and so lucrative, why bother trying to understand all those places where people talk funny and eat weird food? But shunning foreign markets is a mistake, and here's why.

You lower your risk. You've probably heard pundits say that the overseas markets now march in virtual lockstep with Standard & Poor's 500-stock index. In fact, in this chapter, Salomon Smith Barney's Leila Heckman has said, "The diversification argument holds a little less today than it used to, if you're hoping to reduce overall risk by investing abroad." Some experts assert that in today's world of CNN and the Internet, if investors get jittery in the U.S., which makes up half the total value of all stocks worldwide, it's only natural for the rest of the planet to panic. So when Wall Street sneezes, Copenhagen, Caracas, Kuala Lumpur and Cairo catch cold.

Sure enough, in the third quarter of 1998, when the U.S. fell about 10%, the other 22 countries in the Morgan Stanley capital international world index lost an average of 15%; not one major market anywhere in the world rose as ours was falling. That's roughly what happened in 1987 and 1990, as well as in the bear market of the 1970s. It seems that just when you most need global diversification, it's most likely to fail.

Nevertheless, the true test of an enduring investment strategy is not whether it works at any given time, but whether it works over time. And international investing does. The fact is, you won't lower your risks by keeping all of your money in the U.S.; you will raise them.

While foreign stocks may drop in temporary tandem when U.S. equities crash, it's a different story in the long run. Finance professor Bruno Solnik, who helped pioneer the case for international investing back in 1974, recently wrote in *Investment Policy* magazine: "Contrary to some media statements, this international correlation has not increased markedly over the past 25 years." Over the longer term, the similarity between U.S. and foreign-stock returns has remained relatively stable and surprisingly low. In the past five years, despite the way 1998 made most markets appear to be joined at the hip, only about 60% of foreign-stock returns have moved in sync with the U.S. market. And since 1974, a mere 45% of the long-term movement of foreign markets has been correlated with our own. That suggests that overseas stocks should smooth the bumps of your portfolio in all but the most turbulent times.

No market is an island. In a survey of what they concluded were the world's 35,639 regularly traded stocks, the investment researchers at Wilshire Associates in Santa Monica, Calif. reckoned that only 12,863 were based in the U.S. That means nearly two-thirds of all investment opportunities are based outside our borders. "Do you really think," asks Rick Spillane, who oversees international investing for the Fidelity funds, "that there are no good companies worth owning out there?" Let's say you think cellular telephones have great promise; why limit yourself to Motorola when you could also consider Nokia of Finland or Ericsson of Sweden? Likewise, if you're excited about enterprise software, should you stick to Oracle when you can also buy SAP of Germany? And if you simply love cheap stocks, why hunt, perhaps vainly, in our still pricey market when bargains abound elsewhere? Not long ago, Chris Browne, co-manager of Tweedy Browne Global Value Fund, said that 15% of the 111 Japanese stocks in his portfolio were trading below the value of their cash on hand. In other words, the money these firms had in the bank was worth more than their stock prices—and you got the businesses for free.

David Fisher, who has been investing in emerging markets since they were called Third World countries, oversees $16 billion of emerging markets stocks for pension funds and other institutional investors at Capital International in Los Angeles. "A year ago," Fisher recently said, "our analysts and portfolio managers were bumping into people from other investment firms everywhere they went. Now most of those folks are gone, and we're competing with industrialists from Europe and the U.S. who are buying entire companies. That tells me we'll look back on this period as an absolutely wonderful investment opportunity. I sleep real well at night."

At the time, Brazil's stock market had lost 57% since its peak in mid-1997; Mexico was down 60% since 1994; Thailand had tumbled 91% since 1994; and Indonesia had shrunk by 95% since 1990. If you'd invested in those markets at their peak, your pain was acute. But now is not the time to turn your back on them forever, not at today's lower prices.

What history really shows. It bears noting that over nearly the past 10 years, the average foreign-stock fund returned just 7.63% annually, while the average U.S. stock fund earned 13.78% annually. But try to imagine that it's 1988 and you're Japanese. Your stock market is the most lucrative in the world; your companies are the envy of management gurus everywhere. Buying stocks outside Japan (especially in a then decrepit economy like the U.S.) strikes you as the dumbest idea since sushi vending machines. So you put all your money in Japanese stocks. Now fast-forward to 1998: After Japanese stock prices have skidded for a decade, you've lost more than 50% of your stake.

The real lesson to draw from history is not that you should never invest in foreign markets like Japan; it's that the Japanese should never have kept all their money at home. And neither should you. Because you can't possibly know what the future holds here or anywhere else, it's imperative to spread your bets. With 50% of the planet's total market value outside the U.S., even if you have 13% of your portfolio overseas—the average for an American fund investor—you're taking a big gamble that your backyard will continue to be the world's best place to invest.

If you're ready to shop elsewhere, here are some tips: Look for foreign mutual funds with annual expenses under 1.5% and portfolio turnover of 75% or less (which will keep the fund's trading costs low). A few good choices: **Acorn International**, **Fidelity Diversified International**, the new **Longleaf Partners International**, **Scudder International**, **T. Rowe Price International Stock**, **Vanguard International Growth** and **Vanguard Total International Stock Index**. If there are specific countries you'd like to target, consider the tax-efficient webs, which are index funds for 17 individual countries listed on the American Stock Exchange and available through full-service, discount and Internet brokers.

MUTUAL FUNDS FOR THE LONG HAUL

Sure, choice is good, but this is ridiculous. Investors now face a baffling array of more than 9,000 stock and bond funds. Do all those choices mean that today's investors really have more and better ways to achieve superior returns? Of course not. What's driving the proliferation of funds isn't a wealth of innovative investment ideas; it's the fact that sponsors figure the funds will sell. Unfortunately, that guiding principle has created a chaotic marketplace, where portfolios that can deliver truly outstanding long-term results often get lost in a crowd of inferior alternatives.

How can fund investors simplify their shopping? To help you, we have assembled our own all-star lineup of superior stock portfolios that span a wide range of investing styles. This is not a tipsheet of hot funds that have recently topped the performance charts, nor is it a mechanical screening system based on a rigid set of statistical criteria. It is a list of the best funds around, as determined by MONEY's staff. That said, we did ground our search in a rigorous quantitative analysis of fund performance. But electrifying figures alone didn't guarantee a place on the list. Like stock pickers who start with a statistical screen and then probe deeply into each company's business, we went well beyond the numbers. We used the knowledge and experience of the MONEY reporters, writers and editors who regularly cover funds to assess each fund's investment strategy and each manager's skill at executing that strategy.

We can't promise, of course, that these funds will always rise to the top of the performance charts. But we can say that as a group, these funds share most, if not all, of the characteristics that lead to long-term success: low to moderate expenses, a well-defined investing strategy and experienced managers with plenty of talent.

♦ **Acorn** (Managers: Ralph Wanger, Charles McQuaid) In a mutual fund universe that's filled with baby-faced managers, Wanger stands out in part because he's been at the game nearly 30 years. But more than longevity separates Wanger from other small-stock skippers. Foremost is his singular strategy of exploiting idiosyncratic "themes." A constant theme has been finding companies that meet his "quit" test—that is, businesses so exciting that he'd consider leaving his fund to join them.

♦ **American Century–20th Century International Growth**
(Managers: Henrik Strabo, Mark Kopinski) While most international managers choose countries first and then hunt for stocks, Strabo and Kopinski are strictly bottom-up stock pickers. And true to American Century style, they prize rapid and sustainable profit growth above all. Pick virtually any long-term period and this fund's performance ranks among the top 10% of its peers.

♦ **Babson Value** (Manager: Nick Whitridge) Whitridge succeeds by avoiding the classic value trap of buying shares too early and watching them languish. How? He screens for companies with low P/E and price-to-book rates, plus rising earnings. He figures that by looking at both valuation and growth prospects, he can spot companies that are ready to attract Wall Street's notice.

♦ **Baron Asset** (Manager: Ron Baron) Baron takes the concept of getting to know a company further than most managers—he even toured prisons before investing in jail operator Youth Services of America in 1995. Some of his small-company winners have grown so much that they are now mid-caps. But Baron hangs on to such shares as long as he believes their prices can still rise.

♦ **Berger Small Cap Value** (Manager: Robert Perkins) Before opening this fund to the public in 1997, Perkins ran it for fund manager friends and wealthy investors who wanted him to invest their money. Perkins buys stocks when they drop to their 52-week lows.

♦ **Brandywine** (Manager: Foster Friess, team) With 30 analysts, this fund has roughly one analyst for every three stocks in the portfolio. Friess runs the fund with a system he calls pigs in a trough—that is, the analysts compete for dollars to invest and they must sell a holding to buy a new one. But Friess also makes macro calls, such as when he dumped his tech shares in the wake of the Asian crisis. Brandywine is volatile, but its long-term record is superb.

♦ **Brazos/JMC Small Cap Growth** (Manager: Team) A new fund with a distinguished pedigree. Prior to launching this portfolio in 1997, John McStay and the other managers had built a solid record picking underpriced growth stocks for institutional accounts.

♦ **Brinson Global** (Manager: Gary Brinson) The whole-planet portfolio: cash, stocks and bonds, here and abroad. Brinson's pioneering mid-1980s research on asset allocation transformed the way large institutions deploy their money. A guiding principle: "To get the most favorable combination of risk and return, you have to draw from the complete global mosaic." Brinson and his team tilt the fund away from markets they view as overvalued.

♦ **BT Investment International Equity** (Managers: Michael Levy, Robert Reiner, Julie Wang) The three managers look for undervalued foreign stocks from every angle, running top-down and bottom-up screens and playing themes like corporate restructuring. Over a recent five-year period, this fund outpaced 98% of its peers.

◆ **Capital World Growth & Income** (Manager: Team) The Los Angeles-based American Funds group runs this global portfolio, using its distinctive research-intensive team approach. Over a recent three-year stretch, World Growth & Income outperformed 92% of its peers at 97% less risk.

◆ **CGM Focus** (Manager: Ken Heebner) Heebner's best-known fund—CGM Capital Development—is closed to new investors, but you can still get his maverick stock picking through this newer offering. He moves quickly—"I'm prepared to make a decision in an hour"—basing his buys on anything from a tidbit of industry news to his feel for major economic trends.

◆ **CGM Realty** (Manager: Ken Heebner) All real estate, all the time—and all in Heebner's favorite two dozen property stocks. A good way to get real estate exposure, as long as you can tolerate the volatility.

◆ **Clipper** (Managers: James Gipson, Michael Sandler, Bruce Veaco) These guys are value purists. They look for companies selling at sizable discounts to their cash flow, typically limiting themselves to 20 or so stocks. And when they find companies they really love, they'll go with huge positions. But when the trio can't find the values they want, they patiently wait with cash and bonds until the right opportunities come along.

◆ **Colonial Small Cap Value A** (Managers: James Haynie, Michael Rega) Many value managers focus on the industries that offer the best buys. But Haynie and Rega try to include the most undervalued stocks in all major market sectors. So Colonial usually holds more tech and health-care stocks, making it riskier than its peers. Then again, its returns have been superior too.

◆ **CRM Small Cap Value** (Manager: Team) The managers of this fund ignore Wall Street, and their portfolio proves it. Among their 1998 top holdings were United Stationers and ChoicePoint, a company that does background checks for employers. The fund's record is short, but the managers have returned almost 19% annualized for private clients in similar portfolios over the past 15 years.

♦ **Dodge & Cox Stock** (Manager: Team) Nothing flashy here. The managers pick up blue-chip stocks that have been laid low—and hold them until the firms rebound. And the fund consistently beats about three-quarters of its large-value competitors.

♦ **Dreyfus Appreciation** (Manager: Fayez Sarofim) Since assuming command of this fund in 1990, renowned growth investor Sarofim has taken its portfolio beyond large-caps to megacaps. He invests in humongous household-name multinational companies, like Coke and Merck, that can churn out above-average profits over the long term. Low turnover minimizes taxable gains, making this portfolio a good choice for taxable accounts.

♦ **Europacific Growth** (Manager: Team) This American Funds portfolio is the biggest foreign-stock fund and one of the oldest. But neither size nor age has slowed it down; choose a time period and it usually bests most of its peers. The fund invests in more than 300 foreign blue chips, which it clings to for four years on average.

♦ **Fasciano** (Manager: Michael Fasciano) Here's another fund that doesn't get the attention it deserves. Manager Fasciano scoops up reasonably priced small firms with the potential to double earnings or sales within five years. Into 1998 he'd topped about two-thirds of his small-blend peers over the past 10 years while taking less risk than 99% of them.

♦ **FBR Financial Services A** (Manager: David Ellison) Call Ellison the king of banking. He steered Fidelity Select-Home Finance to the second-best 10-year record among all funds before leaving to launch this portfolio in 1996.

♦ **Fidelity Diversified International** (Manager: Greg Fraser) This top-performing fund uses a computer-driven approach in a fund company that was largely built on instinctive stock jocks like Peter Lynch. Fraser does tweak his quantitative model with subjective factors, such as political trends, and the recipe works.

♦ **First Eagle Fund of America** (Managers: David Cohen, Harold Levy) Cohen and Levy begin their stock search every day by going through the newspaper. They look for stories of companies undergoing management changes, spinning off divisions, introducing new products or announcing buybacks. The pair then assess a company's cash flow to see if they consider it a buy. Over recent three-year and five-year periods, First Eagle out-gained 98% of other midcap value funds.

♦ **Franklin California Growth** (Managers: Conrad Herrman, Frank Felicelli, J.P. Scandalios) Hermann and company invest only in small- and midcap growth companies that are based in California or that do most of their business there. But they see that policy as a plus, not a burden. For example, when they seek fast-growing tech stocks, they find all they need in Silicon Valley, just 20 minutes from Franklin's San Mateo offices. "We read the local papers and socialize and interact with executives at the companies," Herrman says.

♦ **Franklin Small Cap Growth 1** (Manager: Edward Jamieson, team) The key to this fund's success: Manager Jamieson can draw on the ideas of 25 or so Franklin analysts who follow specific sectors and query customers and suppliers of industries in their areas for ideas about little-known firms. Jamieson and his colleagues' strategy of buying small companies with P/E ratios lower than their growth rates has propelled the fund to an impressive record.

♦ **Fremont U.S. Micro–Cap** (Manager: Robert Kern, team) Kern loves microcaps because there are so many—more than 5,000—that bargains almost always abound. He looks for companies with market values of $10 million to $400 million whose innovative products or services provide big growth potential.

♦ **Gabelli Asset** (Manager: Mario Gabelli) Gabelli takes huge positions in sectors he believes are undervalued—and hangs on even when the market tells him he's wrong. Gabelli was labeled a has-been in '95 and '96 when this fund lagged, owing mostly to its big stakes in cable and media stocks. Gabelli toughed it out, and when entertainment stocks surged in '97 his fund scored S&P 500-topping 38.1% gains.

♦ **Gam International A** (Manager: John Horseman) Horseman takes an international gunslinger approach, shifting from stocks to bonds and from one region to another, depending on where he sees the best value. A year ago, the fund ranked No. 2 in its category over five years.

♦ **Hancock Financial Industries A** (Manager: James Schmidt) This relatively new sector fund made our list because Schmidt's eminently successful flagship portfolio, Hancock Regional Bank, was closed to new investors. That's okay; we'll take Schmidt wherever we can get him.

♦ **Harbor Capital Appreciation** (Manager: Sig Segalas) A growth-stock purist, Segalas sticks to rapidly growing mid- and large-caps. He's quick to dump stocks that sour. During 1998, the strategy had earned a three-year return of 31.5%.

♦ **Homestead Value** (Managers: Peter Morris, Stuart Teach) The fund's small size, relatively focused portfolio, low costs and patient management (turnover is a mere 10% a year) create an uncommonly inviting environment for midcap investors.

♦ **Hotchkis & Wiley International** (Managers: Sarah Ketterer, Harry Hartford, David Chambers) There's something to be said for nepotism. John Hotchkis tapped daughter Sarah Ketterer to manage this fund in 1990. Since then, she and her co-managers have earned top returns with very little volatility by investing in stocks with scrawny P/E and price-to-book ratios.

♦ **IDS Growth A** (Manager: Mitzi Malevich) This fund doesn't invest by the numbers. Malevich looks for what she calls visionary managers who will stay ahead of the curve—and she says she plans on keeping her picks "forever." (Her average holding period is actually about four years vs. one for the typical growth manager.)

♦ **Janus Special Situations** (Manager: David Decker) There's a lot that's special about this fund. Decker looks for special stocks: out-of-favor mid-size and large companies that are right on the brink of rebounding, thanks to a restructuring, management change or redeployment of capital. And it has generated some pretty special returns.

♦ **Kemper–Dreman High Return Equity A** (Manager: David Dreman) Dreman has an uncanny sense for stepping into—and ducking out of—the right sector at the right time. During 1998, the fund's five-year returns had topped 95% of large-value funds' returns.

♦ **Legg Mason Value Trust** (Manager: William Miller III) Miller holds on to his rebounding winners long after others would cash out. The fund has consistently ranked in the top percentile of its large-value category.

♦ **Longleaf Partners Realty** (Managers: C.T. Fitzpatrick, O. Mason Hawkins, G. Staley Cates) Operating out of Memphis, Hawkins and Cates have established themselves as two of the fund world's top value investors, buying only companies they believe are selling 40% or more below their intrinsic worth. At this fund, along with co-manager Cates, they apply their value discipline to hotel, restaurant, mining and other property-related outfits, including REITS.

♦ **Lord Abbett Developing Growth A** (Manager: Stephen McGruder) McGruder looks for high growth, market leadership and decent prices in small and microcap stocks, holding on to them until they start behaving like, in his words, "tomorrow's blue chips." Under his management, the fund has landed in the top 2% of the small-growth group.

♦ **Mairs & Power Growth** (Manager: George Mairs) At age 70 last year, manager Mairs had been around a long time—and so had a lot of his stocks. Three of his top 10 holdings had been in the fund for 29 years or more, and Mairs & Power Growth had beaten 96% of all funds for the past decade. Most of Mairs' picks are in or around the fund's home state of Minnesota. Although this fund is not available in all states, it was just too good to leave off our list.

♦ **Map–Equity** (Managers: Roger Lob, Michael Mullarkey and John Stone) Each manager uses a different strategy for finding undervalued stocks. This makes for one sturdy three-legged stool. They deliver top returns with below-average risk for midcap blend funds.

♦ **Marsico Focus** (Manager: Thomas Marsico) This fund is barely a year old. But Marsico runs it using the same strategy that led him to market-beating gains in his nearly 10 years at the helm of the Janus Twenty fund. He makes big bets on 20 to 30 large stocks that he believes have the strongest growth prospects over the next three to five years.

♦ **MFS Massachusetts Investors Trust A** (Manager: Team) America's oldest fund (founded in 1924), MIT proves that an old reliable investing strategy—buying big stocks at reasonable prices—can still excel in the '90s stock market.

♦ **Montag & Caldwell Growth 1** (Manager: Ronald Canakaris) Here's your chance to get a great growth manager on sale. Since 1980, Canakaris has dazzled at Enterprise Growth Fund by sticking to blue chips with above-average earnings growth. Here, you get the same manager following essentially the same investing strategy but without Enterprise's 4.75% sales load.

♦ **Neuberger & Berman Partners** (Managers: Michael Kassen, Robert Gendelman) Over a recent five-year period this fund topped more than 90% of midcap growth funds by snapping up slumping growth stocks and other undervalued companies.

♦ **New Perspective** (Manager: Team) This giant global fund has been around since 1973. Investing in hundreds of American, European and Asian growth companies with global reach, New Perspective has beaten 85% of its peers over most of the past decade.

♦ **Nicholas** (Managers: Albert and David Nicholas) Albert Nicholas founded this fund in 1969; son David was named co-manager in '96. They follow a growth-at-the-right-price strategy and stress patience.

♦ **Oakmark** (Manager: Robert Sanborn) This flagship fund from Chicago's Harris Associates was founded in 1991. By 1998, it had posted returns that ranked in the top 4% of large-value funds for the previous five years, while taking less risk than 83% of them.

♦ **Robertson Stephens Value + Growth** (Manager: Ronald Elijah) Tech savant Elijah spots trends, then makes huge bets on the industries that can exploit them. This strategy racked up a three-year return of 22.1% into 1998.

♦ **Royce Premier** (Manager: Chuck Royce) A renowned value investor, Royce has been digging for bargain stocks with little debt and low price/earnings for more than 25 years. His small-cap portfolio is built for comfort, not speed.

♦ **Schwab 1000** (Manager: Geri Hom) This index fund, which owns the 1,000 U.S. companies with the largest market value, keeps your tax bill low by taking losses to offset gains. Low annual expenses are a bonus.

♦ **Selected American Shares** (Manager: Chris Davis) Shelby Davis and his son Chris made their reputations as great value investors at Davis New

York Venture. But there's no reason to pay Venture's load when you can get the same Davis style with no admission charge at Selected American. Ever since Chris joined Shelby as co-manager in 1994 and then assumed the reins of Selected American in 1997, he's played what his dad calls the best game in town—buying companies that can grow earnings at 15% or more annually but that sell at P/Es of 10 or so.

♦ **Smith Breeden Equity Market Plus** (Manager: John Sprow) Sprow uses a complex strategy that involves putting a portion of the fund's assets into S&P 500 futures contracts and then plowing much of the rest into mortgage-backed securities.

♦ **Sogen International** (Manager: Jean-Marie Eveillard) The perfect fund for soothing market jitters. The independent-minded Eveillard looks around the world for obscure issues that are selling at bargain prices. But Eveillard's chief goal is preserving capital.

♦ **Sound Shore** (Managers: Gibbs Kane, Harry Burn) "We like to go wherever Wall Street isn't," says Kane. He and Burn look for beaten-down growth stocks and overlooked jewels where others often choose not to look at all.

♦ **SSGA Emerging Markets** (Manager: Joshua Feuerman, team) The initials stand for State Street Global Advisors, a firm that specializes in quantitative investing strategies. In this case, Feuerman and his fellow quants rely on computer models to identify companies in emerging markets with expanding profits.

♦ **SSGA Growth & Income** (Manager: Emerson Tuttle, team) Another State Street Global Advisors quantitative fund, this one hunts down large companies whose earnings are growing faster than Wall Street expected.

♦ **Stein Roe Young Investor** (Managers: Erik Gustafson, David Brady) Launched in 1994, this fund was designed to put most of its money in companies that cater to teenagers and other children. The premise has done more than just attract youthful shareholders; it's led Brady and Gustafson to such stellar blue-chip performers as Disney and Coke as well as more off-beat kiddie stocks like Orthodontic Centers of America, up 26.5% in the first year since the fund bought it in 1997.

♦ **Strong Opportunity** (Managers: Dick Weiss, Marina Carlson) This duo hunt for midcap companies selling at a discount to the price they would fetch in a takeover.

♦ **Strong Schafer Value** (Manager: David Schafer) For Schafer, value means a stock that's growing faster than the S&P 500 but selling at a P/E lower than the index's. He limits volatility by investing no more than 2% of his assets in any one of his 50 or so stocks. And he keeps about 7% to 15% of assets in foreign issues.

♦ **Templeton Developing Markets 1** (Manager: Mark Mobius) With 30 years of experience, Mobius is the poster boy for emerging markets. Perpetually on the move, he scours the globe for stocks selling at discounts to their peers—and has one of the category's best long-term records to show for his efforts. His fund is definitely not for the timid investor. Mobius isn't afraid to pour money into embryonic markets, and the portfolio can get slammed. But if you buy the long-term case for emerging markets, no one knows them better than he.

♦ **Templeton Growth 1** (Manager: Mark Holowesko) A value-investing disciple of Sir John Templeton, Holowesko was among the first managers to recognize that corporate restructuring in Europe—like that in the U.S. in the mid-'80s—would send European shares soaring. Thanks to such insights, Templeton Growth's returns have consistently ranked in the top 10% of its peers over the past 10 years. Not bad, considering that Holowesko typically keeps 20% of assets in cash and Treasuries.

♦ **Torray** (Manager: Robert Torray) Torray typically invests in fewer than 50 stocks and plans to hold them indefinitely. Some of his picks may take a while to pan out, but his patience tends to pay off.

♦ **T. Rowe Price Dividend Growth** (Manager: William Stromberg) Stromberg's strategy of buying companies with solid earnings growth, reliable cash flow and rising dividends has generated gains close to those of the S&P 500 over the years while keeping the fund less volatile than its large-value peers.

♦ **T. Rowe Price Equity-Income** (Manager: Brian Rogers) "I've found that most investors don't want as much risk as they say they do," says

Rogers. So Rogers has run Equity-Income for more than 12 years with the goal of keeping volatility low. One way he limits risk is by latching on to otherwise sound stocks that have run into trouble—temporarily, he hopes. Loading up on slumping issues helps limit the damage to the fund when Rogers makes a mistake. "These stocks are already a disappointment," he says. "So even if we're wrong, they don't have much farther to fall." Of course, he made our list by being right far more often than he's wrong.

◆ **T. Rowe Price International Stock** (Manager: Team) This fund's seven managers take a cautious, highly diversified approach, holding 300 to 400 stocks in 33 countries. The long-term results of their conservative stance are tough to beat.

◆ **T. Rowe Price Mid-Cap Growth** (Manager: Brian Berghuis) One of the first managers to launch a fund devoted to medium-size growth stocks, Berghuis remains a master of that universe. His returns have ranked in the top 5% of midcap growth funds for years. Better yet, he achieved those results while taking less risk than 99% of his peers.

◆ **T. Rowe Price Small Cap Stock** (Manager: Gregory McCrickard) McCrickard took an unremarkable fund that T. Rowe bought from USF&G and in six years built a record that beat 80% of small-blend funds. He looks for small undervalued stocks as well as growth shares selling at reasonable prices, a mix that has helped keep the fund less volatile than almost all its peers.

◆ **Tweedy Browne American Value** (Managers: Chris Browne, Will Browne, John Spears) Tweedy's veteran trio snap up true-blue value stocks (mostly U.S. but up to 20% foreign) in a solid traditional style—typically, firms selling at extremely low P/E and price-to-book ratios. Given this mid-cap value fund's low turnover and its peer-beating record, it's a prime pick for taxable accounts.

◆ **Tweedy Browne Global Value** (Managers: Chris Browne, Will Browne, John Spears) This is the global version of Tweedy's American fund, collecting value stocks from around the world.

◆ **Vanguard Index 500** (Manager: George Sauter) With razor-thin expenses and a 23-year record, this is simply the best way to ride the S&P.

♦ **Vanguard International Growth** (Manager: Richard Foulkes) London-based Foulkes focuses on big foreign blue chips with brawny balance sheets and great growth potential, typically spreading his assets among 25 or more countries ranging from South America to the Netherlands to Japan.

♦ **Vanguard Specialized Health Care** (Manager: Edward Owens) You don't usually think of sector funds as models of stability, but this one is. Owens' tried-and-true risk reducer: Instead of making big bets on whichever health-care sector is hot, he spreads his assets across a range of firms, including drugmakers, hospital chains and medical-device manufacturers.

♦ **Vanguard U.S. Growth** (Managers: David Fowler, J. Parker Hall) Fowler and Hall look for large companies boosting earnings faster than the S&P 500 but selling for less than rival firms. The managers' skill at finding bargain growth stocks has paid off with remarkably consistent low-risk returns over 10 years.

♦ **Vanguard Windsor II** (Manager: James Barrow) Shunning the pricey growth issues, Barrow and his team look for stocks with low P/Es and high dividends. Barrow's philosophy: "Over time, good cheap stocks will rise in value."

♦ **Warburg Pincus Growth & Income** (Manager: Brian Posner) This fund was struggling when Warburg lured Posner from Fidelity Equity-Income II to turn it around. We're betting his strategy of buying out-of-favor stocks with strong cash flow can generate the kind of numbers that made him a star at Fidelity.

♦ **Wasatch Growth** (Manager: Samuel S. Stewart Jr.) Stewart, a finance professor at the University of Utah, has stashed nearly 40% of assets in tiny issues (average market value: $356 million) because he believes they offer the most growth at a reasonable price. His refusal to buy companies with unpredictable long-term earnings means that you won't find many tech stocks here.

♦ **Weitz Value** (Manager: Wallace Weitz) Warren Buffett's not the only wizard of Omaha. Weitz, who runs this fund out of the same city, has compiled a remarkable record, recently topping 87% of his peers over 10 years while registering lower volatility than 97% of them. It's not for style purists.

As Weitz has searched for stocks selling at discounts to their asset values, the fund has drifted from midcap blend to large growth to large value to midcap value status.

♦ **Westwood Equity** (Manager: Susan Byrne) "I'm not looking for companies that are already doing great," says Byrne, "just companies that are doing better than people think they should." To fill her portfolio of 50 or so stocks, Byrne starts with a 1,500-company universe of medium- and large-size names that she reviews quarterly, searching for firms that have just beaten analysts' earning estimates. Ideally, her choices have low debt and high return on equity. To keep risk low, Byrne tries to buy stocks that look cheap when measured by factors like price-to-sales ratios. The result is a portfolio packed with potential overachievers.

♦ **White Oak Growth Stock** (Manager: Jim Oelschlager) Jim Oelschlager worked in comfortable obscurity in Akron, managing billions of dollars for large institutions, until he launched White Oak Growth Stock in 1992. Then a three-year string of chart-topping returns made him a hot name in the fund business. Like Warren Buffett, Oelschlager puts a lot of money into a few good stocks. But unlike Buffett, Oelschlager has a taste for high-growth industries like technology. He rarely holds more than 25 issues, so a few big winners can turbocharge the fund. But his style makes for some bumpy rides too. White Oak is more volatile than about 90% of large-company growth funds, but it has delivered outsized rewards too.

BOOST YOUR YIELDS TODAY

If you count on income from your investments, you may feel as though you've taken a pay cut because since 1997, interest rates have sunk from a high of 7.17% to under 6%. "The easy 7% and 8% yields are gone," says Marilyn Cohen of Envision Capital management in Los Angeles. "Get over it." Instead, focus on this: With low inflation, you're doing okay. For example, at the time last year when inflation was 1.7% and interest rates were 5.9%, your after-inflation return on a 5.9% Treasury bond was around 4%—about the same real return you got when rates were at 7% and 8% and inflation was around 4%.

Treasuries, of course, have a lot to offer beyond yield. They are effectively defaultproof—your interest and principal are guaranteed if you hold until maturity. Further, they are exempt from state and local taxes. Depending on where you live, that's a break that can substantially boost what goes into your pocket.

One temptation to avoid: locking in today's rates for as long as possible because you think yields will keep declining. Longer-term issues don't usually pay you much more than short-term ones. And longer maturities mean more price volatility, which endangers your capital if you have to sell. Says Ian MacKinnon, head of fixed income for the Vanguard Group in Valley Forge, Pa.: "You give up basis points by putting your money in two- to 10-year securities instead of longer issues, but you also cut your risk almost in half."

To get maximum income with minimum risk, ladder your portfolio with maturities ranging between two and 10 years. Cohen suggests buying mostly five- to seven-year maturities. You'll save commission costs if you buy through your local Federal Reserve bank or call Treasury Direct in Washington, D.C.

Preferred stocks are worth your consideration too. Like bonds, preferreds deliver a fixed payout, are graded by the rating agencies for their financial security and can be called for redemption years before their maturity date. But, for today's income investor, they have two distinct advantages over bonds. Explains Richard Lehmann, publisher of the *Income Securities Advisor*: "Their yields are higher and they won't react as strongly if interest rates turn around."

As expert William Gross advised in the section "Wall Street's Picks and Predictions," you also should check out municipal bonds. Many are exempt from federal, state and local taxes, so your real return might beat Treasuries by a few points. But for safety's sake, confine yourself to issues with an A or higher investment-grade credit rating and stick to general-obligation, or G.O., bonds, which are backed by the taxing power of the city or state issuer. Mutual funds are the easiest way to buy these bonds.

SAFE HAVENS FOR MONEY YOU NEED SOON

Kip Rupple can hardly remember a day in the fall of 1997 when his heart wasn't in his throat. Rupple, the sales manager of a Ford dealership in Waukesha, Wis., and his wife Juliann were ready to build their dream house. They'd been salting away money every month for years. And with the market on a tear, they left that money in the aggressive Strong Opportunity fund, even though they knew there was a good chance they would soon need to make a big down payment.

Then the Asian crisis hit, and Rupple began to worry that he'd missed his chance to take his nest egg out of the market. "I'm not a rich man," he says. "If I'm down even $1,000, it makes a difference."

It could have made a big difference—at one point, Rupple was down 20%. But he held on, the market rebounded, and he got out with his shirt. In retrospect, he says the weeks of trepidation weren't worth it. "Had I been thinking," he says, "I probably would have pulled the money out earlier and moved it into savings."

Taking stock market risk is okay—in fact, it's essential—when you're money is earmarked for long-term use. But can you afford to gamble on the market when you're about to buy a house or pay the tuition?

We wouldn't. There are plenty of alternatives—not mattresses or passbook savings, but choices that will keep you ahead of taxes and inflation. Which you pick depends on how much you're investing, and when you'll need it back.

Up to six months. If you look hard enough, you can find competitive deals in both insured bank money-market accounts and money-market funds.

Six months to one year. If you're comfortable locking up your money, federally insured certificates of deposit are a good bet. But shop carefully. The average one-year CD was yielding 5.07% in late May last year, according to *Bank Rate Monitor*; at the same time, one bank was paying 6.03%.

Bond funds also merit consideration. But six months to one year puts you in ultra-short-term territory, and Morningstar analyst Eric Jacobson cautions that some top-ranking funds have taken on too much credit risk to make them suitable cash alternatives. So check out the fund carefully before you hand over your money. And if your tax bracket is 28%-plus, be sure to consider tax-exempt alternatives.

One to three years. Again, look at short-term bond funds. The **Vanguard Fixed Income Securities Short Term Corporate Portfolio** is a consistent standout, primarily because of its low expenses.

Prime Rate Funds also bear a look. These are pools of floating-rate bank loans that pay shareholders dividends. On the upside, they're quite stable.

On the down, they're fairly illiquid (you can usually sell just once a quarter). During 1998 the **Eaton Vance Classic Senior Floating Rate** had an effective yield of 7.06%. In the short term, you don't want to do any better than that.

A NEW TWIST TO SAVINGS BONDS

To boost the flagging sales of savings bonds, the Treasury Department has begun selling an inflation-indexed version. As with the 10- to 30-year inflation-indexed Treasuries on the market, the allure of the I-bond (as it's called) is a guarantee that your return will outpace inflation. With inflation low, the I-bond's payout is unlikely to beat that of a regular savings bond. But in times when inflation picks up, so will the bond's appeal.

I-bonds are similar to traditional Series EE savings bonds. They're sold by most banks and credit unions, and interest is exempt from state and local taxes. The difference lies in how the interest is calculated. The rate on a Series EE bond, which adjusts every six months, equals 90% of a five-year Treasury yield. Interest on the I-bond will equal the inflation rate plus a fixed rate of return. Once you buy an I-bond, that fixed rate stays the same until the bond stops earning interest after 30 years. But your total interest rate changes every May and November based on the current inflation rate.

"Because the I-bond's rate is reset every six months, there's a lot of upside potential," says industry expert Dan Pederson, author of *Savings Bonds: When to Hold, When to Fold and Everything in Between.* A guarantee that you'll beat inflation for the next 30 years is something bank savings accounts, certificates of deposit and other savings bonds can't match.

CUT ONLINE TRADING COSTS

The price wars and advertising blitzes launched by online brokers have made investors more cost-conscious than ever: $14.95 a trade! $8 a trade! Free trades! But these offers may have you wondering, "How exactly do these guys make money?"

Part of the answer, of course, is technology: Online brokers can process trades cheaply. But that's not the whole story. Online brokers, like their offline competitors, have creative ways to increase their revenues, sometimes at the expense of getting you the best price on your trade.

How cash flows online. A typical online brokerage makes a bit more than half of its revenue from commissions alone. Other sources include interest that is earned on margin loans and on the cash in client accounts. Then there's payment for order flow, the practice by which large stock-trading firms, called marketmakers, pay brokers for directing orders to them.

While payment for order flow looks a bit like a kickback, it's perfectly legal. The real problem for investors is that this practice provides an incentive for brokers and marketmakers to maintain wide spreads—the difference between a stock's "bid" (the price a dealer will pay) and its "ask" (the amount he'll accept to sell).

The marketmaker, a classic middleman, tries to buy a stock at the bid, say $20, and sell it immediately at the ask, perhaps $20.25. The difference is money in the bank. The larger the spread, the greater the marketmaker's cut and the easier it is for him to reward the brokers who steered him the trades—and the worse the price you get.

Plenty of traditional brokerages collect payment for order flow, but *almost every* online brokerage does, says Robert Battalio, a finance professor at Notre Dame. Payment averages a few bucks a trade. And order flow accounts for a far higher portion of an online broker's revenue—perhaps 15% to 20%—than an offline firm's, according to Piper Jaffray analyst Bill Burnham.

A limit order is your friend. Many investors try to cut the spread by using what's called a limit order, an order to execute a trade only at a specified price. (The more common use of a limit order is simply to set the maximum amount you'll pay for a stock. If the stock never drops to your target price, well, you'd already decided you didn't want to buy it at a higher price anyway.) You can place a limit order between the current bid and the ask, hoping to improve on the price you'd get with a market order, which instructs your broker to pay the prevailing price.

Let's say you wanted to buy a stock that had a bid of $20 and an ask of $20.25. If you place a limit order at $20.13, there's a good chance an impatient dealer will lower his ask price, saving you an eighth of a point.

How significant shaving the spread is depends on how much, how often and what kinds of stocks you trade. On 100 shares, shaving a dime nets a little. If you're trading 1,000 shares, it's a lot. Tougher SEC and NASD rules have narrowed spreads in recent years, especially for the largest, most popular stocks. But for a small, thinly traded company—say, an undiscovered $4-a-share Internet outfit that might appeal to the tech sensibilities of an online investor—the spread could be three-quarters of a point.

Even if your tastes run to more liquid stocks, online investors make perhaps twice as many trades as they did when they were offline (we're not recommending that, mind you, but it's reality). So if you're investing online, placing limit orders between the bid and ask is something you should think about. Brokers, however, hate limit orders. Some of the biggest online brokers charge an extra fee, usually $5, for limit orders, a practice that is virtually unheard of in the brick-and-mortar brokerage business. Now, $5 is not a lot of money, but if you are choosing brokers on the basis of price, you have to factor in this extra cost.

Whose interest? It's not hard to see why some brokers levy a surcharge. First, limit orders are more labor intensive. "We can execute a market order immediately," says Mike Anderson, president of Ameritrade. "But with a limit order, we have to put it on a shelf, so to speak, and check back to see if we can fill it every time a price moves. And if the order isn't fillable, we get no revenue at all."

Second, limit orders reduce brokers' take on order flow. Because limit orders tighten spread, marketmakers don't pay as well for them. Therefore, many online brokers levy a charge in order to dissuade you from a trade that might be in your best interest but not in the broker's.

Ameritrade president Anderson predicts that order-flow payment will disappear in a few years as spreads continue to tighten. Until that time, however, you can help the process along by using limit orders.

There are risks, however. Unlike market orders, no limit order is guaranteed—that's the benefit you give up by naming your price. It's possible that a fast-moving stock could entirely skip your price.

If you're going to buy a stock, get a real-time quote and try to get between the bid and ask prices by using a limit order. But don't let the spread, or lack thereof, dictate your decision. As James Angel, a finance professor at Georgetown, says, "It's okay to be cheap, but you'll wind up hurting yourself if you get greedy."

WALL STREET RESEARCH ON THE WEB

Financial Websites have been rolling out more sophisticated data and tools so fast that quarterly earnings numbers, fundamental data and price histories, real-time quotes, stock screeners and charting programs are now de rigueur on subscription sites and on more and more free ones.

The next frontier is genuine Wall Street research—the buy, sell and hold recommendations that are, for better or worse, what distinguish full-service brokers from discounters. But these initiatives so far have come with big limitations. The sites are mostly the handiwork of online brokerages, which provide only one company's opinion (its own, or an exclusive provider's) and carry either a hefty monthly subscription price or restrict access to customers with large balances. That has left the Web conspicuously missing a timely Wall Street stock report clearinghouse that's open to all investors.

Until now. Multex, a company that has provided a research clearinghouse to institutions for five years, recently launched the Multex Investor Network (www.multexinvestor.com), a paid site (with some neat freebies) that's designed to appeal to serious online investors. The heart of the site is a database of 200,000 research reports from 214 contributors, including brokerages such as Hambrecht & Quist, BT Alex. Brown and Everen Securities, as well as independent researchers Baseline and Value Line, among others.

After registering with your name, e-mail address and a password, you can search the database without charge. Type in a company's ticker symbol, select an industry category or highlight a research provider, and the site will return a free summary of analyst consensus on a stock, as well as a hit list of recent reports, giving the name of the research company and the report's date, length and title, which often indicates changes in recommendations or earnings estimates. If you find a report you want to buy, just click on its link, and you'll be led to the download process (most files are formatted for Adobe Acrobat). Price is generally determined by length; most reports are under five pages and sell for less than $25.

While the Multex network is a big step in the democratization of quality investing information, gaps do remain. For every top-performing research department that is in the network, there are others that aren't. And while the pay-per-download model can be a bargain, it takes discipline. You could easily rack up profit-destroying fees having Wall Street's mandarins double- and triple-vet your every move.

Happily, Multex has left an admirable stash of goodies available on the free part of its site. There are solid stories on market sectors, frequent updates on upgrades and downgrades, and investment ideas culled from analysts' top picks. These offerings make Multex worth a regular visit when doing investing research online.

♦ **CHAPTER 2**

BUILD UP A BIG, SAFE NEST EGG

ertain ideas are always worth emphasizing. Year after year, therefore, the *Money Adviser* has offered readers a valuable comparison to put them on the path to smart saving. Whether you're taking it in as new information or as a refresher, this example warrants your attention:

Suppose you set aside $500 a month for 30 years. If you stash it in a safe money-market fund that earns an average 6% a year, you'll end up with about $555,000. But what if you put that money in a growth-oriented blend of mostly stocks, plus bonds—or mutual funds that invest in those securities? With an average return close to 10% annually, a reasonable expectation for that portfolio over 30 years, you'll build a nest egg of $1 million. No problem, then, right? Why not go for gains that will just about double the money you'll have available in your retirement? Is there a catch? Well, yes, risk. The price for nearly doubling your return would be much greater uncertainty in the short run. With only a moderately risky growth portfolio, you should still be prepared to ride out market drops that could be as nerve-wracking as 20% over the course of several months or even weeks.

Risk is a key consideration in growing and guarding your nest egg. Whether you're just starting to amass your wealth or are within short range of retiring with it, this chapter will help you get the most out of your money. The important decisions you'll be making through the years will depend significantly on your age, where your financial assets are concentrated, the state of the economy and your tolerance for risk. The ups and downs of the stock and bond markets are two factors you should consider in investing your money. But you should also make gradual adjustments in your asset mix to match your changing needs for capital growth, steady income or a combination of both.

Your personal level of tolerance for risk is important. But it's critical, too, to know what chances to take at various stages of your life. The key to smart asset allocation is simple. Begin by carefully analyzing your investments and other aspects of your financial situation to determine the degree that each exposes you to the following types of risk.

Risk from inflation. When prices go up, the purchasing power of an investment goes down. For example, an annual inflation rate of 5% over 15 years will reduce the value of $1,000 to $480. Therefore, investors who are overcautious and hoard assets in low-yielding vehicles such as savings accounts and money-market funds may not earn enough to outpace rising prices. Rising inflation also lowers the value of future income generated by investments with fixed payments, most notably long-term bonds.

Risk from interest rates. Rising interest rates will cause investments to drop in price. Higher rates make yields on existing bonds less attractive, so their market values go down. Rising rates also hurt stocks by making their dividend yield less appealing. Moreover, risk will increase for people who invest borrowed money through margin accounts or have other kinds of floating-rate debt, because higher interest rates cut into their net profits.

Risk from the economy. Slower growth in the economy will cause investments to fall in price. It will have an impact on shares of small growth companies because they need a booming economy to maintain robust earnings gains. Cyclical companies, such as automakers and chemical producers, can't easily cut costs during a recession, so their stock prices may fall. And economic slumps can undercut junk bonds, issued by financially weak companies that might default.

Market risk. Political developments and Wall Street fads are among the factors that can hurt investment markets. Other contributors to market risk include tax-law changes, trade agreements, program trading and the idiosyncrasies of investor psychology; each helps account for much of the stock market's day-by-day volatility. Gold also carries considerable market risk because its price moves sharply when political or military upheavals in other nations encourage the flight of capital.

Specific risk. This covers occurrences such as poor management or bad luck that may affect only a specific company or industry; high-flying growth stocks are particularly vulnerable to earnings disappointments. You amass considerable specific risk when you buy stock in a company with a heavy debt burden or invest in specialty stock funds, often called sector funds because they concentrate their holdings in a single industry such as technology. Specific risk also includes the chance that government regulation will hurt a particular group of companies.

LEARN TO ASSESS YOUR ASSETS

Once you determine the major risks in your portfolio you can correct problems by redeploying assets. But when you take inventory, don't limit it to investments in your brokerage account. Your earning power may be your most valuable asset, and your home equity next best. You may have significant assets invested in a company pension plan or insurance policies with cash value. And if you own a business, you must assess any risks that could lower its value.

Risk can creep up on even vigilant investors. Your retirement-plan holdings may grow more quickly than you realize. And this success can be accompanied by a problem. That's because growth in one asset can throw a portfolio out of balance if other investments don't keep up. If a prolonged bull market boosts the value of your stockholdings, you may need to sell some shares to restore the balance between stocks and other assets. Correspondingly, if a single stock does extremely well, you have to consider whether it's time to sell some shares. Be especially on guard against loading up on your company's stock through retirement and savings plans. If the company runs into trouble, both your job and your stock could be endangered at the same time, and if you live in a one-company town the value of your home may also be tied to the fortunes of the firm.

To evaluate your own situation, you will need to conduct a survey of your investments and other aspects of your finances. Here's a rundown of the strengths and weaknesses of various assets.

Stocks and stock funds. They are vulnerable to the possibility that nervous investors will panic for some reason and drive down share prices. That's an example of market risk. There are other risks, too. Inflation, interest rates and the economy can affect different stocks in different ways. A boost in the inflation rate lowers stock prices because it may cut the purchasing power of future dividends to stockholders. Also, inflation usually coincides with higher interest rates, and they move investors from stocks to bonds. Because firms such as retailers, consumer-product manufacturers and service companies can pass along cost increases to customers relatively easily, they are more likely to prosper during periods of high inflation.

Slowing economic growth tends to hurt some firms more than others. Manufacturers with high overhead, known as cyclicals, cannot easily cut costs when a recession slices sales. So their earnings quickly tail off. Many small growth companies also require an expanding economy to sustain their earnings growth and stock prices. By contrast, firms that sell necessities such as food or clothing often shine in a lackluster economy, and their shares tend to hold up relatively well. Since overseas stocks are partly immune to changes in the American economy and markets, they may stand firm while U.S. stocks sink. Unlike domestic issues, however, foreign shares carry currency risk. A weaker dollar abroad helps to inflate returns that are earned on overseas assets, while a stronger dollar deflates them.

Bonds and bond funds. Their prices fall when interest rates rise. But the extent of the drop depends on a bond's maturity and the amount of its coupon. Short-term bonds fall slightly when interest rates move upward, and a high coupon also offers some protection against climbing rates. At the opposite extreme, zero-coupon bonds fall sharply when rates head higher. A recession generally brings lower interest rates, which boost bond prices. But some issues react negatively to the threat of an economic slowdown. So-called junk bonds, in particular, may lose ground because investors fear that financially weak firms will default and fail to make payments of interest and principal to bondholders on time. U.S. Treasury and high-grade corporate bonds gain the most during hard times because income investors seek them out as safe havens.

Real estate investments. Although they tend to keep pace with inflation over time, they present other hazards. For example, if you own a rental property, you run the risk that you won't find a tenant. A real estate partnership that owns several properties in different regions can reduce

RATE YOUR NEST EGG'S RISK EXPOSURE

Most people shield some of their fund investments against different types of risk. But few balance all of their assets so that they are well protected. This quiz can help you identify your points of vulnerability. With each question, you will accumulate points for one or more of the five major investment risks that are described in the main text. Write the points in the boxes below. Then total the points for each risk, and interpret your scores as follows: Fewer than five points is low. Five to 10 points is moderate. Above 10 points is high. While you may want to vary your exposure to different categories of risk, depending on your personal circumstances and outlook for the financial markets, any score that comes in above 10 points should set off alarm bells.

Once you have identified vulnerabilities, you can take steps to shore up your defenses. Say that you score high for inflation risk and low for market risk. You might balance your portfolio better by switching some cash from money-market funds to those invested in stocks. While your risk of a temporary decline in the value of your portfolio will increase, you will have a better chance of outpacing inflation.

In answering the questions, don't make the mistake of overlooking funds located in 401(k) accounts, IRAs or any other savings or deferred-compensation plans. It may be difficult to pin down the value of some assets. For instance, you may have a universal life policy with an important investment component. Just make the best estimates that you can. It isn't necessary to be exact. But it is important that your inventory be as complete as possible.

QUESTIONS

Questions	INFLATION RISK	INTEREST-RATE RISK	ECONOMIC RISK	MARKET RISK	SPECIFIC RISK
◆ Are your assets diversified among fewer than four of these five categories—stocks, real estate, gold, bonds and cash? If yes, score one point for each risk.					
◆ Are more than 35% of your assets invested in any one of the five categories? If yes, score one point for each risk.					
◆ Is at least 10% of your portfolio in assets such as gold, natural-resource stocks or high-grade collectibles such as rare stamps? If no, score one point for inflation risk.					
◆ Is at least 30% of your portfolio in investments such as growth stocks and real estate, which are likely to produce long-term capital gains that can outpace inflation? If no, score two points for inflation risk.					
◆ Are your real estate and gold investments held primarily in assets such as gold-mining shares and REITs (real estate investment trusts), which tend to fluctuate with the stock market? If yes, score one point for market risk.					
◆ Do you generally keep at least 15% of your portfolio in cash equivalents such as Treasury bills or money-market funds? If no, score two points for interest-rate risk.					
◆ Is more than 30% of your portfolio composed of assets such as long-term government bonds, CDs (certificates of deposit) or annuities that promise investors fixed payments over a period of many years? If yes, then score three points each for inflation and interest-rate risk.					

	INFLATION RISK	INTEREST-RATE RISK	ECONOMIC RISK	MARKET RISK	SPECIFIC RISK
◆ Do highly volatile zero-coupon bonds account for more than 30% of your fixed-income assets? If yes, score two points each for inflation and interest-rate risk.					
◆ Do small growth stocks or junk bonds, which may fall sharply in a recession, account for more than 25% of your portfolio? If yes, score three points for economic risk.					
◆ Do you switch money among different assets to try and catch the highs and lows of different investment markets? If yes, score two points for market risk.					
◆ Do you use dollar-cost averaging or a similar plan that involves adding money to your investment portfolio at regular intervals? If no, score two points for market risk.					
◆ Is more than 20% of your portfolio concentrated in a single industry? If yes, score three points each for economic risk, market risk and specific risk.					
◆ Do stocks or bonds issued by one company (including the one that you work for) or shares in a single mutual fund or limited partnership account for more than 15% of your assets? If yes, score three points each for economic risk, market risk and specific risk.					
◆ Does your share in a privately held business account for more than 30% of your portfolio? If yes, score one point for economic risk and four points for specific risk.					
◆ Does a rental property account for more than 30% of your portfolio? If yes, score one point for economic risk and three points for specific risk.					
◆ Do foreign stocks and shares of domestic companies with significant overseas sales account for less than 10% of your portfolio? If yes, score one point for economic risk.					
◆ Will you need access in the next three to five years to principal in volatile assets such as stocks or long-term bonds? If yes, score one point each for inflation, interest rate, economic and market risk.					
◆ Do you have variable-rate loans such as mortgages or credit-card revolving debt that recently has amounted to 30% or more of the market value of your portfolio? If yes, score four points for interest-rate risk.					
◆ Is 20% or more of your portfolio financed by loans or invested in highly leveraged assets such as options? If yes, score one point each for interest-rate and market risk.					
TOTAL					

such risks through diversification, but it may lose value if tax changes or a recession drive down property values across the country. REITS (real estate investment trusts) and the funds that own them can fluctuate with the stock market as well as with property values.

Gold and other hard assets. The price of gold can shoot upwards during periods of rising inflation. For example, between 1968 and 1988 the consumer price index showed nine annual spurts of 6% or more. During those years, gold rewarded investors with an average gain of 34%. Gold-mining stocks are more volatile than the metal itself and expose investors to other risks. A miners' strike might boost the price of bullion but cut profits at mining companies. Other tangibles present their own problems. While antiques or rare stamps may outpace inflation in the long run, prices of items such as baseball cards are largely subject to collectors' whims.

WINNING PORTFOLIOS ALL OF YOUR LIFE

Why does asset allocation determine most of an investor's returns? According to researchers, the basic reason is that different types of investments don't rise and fall at the same time. By diversifying among stocks, bonds or cash, you can usually offset losses in one asset category with gains in another. For example, in October 1987, when stocks plummeted nearly 22%, long-term bonds rose 6%. The opposite proved true in 1994. Bonds tumbled 3%, while the S&P 500 eked out a 1% gain. While diversification can't guarantee that you'll never lose money, it can reduce your portfolio's overall risk and dramatically improve your odds of reaching your investment goals.

To determine the most efficient mix of investments for a retirement portfolio, experts first look at the correlation among various asset classes. Correlation is the technical term for comparing how different assets perform relative to one another over varying market cycles. You ideally want to build a portfolio of assets that are not closely correlated to one another. That way, you won't get clobbered by all your investments dropping in value at approximately the same time.

What's more, a properly diversified portfolio lets you put some of your money in potentially high-paying assets that otherwise might be too risky. You perform this alchemy by combining them with investments to which the high fliers are only weakly correlated. For example, a portfolio entirely invested in the large domestic stocks that make up the S&P 500 would have gained over 14% a year over the two decades from 1977 to 1997. But you could have earned 16% over the same time with a portfolio invested 65% in S&P 500 stocks, 20% in overseas stocks and 15% in small-company shares. In allocating assets, the pros rely not only on stocks' and bonds' past performance but also on estimates of their potential future returns. These predictions are based on forecasts of how market cycles will affect the performance of different asset classes.

How your goals change. As you grow older, start a family and move closer to retirement, your investment goals and taste for risk change. Your portfolio should change along with you. Younger people, for example, can afford to aim for high returns with aggressive portfolios because they have many years to recover from market slumps. But as you get closer to retirement, you need to shift to a more cautious allocation that will preserve your gains. There's a second, equally powerful argument in favor of asset allocation. Academic studies show that about 90% of investors' returns come from the right combination of assets, with the remainder derived from their skill in picking securities and from timely trading. To help you design your own allocation, MONEY surveyed many experts to devise a model portfolio for each of the four major stages in most people's working lives— starting out, building a family, peak earning years and nearing retirement (depicted on pages 72 to 75). Of course, the portfolios described here are only rough guidelines. You should customize your allocations to meet special needs.

Aim high in your 20s to early 30s. At this freewheeling stage, you have about 30 years before early retirement. So you can afford to gun for growth by stashing at least 80% of your portfolio in stocks and stock funds. Go for as much as 100% if you feel comfortable riding out market swings. Those who tend to get queasy in roller-coaster markets might put as much as 25% of their money in bonds and bond funds, which pay interest income that will help stabilize their portfolios. Based on long-term performance, this 75-25 lineup has the potential to return 9% annually.

For beginners with small savings, a single mutual fund that buys large-company stocks is a sound choice. Blue chips tend to offer solid capital appreciation with less volatility than smaller stocks. Nervous investors might want to opt for a balanced or asset-allocation fund instead. These all-in-one fund portfolios typically keep about 60% of their assets in stocks and the rest in

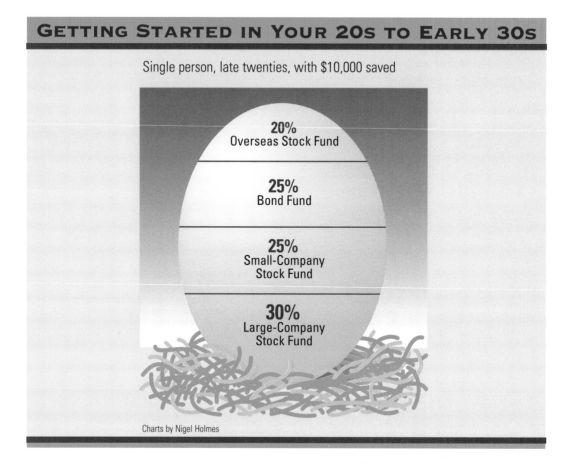

Single person, late twenties, with $10,000 saved

20%
Overseas Stock Fund

25%
Bond Fund

25%
Small-Company
Stock Fund

30%
Large-Company
Stock Fund

Charts by Nigel Holmes

risk-cushioning bonds and other fixed-income investments. Investors who have $10,000 or more ought to assemble a diversified portfolio of funds. Allocate about 30% of your assets to large-company stocks, 25% to small-company stocks and 20% to overseas stocks. Small stocks historically have outpaced their big brothers, though with greater volatility. Overseas stocks can spice up your portfolio because some foreign economies are likely to grow faster than ours over the next decade. The risks you face are political instability and adverse swings in the value of the dollar. But if you can hold on through the downturns, your retirement fund could benefit greatly in the long run.

For a smoother ride to those higher returns, you might include both value and growth-stock funds in your portfolio. Value managers look for out-of-favor companies with share prices that do not fully reflect their earnings prospects or asset values. By contrast, growth-stock managers, as the name suggests, prefer companies with rapidly accelerating revenues and

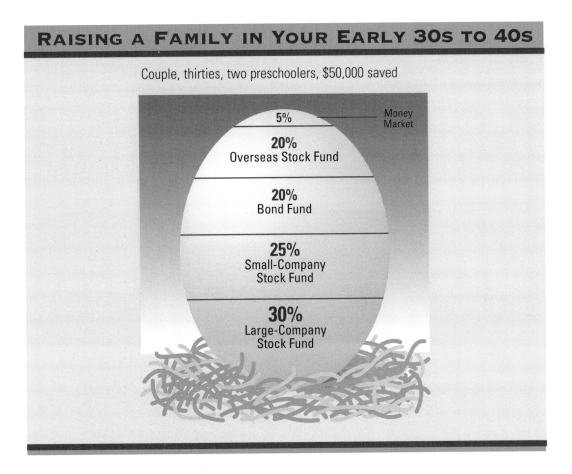

Couple, thirties, two preschoolers, $50,000 saved

5% —————— Money Market

20%
Overseas Stock Fund

20%
Bond Fund

25%
Small-Company
Stock Fund

30%
Large-Company
Stock Fund

earnings, even though their shares typically will command premium prices. You can't really predict which investing style will be more successful in any given year. Studies show that over periods of 20 years of more, however, value has a slight performance advantage over growth.

As for your fixed-income holdings, put about 15% of your money in investment-grade bonds with intermediate maturities of five to 10 years. Studies show that five-year issues produce 96% of the return of 30-year issues with only half the volatility. About 5% of your money should go into a convertible bond fund, which will give you a shot at capital gains, or to a high-yield fund, which takes on extra risk in pursuit of the fatter yields paid by junk bonds. But steer clear of bond funds that carry sales charges or fees that total more than 1% of net assets. Their managers generally can't overcome these high expenses with superior performance. Fees are listed in a fund's prospectus.

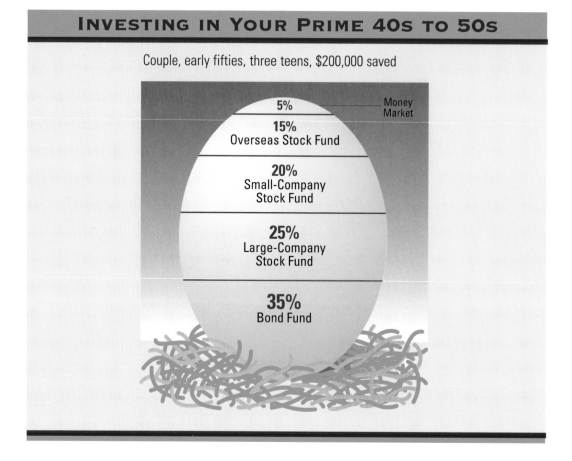

Couple, early fifties, three teens, $200,000 saved

5% — Money Market

15%
Overseas Stock Fund

20%
Small-Company
Stock Fund

25%
Large-Company
Stock Fund

35%
Bond Fund

Bankroll a family in your early 30s to 40s. With young families to provide for and mortgages to pay off, many investors in this age group prefer to reduce their portfolios' risk level. Just don't overdo it. You will be working for another 20 years or more, so you should keep at least 75% of your money in stocks. You can achieve that balance by gradually trimming back your stock funds and moving the excess cash to a money-market fund. Overall, our model is designed to give you average returns of about 8% annually. At this stage, you should further diversify your bond holdings. High earners should consider transferring the money in their convertible or high-yield corporate bond fund to a tax-free municipal bond fund and adding enough money so that it becomes 10% of the portfolio. A taxable alternative is an international bond fund. Fixed-income markets in the U.S. and abroad generally move in different directions, so you will offset a falling market with one that is on the rise. Foreign bond funds, of course,

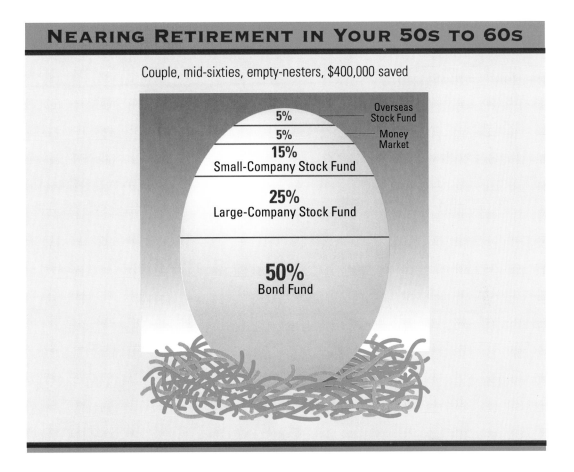

Couple, mid-sixties, empty-nesters, $400,000 saved

5% — Overseas Stock Fund

5% — Money Market

15% Small-Company Stock Fund

25% Large-Company Stock Fund

50% Bond Fund

can respond sharply to currency fluctuations. But the swings will likely even out if you can let your money ride for at least 10 years.

Hit stride in your early 40s to 50s. You have reached your peak earning years—just in time to pay your kids' college bills. Don't let that serve as an excuse to neglect your savings. Stocks should still be the center-piece of your portfolio. But ease back on risk by reducing your exposure to large-company stocks to about 25%, small-caps to 20% and overseas stocks to 15%. This model aims to provide you with average returns of around 8% annually. You can add greater stability to your portfolio by emphasizing value funds. Since value funds focus on bargain-priced companies, they tend to fall less far than their high-flying growth peers during market cor-rections. And the stocks in value funds tend to pay dividends that will bol-ster your returns in down years. In the fixed-income portion of your portfolio, you might seek additional security by cutting international bonds to 5% and exchanging your intermediate-term corporate bond fund for one that holds government issues. Investors in the 28% tax bracket or above, however, will probably do better with tax-exempt bonds. To earn high returns with minimum risk, look for muni funds with annual fees of less than 1% that hold mainly bonds rated A or higher.

Kick back in your early 50s to 60s. With retirement around the corner, you may be tempted to cash in your stock funds and tuck the proceeds into principal-preserving bond funds or bank CDs. That could prove to be a bad move for most MONEY readers. At 50 you still have a lifetime of at least 30 years ahead of you. If inflation were to run 3% a year, that would cut the purchasing power of today's dollar in half in only 12 years. Thus you should still hold a roughly 45% stake in stocks. Such a model portfolio should produce average returns of around 7% a year. In addition, this period of your life is an excellent one in which to move out of international bonds entirely and into U.S. Government issues for greater safety. Truly risk-averse investors might anchor their portfolios with Treasury notes, which mature in two to 10 years, because their principal and interest payments are federally guaranteed. You can opt for a Treasury-only bond fund. But odds are you can do just as well purchasing the Treasuries directly from the Federal Reserve Bank with no fee. We think that's a good deal for investors in any phase of life.

SECRETS OF SUPER STOCK PICKERS

Even at moments when investors face harsh uncertainties, there are a select few who, undistracted by extreme swings in the Dow or the long bond or the yen, can see beyond all the clutter. Instead these individuals forge ahead, making great investing decisions. They are the superstars—the seers, the stock pickers, the money managers who year after year make the right moves. Here, in brief, is what they said in MONEY interviews about how they pick stocks.

The prince. Prince Alwaleed Bin Talal Bin AbdulAziz Alsaud of Saudi Arabia is one of the world's greatest investors. He's made billions investing in everything from Citicorp stock (the $59 million he committed in 1991 was worth $5 billion by 1998) to EuroDisney, Four Seasons Hotels and Apple

Computer. Prince Alwaleed always buys his merchandise on sale. In fact, he may be the world's foremost bottom fisher.

Q. Your Highness, how do you pick companies?
A. We always like to go for a company that has international brands. In other words, it has to be well known, like a Citicorp or Saks Fifth Avenue. But most likely it will be facing difficulties, because of economic crises or cyclical events or new competition.

Q. How do you know that these companies are going to turn around, rather than go bankrupt?
A. Well, this obviously depends on the analysis that we do. Because if a company sometimes is doing bad, it may still do even worse. But you have to understand one thing: When the market penalizes a company, it overpenalizes it. Sometimes it gets hammered badly, in a way that does not correspond to the negative event that has taken place.

Q. Let's talk about some of your U.S. stocks. How in the world did you know Apple was a good buy in 1997? A lot of people said this company is dead.
A. Apple is a typical example of what I do. It's a company I have always liked and admired, and it's an incredible name. Apple is an incredible brand. It has customer loyalty, which is very crucial. It produces good products. So I was waiting for the company to put its house in order.

The legend. Peter Lynch doesn't actively manage money anymore, but you'd better believe his moves are worth watching. Even in quasi-retirement, he keeps a sharp eye on the markets. Lynch was at the helm of Fidelity Magellan for exactly 13 years—from May 31, 1977 to May 31, 1990—and during his tenure, the fund outperformed the S&P 500 2,703% to 573%. Not bad.

Lynch is famous for suggesting that small investors can keep up with the professionals by buying what they know. In other words, if Joe Palooka sees a new type of ice cream flying off the shelves at his local supermarket, he should buy the stock of the company that makes it.

Some have criticized Lynch for this theory, saying that it's 1) too simplistic and 2) specious, since he has had armies of professional analysts helping him. We asked him about those criticisms. "Some people have misunderstood and taken what I have said about this to an extreme," he said.

"You can't buy a stock simply because you see a lot of people buying a product. It's a starting point. But it's a good starting point. If you went to a mall a few years ago, you would have seen the Gap or Wal-Mart or Circuit City. If you do payrolls, you know about ADP. Networking people know about Cisco Systems. For a while I blew it in the mutual fund business. Here I was, sitting right in the middle of this great boom, and I didn't buy Federated and Dreyfus. As far as help from analysts goes, I visited all the automakers myself back in the 1980s; the leading auto analyst hated them, came out against them the week I bought Chrysler." (Chrysler, you may remember, proved to be a huge winner for Lynch.)

The trader. James Cramer appears on dozens of TV shows, writes scores of articles and columns, is co-chairman of TheStreet.com, a fast-rising online business-news service. And, oh yes, he's one great stock picker. In ten years from 1988 to 1998, his $300 million hedge fund had a compound annual rate of return of 24% vs. 15% for the S&P 500.

Q. Jim, when the market began tumbling in late August 1998, you likened the situation to the bear market of 1990. What does that mean?

A. It means you've gotta be really careful. Like 1990, there would come a point when it would be time to buy. But most people would never catch the bottom. So you want to own only the highest-quality stocks and know that you're still going to take some pain. If you are already long on the great ones, stay long. But don't commit any cash.

Q. When you say "the great ones," what do you mean?

A. You have to be able to find the McDonald's and avoid the Boston Chickens, buy the Nikes and skip the L.A. Gears. You don't need to go to business school to do this. You can weed out the flashes in the pan, asking yourself, "Am I certain this company is going to be around in five or 10 years?" I trade, but I also buy and hold. My big picture ideas apply to everyone.

Q. What specifically do you look for?

A. Companies that have proprietary, not commodity, businesses: repeat business, an unassailable franchise, a company that can control pricing. And let's talk about companies that are actually making money, unlike an Amazon.com. Wall Street is looking for execution. That means a company must produce quarter after quarter—it must hit its earnings. Quality growth stocks over time are hard to beat for retail investors.

Q. Are you also looking at trends?
A. Oh, yeah, that works. Look at the U.S. ascendance in financial services. Only three U.S. banks are among the 25 largest banks in the world. By the year 2002 I expect that the first eight will be American. So you can own BankBoston, NationsBank. Or look at autos, where there is also a U.S. ascendance. So you can own Chrysler and Ford. In technology, it's the same thing, so you want to own Microsoft and Intel.

The value guy. Michael Price, fund manager, value investor and CEO cage-rattler extraordinaire, announced last fall that he would never run a mutual fund again. But it's hard to imagine a guy like Price not following the market's every twitch. That and the fact that he has a personal fortune of some $700 million to watch over.

Q. Have you changed the way you pick stocks?
A. No. At various points since 1992, other value guys have said that the market's overpriced. But we have never had a market view. We just came to work every day trying to find opportunities. We found them for a while in the U.S., but as stocks got more and more expensive in '93, '94, '95, '96, more and more of our new cash went over to Europe. We've found tremendous bargains in Europe. We have situations in Europe that are so cheap it reminds me of 1974-75 here. We wait for disasters. We wait for earnings disappointments and we wait for opportunities. If we don't find them, we sit on the cash.

The techie. Ann Winblad is one of Silicon Valley's pre-eminent venture capitalists. She founded her own software company in 1975 on a shoestring, then sold it seven years later for $15 million. These days, she and partners John Hummer, Mark Gorenberg and Bill Gurley run the venture-capital firm Hummer Winblad, which manages $200 million, invested exclusively in software companies.

Demand for technology, Winblad believes, is insatiable. In 1980, nearly 20% of corporate capital spending went to information technology. Today, it's more like 40% and climbing every month. "And the percent of disposable consumer spending going toward technology also looks like a hockey stick over the past 17 years," Winblad says. Because of the burgeoning service business of the Internet, there is almost no limit to this growth in technology, she says. "We are now using digital tools to create efficiencies through the Internet. There is less and less need for bricks and mortar."

Ten years ago, creating a software business was about writing code. Today, Winblad says, it is about coming up with a new way of conducting transactions on the Net. And that is what she looks for in companies. Check out some of the still private companies that Winblad is bankrolling: The Knot, an online wedding registry. No reason to slog out to some department store; with The Knot, you can shop for your friend's wedding online, choosing gifts from a variety of stores. Or National Transportation Exchange, an online service that matches cargo with trucks, ensuring full loads. Or IMX, an Internet mortgage exchange between brokers and bankers.

HOW TO KNOW WHEN TO SELL STOCK

Should I sell my stock? It's the toughest question you face as an investor. And chances are you don't get the answer right as often as you would like. Individual investors routinely "sell winners too early and ride losers too long," wrote researchers Hersh M. Sheffrin and Meir Statman in a 1985 *Journal of Finance* article. They concluded that investors often succumb to fears of loss and regret when making sell decisions. People who don't want to make paper losses "real" hold on to poor performers, and those who don't want to regret a missed opportunity for profits sell winners. A study in 1997 by Terrance Odean, a professor at the University of California-Davis, supports this thesis. Odean analyzed the records of 10,000 accounts at a discount brokerage firm over a seven-year period that ended in 1993. The stocks that investors sold, Odean found, outperformed the stocks they kept by 3.4 percentage points during the following 12 months.

But don't feel bad. The pros struggle with selling too. Want to humble a $2 million-a-year fund manager? Ask about his sell strategy. He laughs nervously, swears he has one, then admits, half seriously, that every sell decision he's ever made is a bad one.

Still, there are times when even the most devout buy-and-hold practitioner can't help thinking about selling. Perhaps a couple of your stocks have posted outsize gains and now represent a big chunk of your holdings. Maybe you're near a goal—college tuition, retirement, a second home—and you need to trim risk. Or you're wondering if this year's losers can rebound. Or you're just doing an annual, semiannual or monthly portfolio review.

Whatever your reason for pondering a sale, don't look at a stock's price and ask simply whether you should unload it. Instead, take time to pose questions and search for answers about the stock's prospects. To help you in your evaluation, we interviewed two dozen of the best fund managers about their sell strategies—and how those disciplines might apply to individual investors who have a long-term focus. We didn't turn up any foolproof formulas, but knowing the kinds of questions these pros ask themselves can help make you a more disciplined, and successful, investor. We've constructed five familiar scenarios that are likely to prompt you to think about selling. A discussion of each follows.

My stock is up big. Does it still offer me what it did a year ago? Is it too big a piece of my portfolio? This is the kind of sell dilemma we would all like to face. Oakmark Select Fund manager William Nygren says you should always have in mind a target price you feel reflects the potential you saw when you bought the stock. Some managers swear by these sell targets. They hit one and get out. But that often leaves money on the table, and individuals—remember—tend to cut loose their winners too quickly. Nygren sees the target "not so much as an absolute sell signal, but as a benchmark when periodically re-evaluating your investment rationale." If earnings come in better than expected, he says, "or if similar companies sell for more than expected in the private market, raise your target."

Another exit strategy comes from Ariel Growth Fund manager John Rogers. He thinks the time to get out is when everyone else is getting in. "We rely on all sorts of benchmarks that individuals can use," says Rogers, a value investor. "If a stock starts showing up on a lot of brokerage firm buy lists, or if a lot of fund companies start owning it, or if the company gets mentioned a lot on television or in newspapers or magazines, we start selling."

If you have a stock that's gone up eight times over, it probably represents more of your holdings than prudence dictates. Charles Mayer, manager of Invesco Industrial Income Fund, says he never lets a stock amount to more than 3% of his portfolio. That translates into a minimum portfolio of 33 stocks. Most benefits of asset allocation can be gained with fewer than 20 stocks, and you likely don't have time to keep tabs on many more. So you may set a higher limit than 3%, but we suggest no higher than 10%.

That doesn't mean you dump a stock that's been great to you. Selling a winner isn't an all-or-nothing proposition. Say a stock has doubled or tripled, but you're worried that it may be too expensive. In that situation, says John McStay, manager of Brazos/JMIC Small Cap Growth Portfolio, "we'll cut our position in half. We've locked in a profit but can still benefit if the stock keeps rising."

Remember, though, that when you sell a winner, you're going to give up a big chunk of your gain in taxes (unless you're trading in a tax-deferred account). "We give a stock a haircut when we think about selling it," says Chris Davis, manager of Davis New York Venture Fund. "If we bought it at $20 and it's now at $100, then we think as if we're really selling it for $84 [$100 minus $16, or the 20% tax on $80 in capital gains]. If we'd buy it at that price, then we should not be selling it."

Correspondingly, to come out ahead, your next stock not only has to outperform the old one—it has to beat it by enough to recoup your tax bill and transaction costs as well. Generally, the bigger the gain you have in a stock, the more reluctant you should be to pull the trigger. Let's say, for example, you own a stock that has quadrupled in value over several years, from $10,000 to $40,000, giving you a $30,000 gain. If you sell that stock and pay brokerage commissions and a 20% capital-gains tax on the profit, you'll have less than $34,000 to reinvest (depending on brokerage costs). A new investment would have to earn roughly 15% more per year, over five years, than your old one would to make the switch worthwhile. By contrast, if you had a 50% gain in your original $10,000 stake, the tax bite ($1,000) would be far smaller, so a replacement investment would have to earn only 6% more annually to put you ahead.

My stock is falling. Is it temporary? Should I buy more? Or is there a long-lasting problem? Odean's study suggests that the biggest mistake people make is hanging on to losers. But panic is an investor's enemy, and buying on dips—"averaging down" your purchase price—is a time-tested investing method. What do you do? Here are a couple of strategies to consider.

McStay generally sells a stock if it declines 20%. If the market is falling, he'll cut his losers more slack, but in a strong market, even a 10% decline may prompt him to bail. "We have learned," says McStay, "that our inclination is to make a mistake that we call 'macho analysis'—to tell ourselves that as soon as the rest of the world knows what we know, the stock will come back."

Because you, unlike most fund managers, don't have to chase short-term performance numbers, a rigid sell rule may not be a necessity. But be careful not to commit the sin of pride that McStay's dump rule is designed to avoid. That leads us to a second strategy: If a stock drops 15% or more in a flat to rising market, re-evaluate. Do you have real doubts about its long-term prospects? There's no easy answer, of course, but if you conclude that your loser isn't coming back, you can take some solace in the tax break that selling it will bring. Uncle Sam allows you to offset capital gains with investment losses in the same year and, if you don't have any gains, you can apply as much as $3,000 of losses against ordinary income or carry them forward for use in another year.

My stock is going nowhere. Should I be doing something better with my money? The question of how long to wait for a stock to soar is especially relevant to investors who don't always have cash to invest in their next big idea. "Often my decision to sell is prompted by a desire to buy something else," says Mariko Gordon, manager of the Daruma Mid-Cap Value Fund.

Selling middling performers to make room for better ones drives the organization structure at Brandywine Fund, whose two dozen research analysts are divided into eight teams that vie for the fund's asset base. You don't have eight teams of analysts, but you can still conduct an internal competition for your money. If you conclude you don't have a better idea, consider spreading the money tied up in your going-nowhere stock among your existing best ideas, if that won't overly concentrate your portfolio. Or just sit tight. An idea will come.

My stock has done okay, but some of the fundamentals have changed. Investors pay too much attention to news events that have little to do with a company's value, says Richard Howard, manager of T. Rowe Price Capital Appreciation Fund. In particular, he thinks the significance of political events and changes in company management tend to get overblown.

The key is to discriminate between meaningful developments and temporary distractions. Here are two fundamental shifts that you absolutely must heed: changes in a company's core business and a falloff in its market position. The former are especially common now, given corporate America's merger-and-acquisition binge. Has the company you're looking at, by acquisition or divestiture, changed its focus? In that case, it isn't really the stock you bought. In 1994, Ariel Growth's Rogers invested in Harte-Hankes, a diversified communications company. But in 1998 he sold (after a better than 230% gain) because the company shed its TV and newspaper operations to focus on direct marketing. "Direct marketing is hot," explained

Rogers, but "our reason for ownership is gone." As to acquisitions, Mayer of Industrial Income looks for any signal that a recent purchase has dulled the acquirer's edge. Mayer bought Union Pacific in 1995 at $44 "because it was the best-run railroad in the country. But after they bought Southern Pacific in 1996, we starting hearing of problems with congestion and maintenance." He sold it at about $64.

The market is in a free fall. Any wise investor recognizes that an investment lifetime will include market downturns as well as bona fide bear markets—and probably several of them. Still, sudden shifts precipitate fear. We view such a period as a chance to remind ourselves what our investing goals are and to make sure that we haven't moved too far away from them. We're not going to abandon our basic principles—that stocks are the best long-term investment, that buying and holding good companies is far wiser than frantically shuffling in and out of the market. But we also recognize that unless your nerves are so steely or your portfolio so huge that you simply shrug off the market's gyrations, you'll ask yourself, "Should I sell?"

There's no one-size-fits-all answer. There are valid reasons for many investors to consider selling holdings during a market downturn, including the staples mentioned earlier. Start by figuring out how much of your portfolio you're really comfortable having in stocks or stock funds. Lured by the steady upward march of share prices the past few years, some investors viewed stocks as turbocharged bank CDs and committed assets where they simply didn't belong. If you still have money in stocks that you may need within three years—for college bills, a house down payment, emergencies— consider a market setback a wake-up call and cash out, even if means taking a loss. "There's an overwhelming temptation to try to get back to even," says James Stack, editor of the *InvestTech Market Analyst* newsletter. "But keeping money in stocks to recover losses isn't investing, it's gambling."

Even prudent investors may be inadvertently overloaded with stocks, thanks to the market's surge of the past few years. Let's say you started out in January 1995 with 75% of your money in equities and 25% in bonds, and that you let all your gains ride through late September 1998. Since stocks on average returned more than three times what bonds did over that period, your portfolio would have rejiggered to consist of almost 85% equities and 15% bonds. So just when you were probably most concerned about stock prices falling, you would have been holding a much riskier mixture than the one you started out with. In such a case, you need not necessarily start shedding stocks, which could trigger taxes. First, try plowing new cash you're investing (including dividends and interest) into bonds, to get you back to your target mix. "Why take a tax hit if you don't have to," advises American Association of Individual Investors president John Markese.

You also should consider whether your investment losses will be more valuable if you sell. This may be the most complicated reason to sell, but that doesn't make it any less worthwhile. Let's say, for example, that you've got a $10,000 gain in one stock. Realizing that gain by selling would incur a tax bill of as much as $2,000 if you've held the stock for more than a year, or as much as $3,960 if you've held it a year or less and you're in the top income tax bracket. But sell a stock where you have a $10,000 loss, and the two cancel each other out—eliminating the entire tax bill on your winner. The tax savings reduces the impact of your $10,000 setback to as little as $6,040.

That's why, when it comes time to dial back your exposure to stocks, the best place to start is among your losers. (If you still think the investment makes sense, you can sell, take the loss, wait at least 31 days, then buy it back.) Then you pair those losers with winners of equal value. The tax code requires that you start by pairing long-term losses (on investments held more than a year) against long-term gains, and short-term losses (investments held a year or less) against short-term gains. Once you've done that, you can mix short-term and long-term gains and losses. In years when most or all of your gains are short term, your best move is to use long-term losses to offset as many of those gains as possible. That way, you shield gains that are taxable at rates of as high as 39.6% with losses that would otherwise offset winners taxable at no more than 20%.

Obviously, you could end up with more losses than gains. Not to worry, at least not from a tax standpoint. As we said earlier, if your realized losses in any year exceed the realized gains on your investments, you can apply up to $3,000 of the losses against your ordinary income, saving you $930 if you're in the 31% tax bracket. And if you still haven't exhausted the loss, you can carry it forward as many years as necessary to use it up.

Ultimately, of course, a decision to sell should depend less on whether a stock has made or lost money for you than on what the company's prospects are. If a stock's been hammered but you still believe the company's underlying business is sound, holding on may be the smartest move. On the other hand, even if a stock has treated you well, the only issue should be whether it's still worth owning at its current price. "It's best to divorce the sell decision from past performance," says Morningstar analyst Haywood Kelly. "The main question to ask yourself is, 'Would I buy this stock today?'"

Granting company stock options to nonexecutives is catching on in corporate America. Options are so complex, however, it's easy to make mistakes when cashing them in. Here are three questions to ask yourself before exercising your options.

Do I need the money now, or can I wait to maximize my return?
Typically, you become eligible to cash in 20% of your options a year after you receive them, another 20% the following year and so on; you have 10 years to exercise them from the date they were granted. You profit when the market price of the shares at the time you sell them exceeds their exercise, or the price at which the company allows you to buy them. (The strike price is usually the market price at the time you received the options.) If the market price of the shares falls below the exercise price, your options are worthless.

Conventional wisdom holds that you should sit on your stock options as long as possible, assuming that you expect the stock to climb. Odds are that you'll snare bigger profits this way than if you cash in and invest after-tax proceeds elsewhere.

However, there are reasons to cash in options earlier. For instance, if the options (based on today's stock price) make up more than 25% of your investments, consider cashing in some of them to diversify your portfolio and reduce risk. Another good reason: You've lost confidence in the company's prospects.

Will cashing in my options bump up my tax bracket?
Most employees outside of the executive suite receive nonqualified stock options that are taxed as ordinary income. Your tax bill will depend on where you live and your federal income tax bracket, but generally, you should expect to turn over about 40% of your options' profits to the government. The key is to plan ahead so you don't give Uncle Sam a penny more than necessary.

What do I want to do with this money?
Don't cash in your options until you have specific plans for the money, such as paying for college. Otherwise, you'll be more likely to exercise your options in a knee-jerk response to gyrations in the share price. For instance, many workers cash in their options as soon as company shares notch a new 52-week high in the

mistaken belief that the stock won't run up any further. Setting goals will also help you avoid viewing options' profits as found money to fritter away.

QUESTIONS TO ASK ABOUT VALUE STOCKS

Value investors follow the style popularized by Benjamin Graham, co-author of the classic *Security Analysis*, written more than half a century ago. Graham believed in buying undervalued stocks, which he defined as those with low ratios of trading prices to earnings and basic asset value, or those selling for less than the sum an acquirer would pay for the company.

Obviously, it takes courage to be a contrarian value investor. Most of us like to buy stocks when the prices are going up, but value players look for companies that have yet to make their move or, worse, have been beaten down.

Value stocks hold up when the market sours because, as we recently noted, many of them pay dividends that cushion price declines. Moreover, since they are by definition undervalued, they don't have as far to fall as growth stocks. But value stocks aren't just foul-weather friends. A number of research studies show that over long periods of time, value investing beats growth and does so with less risk. Trinity Investment Management, a money-management firm in Boston that specializes in value investing, examined the performance of 3,000 stocks over a 28-year period from 1968 through 1996. The Trinity researchers found that value stocks rose an average of 12.7% annually vs. 9.9% for growth stocks and 11.5% for the S&P 500. Moreover, the value stocks were 18% less volatile than the growth stocks.

Michael Berry, who manages the Heartland Midcap Value Fund and who has studied value investing extensively, goes so far as to advise anyone saving for a distant goal like retirement to forget about growth stocks altogether. "As long as you are a patient investor, value stocks are the only kind you need," he says. He studied 3,000 stocks between 1976 and 1996 and found that in any given five-year period during those two decades, value stocks outperformed the market 92% of the time and outperformed growth stocks 67% of the time.

While Berry advocates sticking solely to value stocks, that view may strike you as extreme. Instead, you may want to follow the advice of Susan Steward, president of Charter Financial Group, a Washington, D.C. money-management firm. She recommends long-term investors put 60% of their portfolio of domestic equities in value stocks or value-oriented mutual funds and keep the rest in growth issues.

To get you expert advice on value stock investing, we consulted top-notch value investors. Like all value hunters, these experts use the traditional tools of low price-to-earnings and low price-to-book ratios to help them find companies that the market has either overlooked or beaten down. They also look for companies selling below their intrinsic worth (essentially what a savvy buyer would pay for the whole company). But an inexpensive stock is no bargain if it deserves its low valuation. That's why our experts have additional criteria to assure themselves that a stock is truly mispriced, not accurately priced. You can apply these standards when you strike out on your own to prospect for uncommon values.

Are corporate insiders buying the stock? Chris Browne, his

brother Will and John Spears, who manage the Tweedy Browne American Value Fund, look for stocks trading at least 30% below the market's price/earnings multiple of 20 times estimated annual earnings. When they find them, they apply this test: Have the company's top executives been buying their own stock recently? Says Chris Browne: "That's a sign that corporate insiders believe the company is turning around." (Weekly, the *Wall Street Journal* lists companies whose top executives have engaged in significant buying and selling.)

Is the dividend yield higher than the market average?

Tony Spare, head of the San Francisco investment advisory firm Spare Kaplan Bischel & Associates, invests in large companies that pay substantial dividends. His criterion is a yield at least 25% higher than the yield of the typical stock in the S&P 500. "This is a strategy that works best for fallen blue chips that have a history of paying steady dividends," Spare says. Why? "Because companies that continue their payouts in tough times are companies that are confident of their future growth."

Is the P/E 10% to 15% below its historical average?

Gibb Kane, co-manager of the Sound Shore Fund, swears by a statistical concept called regression to the mean. Translation: A company tends to trade at roughly the same P/E ratio over time. So when the multiple has sunk to unusually low levels, you can expect it to spring back to the average eventually as a company fixes its problems. "We have found that companies don't change as much as the expectations about them change," he says. The fund manager puts his regression-to-the-mean screen into practice by hunting for stocks trading at multiples that, in today's market, are 10% to 15% below their historical five-year average.

Does the company have a bulletproof brand or position in the market? Unlike many value investors, Randall Haase, manager of the Alliance Quasar Fund, focuses on fallen growth stocks that he believes are poised for a comeback. This is a risky strategy for a value manager because when a growth company falters, it can be a sign that demand for its products has evaporated. To help him avoid the has-beens among the small stocks he specializes in, Haase looks for "companies that sell real products to real people, not the fad of the moment," he says.

Does the stock behave like a cyclical company even though investors don't recognize it as one? Companies whose profits wax and wane with economic cycles have long been fertile ground for value investors. But Bill Miller, manager of the Legg Mason Value Trust, mines industries you wouldn't think of as being cyclical, such as technology. "Technology stocks fill the role that traditional cyclicals like autos and steel once did as the motor of growth in the economy," he says. Miller is partial to technology sectors prone to boom-bust cycles like hard-disk-drive manufacturers and chipmakers. These companies benefit from rapid technological developments that stir demand for the latest cutting-edge devices. But then they nosedive when they are left with too many older, obsolete products they can move only by slashing prices. The trick is figuring out whether a company's distress is temporary.

Does cash account for 5% to 10% of assets? When Michael Berry, the Heartland fund manager, scouts for companies, he follows a simple rule: Cash is king. "Smaller companies are often growing so fast that they suck up all their excess cash," he says. So a company that can finance its future growth from earnings and still have cash left over is strong indeed. It can pounce on new growth opportunities or become attractive as a takeover target. Berry looks for companies whose free cash flow, loosely defined as money left over after the outfit pays all its bills and invests in new equipment for future growth, is ideally 5% to 10% of assets.

STRATEGY FOR STARTING A COLLEGE FUND

Here's a quiz: In which recently created Individual Retirement Account should you park your child's college money, the Education IRA or the Roth IRA? It sounds like a no-brainer. "The typical investor would go with the

Education IRA," one financial planner told us. "After all, it's *called* an Education IRA."

Surprise. For a lot of college investors, that's the wrong answer. Truth is, if you don't need the money within the next five years, you may be better off stashing those college dollars in a Roth.

But wait a minute, didn't Congress create the Roth as a place for your retirement stash? Of course. But if—like many investors—you already save the max in a 401(k), SEP-IRA or Keogh, this alternate use has advantages.

To qualify for either IRA, couples filing jointly must earn no more than $150,000 to $160,000 and singles no more than $95,000 to $110,000. The Education IRA lets you put aside up to $500 a year. This means that if you start saving when your child is still in Pampers, you'll have $22,800 in 18 years, assuming your investments return 10% a year. That should be enough to pay for one semester at a private college in 2016.

By contrast, you can shovel $2,000 a year into a Roth ($4,000 if you're married and file jointly), allowing you to pile up $91,198 over those 18 years.

Another advantage is flexibility. The new Education IRA has more strings attached than a marionette. For instance, if you cash in your Education IRA in the same year you take the Hope credit or lifetime learning credit—two new tax credits aimed at easing the burden of college financing—you'll have to pay taxes on the distributions from the IRA or the credits will be disallowed. You're also forbidden from contributing to both an Education IRA and a prepaid tuition plan in the same year. Finally, your child must spend the money on education expenses by age 30. If not, he can transfer the assets to a younger sibling or another qualified family member—or cash out the account and pay income taxes and a 10% penalty on the balance.

Compare that with a Roth. Once you start drawing down a Roth—which you are free to do after five years—you pay taxes on your earnings but not your original contributions. And if you're 59 1/2, your full distribution is tax-free. And there's no mandatory age at which you're required to tap the money, so even if Junior wins a full-ride scholarship or joins the circus, you can keep the money in the account until you're ready to cash it in or pass it on to your heirs.

That brings us to the final reason. The Roth is in your name, not your child's. Let's face it, retaining control has a definite appeal. Even better, since this money is in your name, most schools won't figure it into their financial aid formula. Technically, it's retirement money. Explains Bradley Bodmer, a principal with the Ayco Co., a financial counseling firm in Albany, N.Y.: "Under the federal methodology, which is the most popular, current retirement assets aren't considered in aid formulas." Some colleges do scrutinize your retirement savings, so this upside is not guaranteed. But even those schools generally expect parents to fork over no more than 5.6% of their assets a year, compared with 35% of a child's.

SOME DEBT CAN BE GOOD FOR YOU

We're not going to lecture you. You know all about the downsides of debt. You know you shouldn't run up a credit-card tab for a trip to Tahiti, and you know that such behavior has helped push bankruptcies to an all-time high. But all the doomsaying and admonishment about debt has obscured a dirty little secret of financial planning. Sometimes debt is good.

In fact, you can go overboard avoiding it. Eschewing debt at all costs, experts say, could actually prove quite costly if it leaves you with no cash in reserve for an emergency. "No one can say, 'I won't lose my job.' Or 'The hot water heater? Nah, that never breaks,'" warns Michael Kidwell, vice president of Debt Counselors of America. "There's always an accident waiting to happen."

Now we're not advocating rampant spending, so don't take this as our blessing to hit the mall (or the road to Tahiti). Instead, we're recommending that you learn to separate good debt from bad debt. Financial planners will talk about "needs analyses" or some other jargon until you're glassy-eyed, but it's not that complicated.

Good debt is what you use to buy anything you really need (a home, a car or education, for instance) but can't afford without wiping out your bank account or liquidating your investments. Of course, you must also be able to afford the payments. (Those same financial planners would suggest keeping total debt and housing payments at no more than 36% of your income.) The final key to good debt is the form it takes: High-rate credit cards, for example, are invariably a terrible way to carry debt.

But those cards notwithstanding, today's low-interest rates on most loans make debt especially affordable. If you have the cash, the decision to borrow hinges on a comparison of what you'll spend in interest with what your savings could earn. Take a mortgage rate of 7.1%. Given the deductibility of mortgage interest, your after-tax borrowing cost would be 5% if you're in the 28% bracket. Earning more than 5% shouldn't be hard. The same goes for a 9.37% 10-year home-equity loan, which amounts to 6.75% after taxes for folks in the same bracket. The interest on car loans, however, is not tax-deductible, so your investments would have to beat the recent 8.84% average outright to make borrowing the right choice.

With these considerations in mind, we looked at the merits of borrowing for three major necessities.

Your home. The chances that you can avoid debt altogether by paying cash for a house are slim. The more realistic question is how much to put toward a down payment. While it may seem logical to plunk down every available dime, that's not always best. What you need to consider are the size of your cash reserves, what you expect your investments to make and your income prospects.

"It often makes sense to make a low down payment on a house," says Robin Leonard, author of *Money Troubles: Legal Strategies to Cope with Your Debt*, "because you'll want as much cash on hand as possible to fix it up."

In addition, if you don't expect to stay put until you pay off your mortgage, focus on what you can afford every month. For instance, if you put 5% down on a $150,000 home at the rates a while ago, your monthly payment would have been $958. But if you'd coughed up another $7,500 to reach 10% down, the monthly payment would have dropped a mere $50 to $908. So if you'd wanted to leave yourself a cash cushion or thought you could earn more than $50 a month on that $7,500, you might have opted for 5% down. In such a situation, if you envision steady raises, that $958 will constitute a dwindling percentage of your income in the years ahead.

A new car. Paying cash for a car is more within the realm of possibility. Again, your goal is to make your savings grow at a rate that outstrips a car loan's interest rate. If you borrow, get a loan from a bank or let the dealer act as a broker. Just be careful to look for the best rate—pay no more than average—not a particular monthly payment, says Keith Gumbinger, vice president at the loan research firm HSH Associates. Gumbinger tells of a shopper who told her car dealer she could spend $200 a month. The dealer steered her toward a $200-a-month offering—at a whopping 22% interest rate.

What about the super-low 2.9%, even 1.9%, loans that dealers tout? Well, in the fine print you'll find that most of those deals last for only two years or so. After that, you'll either have to refinance or the rate will automatically rise much higher.

Some lenders offer car loans with terms as long as seven years, but keep the length as short as you can afford, so the loan will be paid off while you still have the car. That advice applies as well if you're considering a home-equity loan to bankroll your wheels, a move most financial planners frown on because you're essentially betting the ranch you can pay for a car.

Your child's education. Borrowing on your kids' behalf will send many planners—and parents—into a cacophony of tongue clicking. Yes, debt can be far preferable to depleting investments you're counting on for retirement, but to get the best deals on a student loan, let the student borrow, especially if your kid is eligible for a government-backed Perkins or Stafford loan. Last year the Perkins had a fixed 5% rate, and the subsidized version of the variable-rate Stafford topped out at 8.25%; with either one you pay no interest during college. "It's almost stupid not to take out a subsidized loan," says Kal Chany, author of *How to Pay for College Without Going Broke*, "since you borrow for free for four years."

Parents can also take out a Parent Loan for Undergraduate Students, or PLUS, which lets you borrow for all school costs (including books and transportation) minus whatever aid you receive. The interest rate on this variable-rate loan can't exceed 9%. Additionally, thanks to the 1997 tax law changes, parents with less than $75,000 in adjusted gross income ($55,000 for singles) can deduct a portion of the interest on qualified education loans.

TIPS TO PUMP YOUR PAYCHECK

Your major source of investment capital for your nest egg is invariably your paycheck. So if you want more than the skimpy 4% raises that corporate America is offering these days, start polishing up your negotiation skills. Although companies claim they're desperately trying to retain their best workers, hefty pay increases aren't on the agenda—unless you're talking high-tech careers.

"Global competition is forcing U.S. companies to keep fixed costs down," explains Steven Gross, a principal at the William M. Mercer human-resources consulting firm in Philadelphia. "Instead of bigger raises, employers are doling out bonuses and stock options to reward their high performers."

If you're lucky enough to share the wealth of a prosperous company, incentive pay can drop a healthy piece of change into your pocket—and since options and bonuses are cheaper for the company than raises, they may be easier to get. But the reality is that only half of U.S. corporations offer incentives to their managers and professionals, explains Gross. And while more and more companies are giving out stock options, as we just noted, a study by Mercer of 350 major U.S. industrial and service companies shows that only 15% currently grant them to a broad base of employees.

How do you angle for more pay at a time when most companies would rather pile on the perks, including flextime and more vacation? You ask for it. "People should navigate their careers as if they were running their own business, and that business is themselves," says Lewis Kravitz, an executive coach in Atlanta. "Your compensation should reflect your value to the company."

Almost a decade of corporate downsizing, salary freezes, cost cutting and Dilbert cartoons has convinced many of us that we're expendable and lucky to have a job—and maybe some of us are. But in 1998 unemployment hit a 25-year low, and the tight labor market left companies scrambling to find the brainpower and experience they need in order to thrive.

So even if you're not a techno hotshot or the creative force behind your company's latest multimillion-dollar product, you're probably more valuable than you think. For instance, some recruiters say they are swamped with requests for middle managers who can lead project teams that cross functional lines.

Sure, there are timing issues, research requirements and a few negotiation tricks you should know before popping the money question, but you can do it. We'll show you how.

A little knowledge can be a lucrative thing. Before you
launch an intense lobbying effort to fatten your paycheck, build a rock-solid case for why you deserve a raise. And here's a hint: It's not because of the new house you just bought or the enormous tuition bills you face. Quite frankly, these are your problems, not your employer's.

"Your need is irrelevant to the company, even if your bosses like you," warns Robin L. Pinkley, who is a co-author of *Turning Lead to Gold: The Experts' Guide to Negotiating Salary and Compensation.* "To get more money, you must first determine what you're worth professionally—to your company and in the marketplace." In order to prepare for his own salary negotiation, Jim Cichanski, a vice president of human resources at a technology company in Atlanta, logged about 35 hours researching compensation packages for his peers in the same field.

Like Cichanski, start your investigation by priming your network of friends and business associates. "Within six degrees of separation, everybody knows somebody at a company similar to yours," says Eva Wisnik, a New York City career counselor. "Ask what their company would pay someone with your experience."

Professional associations can usually provide salary information that's broken down by years of experience, type of employer, geography and sometimes gender. Some Websites that can help your search: www.careers.wsj.com, www.experienceondemand.com and www.jobsmart.org.

Headhunters are also good for up-to-the-minute salary intelligence. To get plugged in, introduce yourself to recruiters who specialize in your field, suggests Laura Berman Fortgang, author of *Take Yourself to the Top: The Secrets of America's No. 1 Career Coach.* "Say you want a reality check," says Fortgang, "because in this market there's lots of room to move."

If you've got it, flaunt it. Once you have settled on how much you're worth on the street, document your contributions to the company. "Your track record is the best negotiating tool you've got," says Kravitz. "Past accomplishments are excellent indicators of future potential, but if you don't tell your manager what you've done, he's not going to look it up for you."

That's why Kravitz suggests that you keep a "Friday file." At the end of each week, jot down the progress and results of your most significant assignments. Provide details to demonstrate your value to the organization and to track how your job has evolved.

Proving his ability to handle major projects helped Transamerica auditor Robert Schmollinger get more than the average 3% to 5% increase he heard the financial services company was offering. But it took some work. First the 27-year-old checked out several salary surveys to discover that he wasn't making the $58,000 a year that auditors with similar experience were earning. Then Schmollinger started flipping through his datebook to compile his most important assignments, which included serving on the team that implemented a new companywide financial system. Armed with an enviable portfolio of achievements and the salary research, Schmollinger presented his case after receiving a positive review from his boss. "Then I said right out that I wouldn't be satisfied with a standard 3% to 5% raise," he recalls. "But I didn't volunteer a specific number. Instead, I asked that my compensation reflect my job performance." Impressed by his achievements and confidence, Schmollinger's supervisors took his request to the general auditor. Six weeks later, Schmollinger got a sweet 17.4% raise—far more than he expected.

If talking about yourself makes your stomach churn, follow the lead of Kirk Robey, a 48-year-old certified public accountant at EMO Computer Products in Naperville, Ill.: Hire a career coach to hone your presentation skills. "My coach encouraged me to emphasize projects that were extremely important to the company, such as improving banking relationships," Robey says.

But remember, even a winning presentation can be defeated by poor timing. For instance, at companies where raises are tied to annual reviews, waiting for your performance review may not always be the best strategy. "To set yourself apart from the crowd, ask for a raise when you've finished a project and everyone's happy with your work," advises Robin Ryan, author of *24 Hours to Your Next Job, Raise or Promotion.*

Let your boss make the first offer. If the amount doesn't wow you, start lobbying. "Don't respond with a salary range, because you might wind up at the lowest end," advises Pinkley. "Instead, set a target and explain that your figure is negotiable. Then, position yourself as a top performer who deserves more than the average compensation."

Don't take "no" for an answer. No matter how deftly you ask for a raise, chances are your boss will try to stall you. But even canned responses—"That's the salary attached to this position" or "We don't pay Joe that much, and he's been here longer"—can provide a road map to a future raise.

First, clarify whether raises are based on seniority or merit. Unless yours is a union shop, performance is probably the real issue. In that case, suggests Cleveland executive recruiter Jeffrey Christian, CEO of Christian & Timbers, figure out ways to increase your level of responsibility, broaden your skill set or take on higher-profile projects to better position yourself for a promotion that would include a raise. If you really don't think your credentials are the problem, ask your boss what it will take to get a raise. Then set a later date to review the situation. He may come back with an offer of Fridays off or flextime in lieu of more pay. If you're unwilling to accept this, express your appreciation, and if an actual boost of pay seems impossible, suggest other cash benefits that come from a budget other than payroll, such as membership in a health club or a car allowance.

The art of the counteroffer. Of course, nothing tells you more specifically what you're worth than another job offer. So if your research shows that you're significantly underpaid, start shopping around. But any career counselor will warn you that once you go that route, you must be prepared to leave. Counteroffers are flattering, but as David Yearwood, executive vice president and station manager for Fox 41 WDRB-TV in Louisville, explains, when they are introduced during salary negotiations, employers like himself may view them as your threat to leave.

Keeping the discussion nonconfrontational worked out very well for public relations specialist Elhom Javadi. Six months after joining Aspect Development, a software company in Mountainview, Calif., Javadi received an even more attractive offer from Hewlett-Packard. H-P was ready to bump up her pay by $10,000, plus provide a slew of great benefits, such as on-site day care for her three-year-old son Leith.

"It was tough to ask for a raise so soon," Javadi says, so she supported her request by focusing on how well she was performing on her job. Three weeks later her company met Hewlett-Packard's offer. Between the salary increase and the stock options that Javadi already had from Aspect, she decided to stay.

Javadi credits her success to her straightforward, nonthreatening presentation of the attractive H-P offer. "Don't start rattling off all your issues," advises the 29-year-old publicist. "When you're negotiating a raise, stick to finances." And most important, be sure that you want to stay at your current company. When you ask for a higher salary, you're offering total commitment to that job. If more money isn't worth the extra scrutiny, give yourself a break and move on.

PROTECTION FROM THE YEAR 2000 BUG

Mark Yarsike got an early taste of the new millennium back in November 1996 in the gourmet food market he co-owns in Warren, Mich. A customer tried to pay with a credit card that was perfectly valid but happened to bear an expiration date in 2000. That caused the store's 10 computerized cash registers to lock shut for half a day, and for months afterward glitches continued to plague the system. Similarly, in 1997, the computer network that schedules patient appointments at three hospitals and 75 clinics in Pennsylvania shut down—all because one person punched in an appointment for January 2000.

Such computer glitches, called "sightings," have been popping up throughout the U.S. and the world, interrupting enterprises large and small in advance of the dreaded date of Jan. 1, 2000. Millions of computer software programs can't read dates beyond 1999, and armies of programmers from Berkeley to Bombay are working strenuously to scan and correct them, line by laborious line.

Companies that aren't moving openly and aggressively to deal with what is known as the Y2K problem will see their business prospects seriously damaged. What's already clear is that the millennium bug is affecting your finances, determining which mutual funds, brokerages, banks and other businesses will win and lose customers and profits, and which ones deserve both your patronage and your investment. You need to act now to protect your finances.

The countdown to the year 2000 glitch began more than two decades ago, when to conserve computer memory space—which then cost $600,000 a megabyte vs. about a dime today—programmers used only two digits rather than four to represent years: that is, 99 instead of 1999. That's why so many computer systems can't distinguish between 2000 and 1900. The same kind of data error that fouls up mainframe computers also appears in "embedded systems"—the computer chips that control all kinds of machines. Millions of chips must be tested and, if necessary, replaced. When faced with a date beyond 1999, a noncompliant computer system may shut down, just like Mark Yarsike's cash register did. Or, worse, the system may continue operating but spin out inaccurate information.

To minimize the negative impact of the millennium bug on your life, one tactic applies across the board. Keep paper records of this year's statements for all financial accounts and important records, and save all receipts for the final two months of 1999 so that you can reconstruct an account if you discover errors in statements issued in 2000. We also suggest action in the following key areas.

Your investments. You need to know how firms whose stocks and bonds you own, or might buy, are confronting Y2K. "I want my retirement money invested in companies that are moving swiftly to become Y2K compliant," says Cathleen Judge, a securities attorney at Ballard Spahr Andrews & Ingersoll in Philadelphia.

Your broker or mutual fund. A bit more than a year ago, a Securities Industry Association survey of 3,200 brokers, fund companies and other financial services found that while 77% of large firms (those with more than 6,000 employees) were fixing and testing their systems, only about a third of mid-size and small companies were doing so. Among those scheduled to have systems in shape and thoroughly tested in 1999: Merrill Lynch, Charles Schwab, Vanguard, T. Rowe Price and Fidelity. It pays to personally check out the people with whom you do business.

THE INSURANCE MOST PEOPLE NEED

We want to help you make sure you have all the protection you need without paying too much for it. You can compare your coverage against this handy checklist in about an hour.

◆ **Auto.** You should have liability insurance (which protects you against claims by people injured in an accident) and uninsured motorist coverage (which comes to your aid when you're involved in an accident with someone who has little or no insurance) of at least $100,000 per person and $300,000 per accident. That's two or three times more than many states require. But we think it's the minimum you need to protect your assets. To save money on your premiums, consider raising the deductible on the collision and comprehensive portions of your policy, which covers accidental damage and theft, among other things, to $500 from the standard $200. That would mean you would foot a bigger portion of any repair bills. But it could cut your premium costs $50 to $100 a year.

◆ **Life.** If you support a family, you generally need coverage equal to six to eight times your annual salary. If your spouse works, each of you should be insured for six to eight times your annual pay. The coverage won't guarantee your survivors a lifetime of luxury. But it would give them time to adjust to their new circumstances without worrying about bills going unpaid. Life insurance should be used to protect your survivors, not to build an investment stake. That's why we recommend term insurance, especially for people under 40, rather than whole life. Whole life policies initially cost seven to 10 times more per year than term and double as a tax-deferred savings vehicle.

◆ **Homeowners.** By one estimate, 50,000 homes are totally destroyed each year by fire alone. To guard against such a disaster, you want insurance that will pay enough to rebuild. It's sometimes called a guaranteed replacement cost policy. If you simply buy coverage equal to what you paid for your home, or its current market value, you may be buying much less or much more insurance than you really need.

◆ **Liability.** Usually purchased in conjunction with auto or homeowners insurance, a so-called umbrella liability policy could provide valuable protection when you are sued. We suggest at least $1 million worth of such coverage. That's a lot of peace of mind for the price: about $200 a year.

◆ **Disability.** Four out of 10 workers will become disabled by injury or illness for more than 90 days at some point in their working lives. When you are unable to work, disability insurance provides a means of support. Many employers provide it free or for a nominal charge. If yours does not, or if you're self-employed, you'll have to purchase it on your own. The typical annual cost is $650 for a policy that will provide at least 60% of a $50,000 annual income for the rest of your normal working life (generally to age 65).

◆ **Policies you don't need.** To conclude your checkup, cancel any insurance that's not worth the cost. High on the list of dubious ones are credit life insurance and mortgage life insurance, which pay off your debts when you die. A much cheaper alternative is to buy sufficient term life insurance to cover your liabilities.

Your bank or credit union. The Federal Reserve has been making contingency plans to assist banks that may be crippled by computer problems in January 2000. A major upbeat note for both depositors and investors is that even Y2K doomsayers believe that the largest U.S. banks will have their systems ready. But about a year ago federal regulators reported that 500 of the nation's community banks were either doing nothing or just beginning to develop correction plans. And credit unions—to which one out of four Americans belong—were criticized by the U.S. Government Accounting Office for dragging their feet on Y2K problems. Foreign banks were also lagging, and U.S. banks that trade data with them can be vulnerable.

Here's what you can do to reduce the risks of losing access to your funds, being harried by inaccurate statements and encountering delays in clearing checks and deposits. Find out whether your bank has all computer systems reprogrammed and is testing with other banks and the Fed's wire transfer systems. If you can't get this assurance, shift your money. One other tip: Prior to New Year's Eve, withdraw a couple of weeks' spending money in cash just in case your ATM is temporarily down.

Your credit. Given the fact that credit reporting bureaus experience some errors even in the best of times, you'd be wise to obtain copies of your credit report both before and after the century change so that you can promptly spot and correct any Y2K errors.

Your insurance. If your home, auto or life insurance policies are issued by a large national concern, your Y2K risks are minimal. But be wary of small regional insurers, which supply coverage for 30% of Americans. Many of them hadn't even started making fixes at the start of last year.

State insurance commissioners have been surveying companies about Y2K progress, so you may be able to get information on your insurer's status by calling your state's insurance department, as well as plowing through insurance ratings bureaus and, possibly, 10K filings. If you can't obtain sufficient disclosure about your company, ask your agent to state in writing when your insurer will be Y2K-compliant. A noncompliant computer might, for example, cancel a policy running through 2001 because it reads the policy as having expired in 1901.

Your Social Security and Medicare. Social Security benefits are not likely to be disrupted by millennium bugs because the SSA began its Y2K program in 1992, far earlier than even most businesses. A report card on Y2K progress issued in September 1997 by a U.S. House subcommittee gave Ds or Fs to nearly half the federal agencies, but Social Security scored an A-, the highest grade given.

The risk of delays or foul-ups is higher for Medicare benefits. The GAO says that, astoundingly, the Department of Health and Human Services in its May 1997 progress report failed to assess how much systems renovation was needed by contractors who are paid by the government to process the nation's Medicare claims. HHS finally began taking action.

To avoid delays, submit Medicare claims as early as possible this year, and after the first quarter of 2000 check the accuracy of your Social Security Personal Earnings and Benefits Statement, which lists your annual earnings and estimates future benefits. You can get your statement by phone at 800-772-1213, at local Social Security offices or on the Internet (www.ssa.gov).

Your taxes. Seeing the IRS computers frozen might be a dream come true for some folks, but in the long run taxpayers would pay the price. You're still expected to pay scheduled taxes plus any applicable interest even if it takes the agency a year to communicate that to you. And to avoid having a significant refund delayed in 2000 because of a millennium glitch, calculate your 1999 tax withholding—for federal, state and local filings—as close as possible to what you'll owe.

CHECK OUT WEALTH INSURANCE

Like many parents, Barbara Hooke, 70, of Baltimore, wants to leave her children an inheritance—in her case, an estate that is currently worth upwards of $200,000. But a few years ago, Hooke's son Jeff, a 43-year-old investment banker in Chevy Chase, Md., spotted a potentially fatal flaw in his mother's vision of the future. With nursing-home fees averaging $41,000 a year, Jeff realized that a prolonged illness could consume his mother's assets. That's because private health insurance and Medicare don't cover lengthy nursing-home stays or extended home care. What's more, if Barbara's money ran out, the family would have only two choices: Enroll her in Medicaid (the government program that pays nursing-home costs after most of the patient's assets are depleted) or shoulder the costs themselves.

Jeff's concern wasn't merely theoretical: Although his mother is a healthy septuagenarian, his maternal grandmother spent 16 years in a nursing home with Alzheimer's disease, until her death in 1997 at age 97.

With this in mind, Jeff offered to pay the premiums on a long-term-care insurance policy for his mother. Barbara now has a policy that costs $2,400 a year and promises to pay benefits for up to three years—$120 a day for nursing-home care or $60 a day for home care. The coverage will kick in if she becomes severely cognitively disabled or is unable to perform routine daily activities, such as eating and dressing. The annual cost also includes a rider that allows the daily benefit to rise 5% a year compounded, to help keep pace with inflation. "For me, the policy provides a cushion against long-term-care costs that I might otherwise have to pay," says Jeff.

Indeed, many baby boomers are realizing that they may ultimately bear the cost of their parents' long-term care, whether in the form of a forgone inheritance or as out-of-pocket outlays. And some are attempting to guard against those losses by purchasing long-term-care insurance for their elders. Why would an adult child buy the coverage rather than the parent? In a word: cost. Long-term-care insurance premiums typically run about $2,100 a year at age 65, and $4,500 a year at age 75. Adults in their prime earning years may be more likely to have adequate cash flow to meet those costs.

But while buying long-term-care insurance may be a good move for some people, it's folly for others. Whether you're considering buying the insurance for yourself, a spouse or a parent, here are three questions to ask before you look for an agent.

1. Are there enough assets to justify premium costs? A suitable candidate for long-term-care insurance should have at least $100,000 in assets, not counting a home and an automobile. Below $100,000, you may end up paying more in premiums than you'll protect in assets; moreover, if the person to be covered went into a nursing home, he or she would probably soon be able to qualify for Medicaid.

2. What are the chances long-term care will be necessary? According to a survey published in the *New England Journal of Medicine* in 1991, 57% of people who reach age 65 will never spend a day in a nursing home; of those who do, almost half will stay less than a year. People who are at particular risk of requiring extensive care come from families with a history of debilitating illness, such as stroke or Alzheimer's.

3. Can you commit to paying premiums for the long haul? If your policy lapses and you want to reinstate it, the premium will be reset based on the insured's age at the time of the reinstatement. Worse, the person to be insured may fail to qualify for reinstatement if he or she has become sick in the meantime.

If insurance makes sense—and you can afford it—your next step is to do some comparison shopping. Before you buy, ask a financial planner or an attorney who specializes in elder care but does not sell insurance to review any policy you're considering. Long-term-care policies are exceedingly complex and, unfortunately, some insurance agents have been known to employ dubious sales practices. Use these tips to get started.

Tailor the coverage. The two main types of long-term care are nursing facilities and home care. Policies may also cover alternatives such as community-based adult day care and assisted-living arrangements, where the aged have their own apartments but receive on-site help with daily activities. Insurers define their options differently, and policies vary in the services offered under each category. Choose the broadest range of care options you think will actually be used. Although home care is often desired, for example, it may not work out unless family or friends are available to pitch in when the professional caretaker is off-duty. And a home-care-only policy is usually a bad idea, because anyone frail enough to use those benefits may well need a nursing home someday.

Control the premium—carefully. Most companies let you choose a daily nursing-home benefit, typically between $50 and $250, with home care covered at 50% to 100% of the nursing-home rate. Of course, the bigger the benefit, the costlier the premium. Don't pull a figure out of the air. Call nursing facilities and home-care agencies in the city where coverage will be required to find out how much they charge, then peg your daily benefit to those costs.

You can also select coverage for a period ranging from one to six years or for an unlimited time. Financial pros generally agree that you're playing it safe if a policy covers four or five years, since the average stay for seniors who enter a nursing home is a bit less than 2 1/2 years.

Guard against inflation. Since benefits may not kick in for several years, you need inflation protection. If the insured is age 68 or younger, go for the standard rider that increases the policy's daily benefit by 5% compounded annually, which will add 25% to 35% to the premium. If the insured is between 69 and 75, you can probably protect the benefits and get a somewhat cheaper inflation rider by not compounding the annual increase, says Margie Barrie, the sales and marketing director for BISYS Insurance Services, an insurance brokerage specializing in long-term-care policies.

Deal with a financially strong insurer. Look for ratings of "excellent" or better in the publications of rating agencies such as A.M. Best and Moody's, which are available at your local library. After all, the aim of long-term-care insurance is to protect family wealth across generations. So you have to be confident that the insurer will be around to pay the bills, whether the money is needed next year or decades from now.

Compare your options before you buy. Here's how three types of policies stack up.

Tax-qualified: These policies are eligible for tax breaks, including a deduction for part of the premium. But you probably won't get the write-off for your parent's policy because the tax law won't let you claim expenses you pay for someone who is not your dependent. No matter. Virtually no one gets the deduction anyway, because it is so restricted. For example, to be deductible, the allowable premium costs plus other unreimbursed medical expenses must top 7.5% of adjusted gross income.

The benefits in a tax-qualified policy also tend to be limited. Before payouts begin, a doctor must certify that the patient suffers severe cognitive impairment, such as Alzheimer's disease, or be unable to perform two out of five (in some states, six) normal activities of daily living (ADLs) for at least 90 days. ADLs include eating, bathing, dressing, continence, using the bathroom and being able to move from a bed to a chair.

Nonqualified: These policies don't offer tax breaks, but they also don't require a doctor's note to begin benefits. Plus, the benefits typically kick in if you fail in two of six ADLs for any period of time. But some insurers have stopped selling nonqualified policies in favor of qualified ones.

Partnership programs: Insurers in California, Connecticut, Indiana and New York have teamed up with their state Medicaid agencies to develop partnership policies, which may be appropriate for seniors who have less than $100,000 in assets. In general, under these policies you specify how much you want in benefits, say, $80,000. Once the benefits are exhausted, the patient would able to keep up to $80,000 in assets and still qualify for Medicaid.

◆ **CHAPTER 3**

SMART MOVES TO SLASH YOUR TAXES

Throughout this book we will point out moves you should make for great tax savings now and in the future. For example, in the previous chapter we showed how to profit from the changing capital-gains rates and in chapter five, "Retire Rich With These New Rules," we'll explain how to cut through all the confusion about the new Roth IRA and choose the Individual Retirement Account that is best for you. In this chapter, we'll focus mainly on strategies to minimize the money you owe the government when you file your annual federal income tax return. We'll also offer advice on how to avoid the common tax mistakes that result in people paying more than they should toward Social Security benefits and getting back less than should. And, finally, we'll pass along estate-planning tips from experts. The maneuvers they map out will shield your wealth from unnecessary taxes and provide your heirs with the largest possible inheritance.

LESSONS FROM LAST YEAR'S TAX RETURN

If you file away your copy of your tax return as soon as you file the original with the IRS, you're missing an opportunity: Examining your 1997 return can provide valuable insights as you plot your financial moves for this April's '98 return and beyond.

Nearly every line on your 1040 can raise broad issues, but a careful review of only a few spots may help turn the newest tax breaks to your best advantage. Here, for example, are four key lessons to learn from a tax-filing postmortem.

Preserve your eligibility for tuition tax breaks. The new Hope credit can cut your taxes by as much as $1,500 a year for tuition you pay for each college freshman and sophomore in your family. The lifetime learning credit is worth as much as $1,000 a year for courses from an "eligible educational institution"—generally, any accredited post-secondary school that qualifies for a federal financial aid program.

To claim all or part of your credits for your college children, your kids must be your dependents (line 6 of your 1040) and your adjusted gross income must not exceed $100,000 for joint filers ($50,000 for singles).

Here's the trick: For your college son or daughter to be your dependent, you must provide more than half of the child's support. If your child pays most of his or her expenses through student loans, work and savings, he or she is not your dependent—and you forfeit the tax credits on any tuition you shell out. So make sure that your financial arrangement with your kids lets you deduct them as dependents. In some cases, you could get the dependent writeoff by giving your child a bit more cash and still come out ahead after claiming the tuition credits.

Commit to investing for the long haul. Check Schedule D, "Capital Gains and Losses," to see if you had excessive short- or mid-term gains in 1997. If so, make a vow that from now on you'll try to keep your assets for more than 12 months before selling. That way you'll owe tax of 20% on your capital gain (10% if you're in the 15% tax bracket, which is for joint filers with taxable income of less than $42,351 and single filers with less than $25,351). To compare, you face rates as high as 39.6% on assets you own for less than a year before selling.

Beat the tax bite on mutual fund sales. If you use a tactic called specific identification (Specific ID), you'll have the most control over the tax due on the sale of mutual fund shares, also shown on Schedule D. Specific ID is one of four methods that the IRS lets you use to calculate your gain on a fund sale. One method is "first in, first out" (FIFO), which assumes you sold shares in the order you bought them. A second method is single-category averaging, where you average the cost of all your shares, regardless of how long you held them. The third is double-category averaging, in which you compute the average cost per share for your long-term and short-term holdings and sell shares from the category that yields the better tax result.

The fourth method, specific identification, works this way: Say you want to cash in $10,000 worth of shares. Don't simply place a sell order. Instead, go through your statements and identify the shares that cost you the most. Ideally, your costliest shares will also be long-term holdings. That way you would be able to generate the $10,000 by selling the shares that will yield the smallest gain at the lowest possible capital-gains tax rate.

The math can get gnarly, so may want to consult a tax adviser before you make the sale. But once you've pinpointed the shares that will result in the least tax due when sold, write a letter to the fund or broker specifying those shares—by purchase date and price—as the ones you want to sell. Keep a copy of the letter in your records, along with the statement that shows your redemption.

Vital info: You must use specific ID at the time you make the sale. If you wait until you file your return to compute your gain, specific ID is off limits.

The advantage of specific ID can be considerable. Assume that you want to pocket $10,000 on a fund sale and that your fund is trading at $10 a share. You own 1,000 shares that you bought three years ago at $5 a share and 1,000 shares you bought two years ago at $8 a share. By stating at the time of the sale that you wish to sell the lot you bought at $8, your gain will be $2,000 ($10,000 minus the $8,000 you paid for the shares), for a tax of just $400 ($2,000 times 20%). If you don't specify, however, you'll have to use another method, which can result in a steeper tax bill. With first-in, first-out, for example, you'd have a $5,000 gain and a $1,000 tax bite.

One caveat: If you've already sold shares from a fund using an average-cost method to compute your gain, you must stick with that method for every subsequent sale from that fund. But you can use specific ID on a fund from which you haven't made a sale or one in which you've previously used FIFO.

Lobby for a retirement savings plan.

A tax-favored retirement savings plan—the savings incentive match plan for employees (Simple)—recently made its debut on the 1040. This entry is easy for employees to miss, however, because it appears on the same line as retirement plans that are available only to self-employed taxpayers.

Truth is, your employer can set up a Simple if the company has not more than 100 employees and each made at least $5,000 in the preceding year. But the company cannot use a Simple to supplement an existing tax-favored retirement plan.

If your workplace fits that description, ask your boss to start a Simple. Your ammo: Simples are easy to establish—the boss must fill out a one-page form available from many fund companies or online from the IRS Website (www.irs.ustreas.gov). After that, your contributions of as much as $6,000 a year are deducted from your paycheck, before taxes, and shunted into your Simple at a bank, brokerage or mutual fund. Your employer must also match your contribution by 1% to 3% of your salary—a move that boosts your savings and exempts the employer from having to comply with complex pension rules. Be sure to point out to your boss that a 1% to 3% contribution is well within the range of most annual cost-of-living raises, so employees may be willing to forgo that increase in favor of a match.

A $6,000 Simple contribution would shave $1,680 a year off your taxes, assuming you're in the 28% bracket. In addition, your entire stash grows tax deferred.

Of course, if you take money out of Simple before retirement, you'll pay a penalty—up to a stiff 25% if you raid the plan within two years of the time it was set up. But if you follow the rules, you'll come out ahead.

PROFIT FROM THE PROS' MISTAKES

Congress can cut taxes all it wants, but if your tax preparer doesn't know all the rules, you might actually end up paying more. Before last year's filing deadline, for the eighth time since 1987, MONEY sent a financial profile of a hypothetical family to 60 tax professionals who agreed to prepare the family's tax return based on the information provided. Forty-six ended up completing the test, including 31 certified public accountants, 12 enrolled agents and three others who prepare tax returns for a living. The disturbing result: For the seventh time in the history of the test, no two test takers came up with the same bottom line. Worse still, for the third time, no one turned in an error-free form.

What was especially surprising this time around was how widespread—and costly—some mistakes were. The test's author, Mark Castellucci, a C.P.A. from Davis, Calif. and the winner of MONEY's previous tax test, calculated the lowest legal tax at $37,105. Castellucci acknowledges that his computation is not the only possible correct answer, since the tax law itself is ambiguous in some areas. Still, you can't blame ambiguity for the fact that the contestants' answers ranged from $34,240 to $68,912—a chasm of 101%. That means our fictional family could have underpaid its tax by nearly $3,000 or paid nearly double what they owed.

Five situations, in particular, that thrashed our pros are likely to surface at some point on your return. But before we review them, meet the

Johnsons, our fictional family. Ken, 60, a self-employed computer consultant, and Barbara, 45, an architect, have two children: Joy, 20, a full-time college student who lives away from home, and Craig, 12. In addition to wages and self-employment income of $72,775, Ken received a $142,000 payout from his 401(k) when he took early retirement in February 1997; Barbara rolled over a $127,000 retirement payout when she switched jobs in November 1997. The Johnsons' investments include stocks, bonds, mutual funds and real estate.

These were the pros' most common mistakes, starting with the costliest.

Miscalculating the tax due on a retirement payout.
Because Ken was 59 1/2 when he took his $142,000 early-retirement distribution in 1997, he was eligible for special tax treatment known as five-year averaging. This technique lets you pay tax on your payout as if you'd received the money over five years instead of all at once. But four preparers didn't realize Ken could use five-year averaging—even though his birth date was clearly given on the first page of the test—and thus kneecapped him with an additional $26,558 in tax. Another 14 contestants carelessly flubbed the averaging calculation by using a 1996 rate, for a tax overstatement of $420. Two pros erred in favor of the Johnsons by wrongly applying a 10-year average calculation, which lowballed Ken's tax by $1,010. Unfortunately, 10-year averaging is available only to taxpayers born before 1936.

Failing to grasp the new tax rules on home sales. In
May 1995, when the Johnsons bought and moved into their current home, they were unable to sell their former residence, where they had lived for nine years. So they rented out the house for two years, finally selling it on June 30, 1997, for a gain of $35,727. Under the tax law passed in 1997, a couple who sell a primary residence after May 6, 1997 can completely avoid tax on up to $500,000 of profit, provided they had lived in the house for at least two out of the five years before the sale. The Johnsons clearly met that requirement. Yet eight preparers obviously didn't know that the new law applied in the Johnsons' case and thus wrongly counted the gains as taxable, for a painful overstatement of $8,718.

Double-counting the tax due on stock options. On Jan. 21,
1997, Ken exercised nonqualified stock options from his former employer. On that day, the difference between the option price and the stock's fair market value came to $8,000—an amount that was correctly reported on

Ken's W-2. But seven pros didn't realize that the $8,000 was included in Ken's taxable wages and so taxed the amount twice—once as ordinary income and again as a short-term capital gain. Tax overstatement: $2,408.

Overlooking a tax-saving loophole on a 401(k) loan.

When Barbara switched jobs in 1997, she still owed $15,300 on a loan taken from her 401(k) years earlier. So her former employer simply deducted that amount from her account before rolling over the stash to an Individual Retirement Account. Unfortunately, that maneuver exposed Barbara to tax and a 10% penalty on the $15,300. Reason: You have 60 days from a rollover to add an amount to the IRA that is equal to an outstanding loan balance withheld by your employer. If you don't—and Barbara didn't—the amount is deemed a premature withdrawal, subject to tax and penalty.

What an astounding 43 test takers didn't know is that this is a case where Uncle Sam has a heart: It turns out that if you have a medical deduction and a premature 401(k) withdrawal in the same year, you can reduce the early-withdrawal penalty by an amount equal to 10% of your deduction. In 1997 the Johnsons' medical write-off came to $5,066, so they qualified for a $507 exception to the penalty. This reduced the hit from $1,530 to $1,023. Unfortunately, all but three test takers made the Johnsons pay the full penalty.

Important note: The 1997 tax law added similar exceptions to the fine for early withdrawals from IRAs. For example, you may not have to pay the penalty if you take an early IRA withdrawal to pay for medical insurance during unemployment. Such leniency shouldn't encourage you to tap your IRA early, but if you have to dip into the stash, make sure you're not hobbled later by unnecessary penalties.

Misjudging who can be claimed as a dependent.

If your child is a full-time college student under age 24, you can claim him or her as a dependent—provided, as we noted earlier, that you ante up more than half of the child's support. The confusion lies in what constitutes support. Indeed, 30 preparers understated the Johnsons' tax by $724, wrongly thinking the couple were entitled to the write-off. What confused some of them was that in 1997 the Johnsons gave Joy $12,000—a sum that did, in fact, amount to more than half of her total outlays for the year. But since Joy was able to pay her own way with money from a scholarship, a student loan and a part-time job, she invested the entire $12,000 her parents gave her in savings bonds. The key: For the parents' contribution to qualify as support, they must be able to prove that the money was actually spent on items of support during the year—not invested.

True, a mistake that reduces your tax bill might feel less painful than one that results in an overpayment—at first. But remember, it's you, not your tax pro, who pays in an audit. Whatever the errors on your return, one lesson they teach is that what you don't know can cost you dearly.

BIG BREAKS FOR THE SELF-EMPLOYED

If you're in business for yourself, you can indulge in tax write-offs that are forbidden fruit to many employees, from deductions for your car and your computer to nights on the town. In fact, you can write off any cost, as long as it's an ordinary, necessary and reasonable expense of running your business and a client does not reimburse you for the outlay.

But such plums are not always obvious. Although there are more than two dozen possible write-offs listed on the front of Schedule C, the tax form for sole proprietors, squeezing the most from all your tax breaks requires knowing the rules—and carefully planning. If you are self-employed, you should consider these tax-wise strategies.

Your car. When you use your car for business, you can write off each business mile you drive. What you can't deduct is the distance you commute to and from your work. So one of your goals, says Jan Zobel, a tax adviser, is to convert nondeductible commuting costs into deductible business miles. Here's how: Assuming you don't have a deductible home office, the trip from your home to your first business stop of the day is considered commuting; the same is true of the last leg of your drive home. So whenever you can, you should make your first and last business stops of the day near your home. Say, for example, that your office is 20 miles away from where you live. If you open a post office box for your business one mile from your home and make the post office your first stop each day, the other 19 miles of your drive to work will be deductible. Or end your day by doing your business banking close to home or buying from suppliers in your neighborhood.

You may also be able to boost the tax breaks on your car by using the actual-cost method rather than cents-per-mile to calculate your deduction. The actual-cost approach lets you write off your work-related outlays for gas, oil, repairs, registration, insurance and car washes, as well as the full amount of tolls and parking fees you incur on business trips. You can also depreciate a portion of the price of your car. If, say, 60% of the miles you drive are for business, you can depreciate 60% of the car's cost, generally over six years.

Clearly, you should use the deduction method that gives you the biggest write-off. But there's a catch. If you've used actual cost in the past, you have to keep using it as long as you drive that particular car for business. If you've used cents-per-mile, you can switch to an actual cost, but you can't switch back. The upshot: If this is the first year you've used your car in business, or if you've used cent-per-mile previously, keep records to compute the deduction both ways, and go with the one that gives you bigger tax savings.

Major purchases. In general, you must write off your business equipment according to depreciation schedules published by the IRS. Computers, for example, are depreciated over five years; office furniture over six. But an exception in the tax code, known as Section 179, lets you take a generous write-off for business assets that you buy and place in service each year— up to $18,500 in 1998; the amount will rise gradually to $25,000 in 2003. Ask a tax adviser what to write off under Section 179 and what to depreciate over time. The rule of thumb is to use the Section 179 deduction for items that take the longest to depreciate.

One caution for big spenders: The maximum Section 179 deduction is reduced dollar for dollar by the amount of assets in excess of $200,000. If you spent $210,000 in 1998, for example, you can deduct just $8,500 under Section 179.

Business gifts. Since you can deduct only 50% of the cost of business meals and entertainment, consider wooing your clients with gifts rather than dinner. You can fully deduct business gifts up to $25 per recipient per year. Better still, there's no $25 deductibility limit if you make your gifts to a corporation or other business entity rather than to a specific person. For example, if you give 10 $65 theater tickets to a company that's a major supplier, you can deduct the full $650. But don't overreach: If you're audited and the IRS determines that you had actually targeted the gift to a particular person, the $25 limit will be enforced. To help defend your write-off, send a card with the gift, extending your largesse to the firm's entire staff—and keep a copy.

Another way to stretch your gift write-off: If you give a client tickets to an event and don't go along, you can treat the expense either as a gift (limited to $25) or as entertainment (50% deductible), whichever is better for your taxes. If you attend, the cost must be treated as entertainment.

Incorporating. Most businesses start out as sole proprietorships or partnerships because these are simple to establish. As your business grows, however, incorporating could offer significant tax savings. One example: Some so-called C corporations can minimize taxes by splitting the profits between the owner and the corporation because their corporate tax rates on up to $75,000 of income are lower than personal income tax rates. Assume, for example, that you need $100,000 a year to live on and that your retail business is generating $150,000 of taxable income. As a C corp, you can leave $50,000 in the company, where it will be taxed at just 15%, or $7,500. If you took the $50,000 as income, you'd be taxed at your top tax rate, which can run as high as 39.6%, or $19,800. Be aware, however, that you'll owe tax if those earnings are eventually paid out as dividends. To project whether corporate tax breaks are a compelling reason to incorporate, ask your tax adviser. As long as you're self-employed, the consultation will be fully tax deductible.

Home office. It's about to get easier to write off a home office. Under current law if you are, say, a computer consultant whose primary business is to train clients in their workplaces, the office isn't deductible. But starting in 1999, you can deduct expenses for a home office that you use regularly and exclusively to do administrative and managerial tasks, like billing and record keeping. The key: You must have no other fixed location for carrying out these activities. The new rule is much more lenient than the present one, which allows a home-office deduction only if you perform your primary moneymaking function there.

When you consider the tax savings and the convenience, a home office may be more desirable than renting space. For starters, you can allocate a pro rata share of your home's expenses to the office. If you have a 1,500 square-foot house and your office occupies 150 square feet, you can claim 10% of the expenses of running your home. Note: You may be able to boost your write-off based on the number of rooms rather than square footage. Say your house has seven rooms of roughly equal size and you use one for your office. You could deduct 14.29% of your home's expenses for the office. Allowable costs include a portion of your mortgage interest or rent, property taxes, homeowners insurance, general home repairs, security system, trash collection fees and utilities.

You can also depreciate over 39 years the part of your home's purchase price plus improvements attributable to the office. Note that any amount you claim for depreciation after May 6, 1997 will be subtracted from the tax-free profits you're allowed to pocket when you sell your home ($500,000 for married couples, $250,000 for singles) and taxed at 25%. Still, the benefits you reap over the years through depreciation will likely outweigh the tax hit when you sell.

IF YOU CAN'T PAY, DON'T PANIC

April 15 is looming. Your tax return shows a balance due, and you can't come up with the cash. It's time do some damage control.

First, file your return. Failure to file is a far worse offense than failure to pay. The penalty for not filing is 5% a month of your unpaid tax, up to 25%. So if you owe $5,000, your fine is $250 for each month your return is late, up to $1,250. In contrast, the fine for not paying is 0.5% a month, up to 25% ($25 a month on a $5,000 unpaid balance).

Next, if you know you can pay your debt within a couple of months, don't bother to attach an explanation of your tax delinquency to your return. Just be sure to send a check promptly for the balance due, plus penalty and interest to the IRS Service Center where you file. Write "Form 1040, 1998" and your Social Security number on the check.

But if you expect your tax bill to hamstring you for quite some time, take a different tack: If you owe less than $10,000 and will be able to pay it off within three years, attach a form called "Installment Agreement Request" to your return. Enter the largest amount you can reasonably pay each month. And take heart. The IRS grants most installment-payment requests.

If you owe $10,000 or more or need more than 36 months to pay, file your return and then call your local IRS office to explain the problem. The IRS representative will probably want a face-to-face meeting, during which you'll complete a detailed financial statement. If your disclosures show that you can get your hands on cash—say, by taking out a home-equity loan—the IRS isn't likely to cut you any slack. But if you've truly hit a rough patch, you can work out a payment plan.

A SMALL PROBLEM CAN BE BIG TROUBLE

What would you do if the Internal Revenue Service mailed you an unexpected check for $11,515? If you're like John and Toni Ryerson, who received just such a surprise in July 1996, you'd first try to figure out what the check was for and then call the IRS for confirmation. You might even put it in a bank for safekeeping until the situation was straightened out. Simple, right? No way.

Accepting an undeserved tax refund entangled the Ryersons in a nerve-wracking two-year dispute with the IRS. Along the way, they received a bill totaling $15,090 for overdue taxes plus interest and penalties and more than half a dozen harassing notices, including a "final notice" last February saying that the IRS would levy their paycheck, bank account, car or other property.

"It was a mistake that snowballed," says John, 58, a retired computer hardware and software designer.

"We hadn't done anything wrong, so we thought the IRS would figure it out," adds his wife Toni, 54. "We're a lot wiser now."

The big mix-up. After three years in retirement, John and Toni Ryerson finally sold their Boca Raton, Fla. home in 1995 and moved to a scenic hillside in Pisgah Forest deep in the North Carolina mountains. They were looking forward to the area's lively cultural life and abundant opportunities for sports and volunteerism. Plus, thanks to lower housing prices, they'd netted more than $40,000 in profit on the sale of their Florida house. Looking ahead to the day when they might want to sell their new home, the pair passed up the one-time capital-gains exclusion then available to a taxpayer over age 55 in case they wanted to use it in the future. Although the law then gave taxpayers up to two years to pay capital-gains tax on a house sale, John and Toni included the more than $40,000 profit on their 1995 tax return.

That's why the couple mistakenly assumed the $11,515 refund check was the agency's way of reminding them they were eligible to take the exclusion on their gain. "We couldn't be sure, though," says John, "because there was no explanation with the check." To learn more, he dialed the customer service number listed on the refund form, but the representative couldn't help them. "All he had in the computer was the same notice I had," recalls John. "He advised us to wait to hear further."

It wasn't until nine months later that the Ryersons realized that the unexpected refund had been an early-warning sign of trouble. In March 1997, they received a form letter from the IRS asking whether John's 1995 pension payout was taxable. After a 32-year career at IBM, John had converted his lump-sum pension benefit into an insurance annuity paying $42,398 a year for life. The couple knew they'd reported the pension and paid the tax—John was scrupulous when it came to figuring their taxes, and Toni double-checked his entries. They replied in writing that the pension was taxable. "I sensed something was wrong, though," acknowledges John, so he also called the 800 number listed on the letter. The number was different from the one he'd tried a year earlier to ask about the refund, but the result was the same. The computer records available to the phone representative contained only the correspondence John had already received. "What's the use in calling when all they can tell you is what you already know," he says in exasperation.

The bombshell. Instead of telling John to wait for a written response to his letter, the IRS service representative should have referred him to the Problem Resolution Office—the official IRS resource for beleaguered taxpayers—for further assistance. For their part, the Ryersons should have consulted a tax accountant or attorney. They didn't, says John, "because we had not violated any tax law. I felt aggravated but not really vulnerable."

The bombshell came in June 1997, when the couple were notified that their 1995 return did not include an annuity payout of $42,398 that had been reported by John's insurance company. The IRS demanded either an explanation or $15,090 to cover tax, interest and a stiff 20% penalty for nonreporting of income. That's when the Ryersons realized that the unexplained refund was for the tax they'd paid on the pension, not the capital gains from the sale of their Boca Raton house.

But why had the agency refunded tax that the couple rightly owed? No one at the time had an answer. Nevertheless, the couple agreed they should pay back the $11,515 refund because it was tax they actually did owe. But they didn't feel they should ante up $3,575 in interest and penalties, since the IRS had sent them the check and, despite many phone calls and letters, could not explain why. John then wrote a letter appealing those assessments and sent it to the local service center listed on the bill they had received.

The IRS answers. Within a week, the couple received a letter from the IRS agreeing that the $2,304 penalty was undeserved and would be removed. The letter said, however, that the $1,271 interest assessment would be evaluated by another office.

A month later the couple got a four-page letter explaining why the IRS would not remove the interest due on the mistaken refund. It said that the problem originated when John reported his 1995 annuity payout on both lines that cover pensions on a 1040 return: line 16a, which is labeled "total pensions," and line 16b, which reads "taxable pensions." (The 1040 instruction booklet tells taxpayers to record fully taxable pensions on line 16b only.) The double entry caused the IRS computers to "zero out" his pension, resulting in the unexpected refund.

However, when the IRS compared its records with John's 1099-R (retirement) income statement from the insurance company, it appeared as if he had never declared the $42,398 payout on his 1995 return. It would not remove the interest charge because the Ryersons had made the initial filing error. The IRS representative also felt that the Ryersons hadn't tried hard enough to correct the resulting IRS error.

Irate, the couple paid the $11,515, but once again contested the interest assessment. Meanwhile, the IRS started threatening to levy the Ryersons' property. Although the case was in appeal, they received three notices by certified mail warning that the agency would put liens on their property unless the interest debt was settled.

The couple then called their congressman, Charles Taylor, who notified the IRS. "He found out they'd lost the appeal documents," says John. "Can you believe this? They're threatening our property, the appeal is stopped dead, and no one at the IRS even calls me?"

The Ryersons resubmitted their appeal, but by now they were worried that an IRS action would taint their credit record. So they reluctantly sent a check for the interest—which had oddly diminished to $1,236 on a notice that was dated Jan. 29, 1998. Despite their attempt to end the harassment once and for all, a "final notice on intent to levy" arrived on Feb. 2. "At that point, we called our congressman again and even our senator, Lauch Faircloth," says John. Congressional intervention seemed to stop the levy notices, but it took two more months for the couple to receive a letter abating the interest and closing out their debt with the IRS. They finally received a check from the IRS returning their interest payment in mid-May. "A lot of people probably give up and just let them keep the money," says John. "I think that's what they're counting on."

IRS spokeswoman Jodi Patterson agrees that the agency mishandled the Rysersons' case but insists the agency is trying to do a better job of seeing problems from the taxpayer's point of view. Indeed, recent IRS reform legislation should help thwart agency abuses. In Tax Court, for example, taxpayers would be presumed innocent until proved guilty, as they are in the rest of our judicial system. But most run-ins with the IRS never wind up in court. To spare yourself extra cost and unnecessary anxiety when dealing with the IRS, tax expert Martin Kaplan, a C.P.A. with 20 years experience representing clients in tax disputes, suggests the following cautions:

♦ **Never cash a refund check you aren't sure you deserve.** Don't try to second-guess the IRS, urges Kaplan. If you aren't expecting the money, either put the check in the drawer, pending an explanation, or send it back to the address it came from. Depositing an unexpected check can create serious consequences, as the Ryersons found. Once the IRS discovers the mistake, the agency will demand that you pay interest from the date you cashed the refund check. You may even be assessed a penalty for accepting cash you had no reason to think was yours.

♦ **Reply to every notice in writing.** Call if it makes you feel better to talk to a human being, says Kaplan, but always send follow-up letters by certified mail to the address on the notice. Include photocopies of every relevant document, including your 1040 and any correspondence you've had to date. Don't assume the IRS has copies of anything, including your return. By the time a problem crops up, says Kaplan, "your paper return is stored in a warehouse."

♦ **Pay any tax you owe immediately.** You can withhold disputed interest and penalties, but to show good faith (and stop the clock on further assessments), pay any overdue tax right away. Keep in mind, says Kaplan, that each tax year stands alone. As the Ryersons learned, "If you figure a tax liability from one year can be covered with a tax payment submitted with another year's return," says Kaplan, "you'll just dig yourself in deeper."

♦ **For help, try the Problem Resolution Office.** True, congressional offices have pipelines to the IRS, says Kaplan, but your case better be air-tight or the agency may view the intervention from Capitol Hill as unfair pressure and stiffen its attitude.

♦ **In certain cases, hire a pro.** If your position is questionable or there's big money at stake, consider using a tax professional. Even if you prepared your returns yourself, most C.P.A.s will represent you, and the IRS has special phone numbers reserved for professionals. You'll have to pay $100 an hour or so for four or five hours' work, but it will be worth it. In high-stakes cases, you need an expert negotiator who's partial to your side and has experience arguing taxpayer cases with the IRS.

SOCIAL SECURITY TIPS FOR ALL AGES

Americans are obsessed with income taxes, but there's a parallel tax universe that can be just as costly. This often overlooked world is made up of

Social Security and Medicare taxes, levies on Social Security benefits and penalties for trying to work and collect benefits too. It operates with its own set of unnatural laws. Learning to use these arcane rules to your advantage can make both your working years and your retirement more profitable. Here, we will spotlight the quirks and mysteries of Social Security. Our goal is to arm you with information you can use either to reduce your Social Security taxes if you are still working or to boost your Social Security benefits if you have already retired.

If you're paying into Social Security. Many people pay more FICA, or payroll, tax than income tax. The FICA tax is made up of two separate levies. The Social Security tax is 12.4% on your wages, up to a maximum that can rise each year. In 1999, you will pay no Social Security tax on wages over $72,600. The Medicare tax is 2.9%, with no wage limit. (If you're an employee, you pay 50% of the FICA tax; your employer pays the other half. Self-employed people pay the whole wad, which for them is called the self-employment tax.) But there are things you can do to limit the damage. For starters, not all earnings are subject to FICA withholding. For example, any money you put into a flexible spending account (FSA) at work escapes FICA taxes. The recent transportation bill also provides some modest relief. This new law lets you take a transit voucher, free of income and Social Security tax, in lieu of salary. The most you can take tax-free is $65 a month, for a FICA tax saving of $60 a year.

Business owners can't reduce self-employment tax with an FSA. But they can ease the bite by hiring their children—provided the children do legitimate work—and writing off the kids' salaries as a business expense. Moreover, if your children are under age 18, they owe no FICA tax on the wages you pay them.

If you're receiving benefits (or will be soon). Few retirees feel like high-bracket taxpayers, but it doesn't take much income to subject your Social Security benefits to taxes. Since 1994, couples with a base income of $32,000 to $44,000 ($25,000 to $34,000 for singles) pay tax on up to 50% of benefits. If your base income exceeds $44,000 for couples ($34,000 for singles), up to 85% of your benefits may be taxable. (Base income is your adjusted gross income—AGI—plus any tax-exempt interest you received and half of your Social Security benefits.)

If your Social Security benefits are in danger of being taxed, planning can limit the damage. For example, let's say that to provide necessary living expenses, you are taking large IRA withdrawals and selling some stock every year, and because of that extra income, your benefits are being taxed. If that's the case, you may be able to stay under the tax threshold in alternate years by taking out more than you need one year, less than you need the next.

Deferring interest income can protect your benefits too. For example, you can move cash into Series EE U.S. Savings Bonds, which are competitive with other vehicles for cash but let you defer income until you cash in the bonds. Or you can lock into CDs that mature in a year or more. In years when you take capital gains, you can wipe them off by selling off losers.

If you wait for benefits. You can start collecting benefits as soon as you reach age 62, but you'll get less than you would by waiting until you're 65. At 62, for example, your benefit will be 80% of the full amount. Still, receiving three extra years of benefits generally puts you ahead. It typically takes about 12 years—until age 77—for the fatter checks you would get at age 65 to catch up. If you invest the early payments instead of spending them, the break-even point is even further way.

But there are many instances where waiting until age 65 to claim your benefits pays off. One example: if you plan to keep working and are earning more than the limits on supplemental income for Social Security recipients, which we will describe in a moment. It can also pay to wait if your income will be high enough to trigger tax on your benefits. In both cases, you may be better off dipping into savings or investments for any extra money you need, rather than starting to draw Social Security early.

If you work after retirement. Taking Social Security benefits while you continue to work can dent your pocketbook. In 1999, retirees ages 65 to 69 will lose $1 in benefits for every $3 earned over $15,500. (Only earned income is counted. Dividends, interest income and rents don't jeopardize benefits. If you're self-employed, only net earnings come into play.) Recipients who are under 65 forfeit $1 of benefits for each $2 earned over $9,600. Once you reach age 70, you are free to earn as much as you like without losing any Social Security money.

So before you take a post-retirement job, it makes sense to compute how much the money you earn will cost you in tax and loss of benefits. Suppose you make $2,000 above the $9,600 threshold, and that extra income bumps you into the 28% tax bracket. First, you will pay 7.65% FICA tax on the extra $2,000, or $153. Next, you pay an extra $1,039 of income tax because you're in a higher bracket and more of your Social Security is taxable. Finally, you must give back $1,000 of your Social Security benefits. Your cost of making that extra two grand: $2,192.

PRESERVE THE WEALTH IN YOUR ESTATE

If you know how to work the rules, death taxes—those steep federal levies that erode your wealth as it passes from one generation to the next—can be avoided or at least substantially reduced. And don't assume you'll never be rich enough to have a taxable estate. Even though the 1997 tax law will soon let you leave your heirs as much as $1 million worth of assets without triggering estate taxes, you still may not have all the tax protection you need. In fact, when you add up such assets as your 401(k) and other retirement accounts, your home and the death-benefit payout of your life insurance, your estate is probably worth more than you think.

Consider this: Once your estate tops the maximum exempt amount— $625,000 in 1998, rising gradually to $1 million in 2006—the tax rate starts at 37% and increases to 55% on estates over $3 million. "At these rates, it's very possible that much of the wealth you've accumulated over your entire life won't make it to your kids," warns David S. Rhine, national director of family wealth planning at BDO Seidman, an accounting firm in New York City.

To develop an effective tax-slashing estate plan, you'll need the guidance of a trusted estate-planning attorney; otherwise, you risk dying with a plan that only combative heirs and grasping tax collectors will appreciate. You and your spouse should expect to pay about $150 to $500 for a pair of wills, the cornerstone of most any estate plan, and $1,000 to $5,000 for the legal work required to use common tax-skirting techniques, such as the ones we are about to discuss.

Credit-shelter trust. With the hike in the estate-tax exemption, this type of trust (also called a *bypass* or *family trust*) has taken on added luster. That's because a credit-shelter trust ensures that a husband and wife can ultimately double the amount of tax-free assets they leave their kids—up to $2 million in 2006 and beyond.

To understand how such a trust works, consider the fairly typical situation of Doug and Maureen Wulf, both 35, of Denver. For the first few years after they were married in 1990, the couple spent much of their income on travel—logging visits to 26 countries on six continents—and the rest paying down student loans and credit-card debt. Since then, however, they have acquired two priceless assets, tots Conor and Kathleen. Mainly because of Doug's success as a real estate broker earning roughly $200,000 a year, the couple have also amassed an estate worth nearly $2 million, including their $500,000 four-bedroom home, a $560,000 investment portfolio and $450,000 in term life insurance policies—$300,000 for Doug and $150,000 for Maureen. "Our attitudes and priorities have changed a lot since Conor and Kathleen were born," says Doug.

With both a family and their wealth to protect, the Wulfs' estate-planning goals are twofold: first, to ensure that the surviving spouse will be financially secure after the other dies, and second, to preserve as much of the family wealth as possible for their children.

Clearly, the Wulfs could take care of each other by simply writing wills in which Doug leaves everything to Maureen and vice versa. Such a transfer would automatically be tax-free since a provision in the tax law known as the marital deduction lets you bequeath any amount to your spouse without owing tax (as long as your spouse is a U.S. citizen). But passing everything to the spouse merely postpones the tax hit until he or she dies, undercutting the Wulfs' second objective of shielding the family fortune from tax.

To solve the dilemma, Doug and Maureen each wrote a will bequeathing to a credit-shelter trust property valued up to the maximum estate exemption at the time of death. Each stipulated that the trust income go to the surviving spouse and that the principal pass to their kids after the survivor dies.

Assume, for example, that Doug dies first, sometime well into the 21st century. Under the terms of his will, assets worth $1 million will flow into his credit-shelter trust estate tax-free, thanks to the $1 million exemption. The remainder of his estate will pass directly to Maureen, escaping estate tax because of the marital deduction.

When Maureen dies, the contents of Doug's trust will be distributed to their children. No estate tax will be due on those distributions—no matter how much the trust has grown since Doug's death—since the original contribution was covered by the $1 million exemption. In addition, Maureen's estate will qualify for its own $1 million exemption, enabling her to bequeath her own assets, up to that amount, estate-tax-free.

One warning: A credit-shelter trust can be funded only with separately owned assets. So if you and your spouse own most of your assets jointly, you'll need to retitle some of them in one name to ensure that they can pass into the trust as planned. Cautions T.J. Agresti, an estate-planning attorney in Denver: "Failure to look closely enough at how the assets are owned is probably the most common mistake in estate planning."

Generation-skipping trust.
As your circumstances evolve, so must your estate plan. Like the Wulfs, Ron Eastman, 62, and his wife Joanne, 61, of Naples, Fla. have wills that include credit-shelter trusts, which they drew up in 1986. After the Eastmans die, the trust assets will go to their two children, Randall, 38, and Julie, 36. In the years since the Eastmans established that basic estate plan, however, both their family and their fortune have grown. The clan now includes a daughter-in-law and three grandchildren. Meanwhile, Ron and Joanne's estate has exploded to $7.2 million, made up mainly of their 51% share of a sporting-goods dealership they own with their children, their $950,000 primary residence, a $300,000 lakeside vacation home in Minnesota and their stock portfolio.

Obviously, the Eastmans' estate has outgrown their original plan. Since Randall and Julie are already financially secure, the Eastmans have set their sights on sharing their wealth with their grandchildren.

To do so in a tax-savvy way, they've earmarked nearly $2 million for a so-called generation-skipping trust. In such a setup, the trust beneficiaries—generally your grandchildren—must be at least two generations your junior. You can, however, stipulate in the trust document that your own children may receive the trust income and that they can even tap the principal to pay for virtually anything that can be said to benefit the grandchildren, such as housing, health care for the entire family, and college education. As Robert Buckel, a Naples estate-planning attorney, explains: "The trust lets you funnel money to your child, but since you don't actually give the property to him or her, the sum is never included in your child's estate."

In the Eastmans' case, for example, the three grandchildren are the beneficiaries of the generation-skipping trust. But their father, Randall, is entitled to the trust income—and has control over the principal. When Randall dies, the assets remaining in the trust will go to his kids without ever being diminished by taxes in his estate.

Says family patriarch Ron Eastman: "There will be some estate tax on the wealth that I've accumulated; that's inevitable. But I see no reason for estate tax to be paid again when my son dies. Besides, it's important to me to leave something for my grandkids."

One drawback: You'll create an estate-tax quagmire if you leave your grandchildren more than $1 million (or $2 million if you give jointly with your spouse). Above those amounts, bequests to grandkids are subject to yet another levy, the stiff 55% generation-skipping transfer tax, which is separate from estate tax. The generation-skipping transfer tax doesn't apply if you leave assets to the children of a deceased son or daughter.

Family limited partnership. As with the Eastmans, a family business is the largest asset in the estate of Sonny Rianda, 65, and his wife Lillian, 66. The Riandas own a $6 million, 600-acre vegetable farm in Gonzalez, Calif., part of which Sonny inherited from his father in the late '60s. In keeping with family tradition, Sonny's child Michael wants to continue running the farm after his parents die. But the Riandas also want to give their other three children an ownership stake in the farm. Accordingly, the couple's biggest estate-planning challenge was to ensure that the children won't have to sell so much of the land to pay estate tax that there won't be any farm left to run.

Unfortunately, the 1997 tax law provided scant relief for family business owners like the Riandas. True, starting in 1998, a small business owner has been able to claim an estate-tax exemption of $1.3 million, compared with the $1 million exemption that goes into effect for everyone else in 2006. But many family businesses exceed that limit. Besides, the law places so many restrictions on qualifying for the bolstered exemption that "the change is more smoke and mirrors than substantive help," says estate-planning attorney Martin Shenkman in New York City.

So the Riandas are sticking with a classic, albeit complicated strategy known as a family limited partnership. In effect, the Riandas are giving away the farm while they're alive, rather than bequeathing it in their wills or transferring it through a trust. The partnership arrangement lets the couple control the farm as general partners while gradually bestowing interests in the business on their children as limited partners. Since the kids don't control the business, however, the value of their interests is heavily discounted from the fair market value of the farm itself. In the Riandas' case, the discount came to 30%. (The IRS is on the lookout for excessive discounts, so if you consider setting up a family limited partnership, you're well-advised to hire an appraiser who specializes in such arrangements to compute the markdown.) So far, Sonny and Lillian have given their children interests with a fair market value of nearly $3 million—or just under 50% of the farm. But the couple haven't incurred any tax. Here's why: The first transfer, which they made in 1991, had a fair market value of $1.7 million but a discounted value of just $1.2 million. That discounted amount was equal to the estate-tax exemption back then for the two of them. Each subsequent transfer has had a discounted value of no more than $20,000 per child each year. The tax law lets you make annual tax-free gifts of up to $10,000 a year to each of as many people as you wish, $20,000 if you make the gift jointly with your spouse.

Irrevocable life insurance trust. If a life insurance payout will trigger tax on your estate, you may want to consider setting up one of these. When you place your policy in an irrevocable life insurance trust, you give up all your ownership rights—among them the ability to borrow against the policy or change the beneficiaries. In exchange, the policy is no longer part of your taxable estate. So, when you die, the proceeds will go to the beneficiaries, estate-tax-free.

The sooner you create a life insurance trust, the greater its tax-sheltering potential. That's because a transfer to an irrevocable trust is subject to gift tax if its value exceeds $10,000 a year ($20,000 for joint gifts). But with life insurance, you generally compute the gift value by adding up the total premiums you've paid so far or its current cash value, depending on the type of policy. The newer the policy, the greater the likelihood that figure will be under the annual gift threshold. If it exceeds those limits, the excess is subtracted from the maximum estate-tax exemption allowed at your death.

Another reason for prompt action: If you die within three years of placing your policy in the trust, the proceeds are included in your estate.

◆ CHAPTER 4

HOW TO PUSH FOR TOP 401 (K) PERFORMANCE

Without a doubt your best vehicle for long-term growth is a tax-deferred savings plan. You have several options to choose from, including an IRA, but for overall perks, you're unlikely to beat your company-sponsored 401(k) plan. The money you invest in a 401(k) is deducted from your taxable income, so you owe nothing to Uncle Sam until you withdraw it. And most companies that sponsor 401(k)s will buttress your contributions with their own, typically half of the first 6% of your salary that you put in. People who work for nonprofit groups, like public schools, have their own version of the plans, known as 401(b)s, and so do employees of state or local governments, who get tax-advantaged savings in plans called 457s.

If you haven't yet been convinced of the power of tax-deferred savings, consider this: Say that throughout her career a 35-year-old saves 6% of a $60,000 salary in a taxable portfolio of funds. If that money earns 8% a year, she would have about $284,000 by age 65, assuming a 28% federal tax rate. But if she put that same amount in a 401(k), she would accumulate $571,000. She'd have to pay income taxes on the money she withdraws. But since she could take the money out gradually, she'd lessen the tax bite, and she would be able to leave the rest to grow tax-deferred.

Unless you become disabled, you generally can't get your money back before age 59 1/2 without owing a 10% penalty on the amount you withdraw, plus regular income taxes. But most companies let you borrow against your account without penalty or tax as long as you pay the loan back. And if you leave the company, you have several options for holding on to your money without penalty or tax, and—depending on how long you've been in the plan—some of your company's matching contributions as well.

Not that long ago, few people were attached to the idea of the 401(k) company savings plan. Now the plans are as much a part of corporate America as casual Fridays—and even more beloved. Many grateful employees have come to view their accounts as magic moneymaking machines since, by stashing part of your paycheck in them, you can get an instant tax deduction, a matching contribution and tax-deferred growth for your investments. But you can't just sit back and wait for your money to grow. You must be aggressive in making decisions about your 401(k). This chapter will help you take charge and get maximum benefits from your plan.

ALWAYS CONTRIBUTE ALL YOU CAN

The first step to getting the most out of your 401(k) is to make sure you're putting the most into it. Your employer sets the maximum contribution as a percentage of your salary up to the IRS limit of $10,000 a year.

If you can't afford to save the max, at least kick in enough to take advantage of any money your employer is handing out. More than 70% of companies nationwide match some portion of their employees' contributions. "You ought to have your head examined if you don't contribute enough to get your 401(k) matching contribution from your employer," says Malcolm Makin, a financial planner in Westerly, R.I. "But I'm continually amazed at how many people I see who fail to do that."

BE AWARE OF INVESTMENT CHOICES

The typical 401(k) offers a choice of mutual funds. The mix might consist of a money-market fund, a "stable value" account or bond fund, a balanced fund, a growth fund, an aggressive growth or small-company fund, and an international fund. Some large corporations give you a choice of 35 or more funds, but more typically there are fewer than 10 options.

The funds available can be either retail funds (the kind open to investors) or private accounts managed by banks, insurance companies and money-management firms. The retail funds are becoming more common, because fund companies are homing in on the big 401(k) business. The advantage of retail funds is that, by law, they must provide investors with extensive information, including the name of the manager or managers and a detailed prospectus that describes the fund's expenses and investment policies. Most private funds are not required to disclose that much detail.

FOLLOW FIVE KEY RULES

Don't use your 401(k) as a credit line. If you're among the 15% of 401(k) participants who have outstanding loans, you're well aware that most plans allow you to borrow as much as half your vested account balance (up to $50,000) at attractive terms. In fact, they may be a little too attractive. Consider borrowing from your 401(k) only as a last resort, ideally only for a house down payment or medical bills. For one thing, if you change jobs, retire or are laid off, you typically must pay back the outstanding balance in full. Otherwise, that amount will be considered an early distribution on which you will owe tax, plus a 10% penalty if you're younger than 55. Moreover, a loan eliminates one of your 401(k)'s biggest advantages, which is that you don't pay taxes on what you invest until you withdraw it. If you borrow from your 401(k), the money you use to repay the loan is taxed once as income—and again when you withdraw it. Finally, if you stop contributions until your loan is repaid, your 401(k) could be worth at least 20% less by the time you retire, according to a recent study by the General Accounting Office.

The best policy is to borrow against your 401(k) only if you can keep investing while you repay the loan and you've exhausted all other avenues of funding. And, again, make sure what you hope to achieve with the loan is at least as important as living comfortably in retirement. "Too many people tap their 401(k) to buy a boat or truck," says Garrett Ahrens, an investment adviser at Balentine & Co. in Natchez, Miss. "During the time of the loan, your 401(k) could have doubled."

Don't dump your dough when you change jobs. More than half of participants in large 401(k) plans succumb to temptation and spend their account balances after leaving a job, according to Deborah Neilson, president of Communi(k), a retirement communication and educational services firm in Portland, Ore. Bad move. Very bad. Not only does spending a distribution rob you of retirement savings, but what looks at first like a fat check ends up being shockingly lean after taxes, says Martha Priddy Patterson, an employee-benefits consultant at the accounting firm

KPMG. After paying the 10% penalty, perhaps getting kicked up to the 39.6% tax bracket thanks to your 401(k) windfall and paying state tax in a high-tax state like Maryland (8%), you may find that a $10,000 distribution puts less than $4,000 in your pocket. You're far better off leaving your 401(k) balance in your former employer's plan (which you are entitled to do if you've accumulated at least $5,000) or rolling the money over into an IRA. You may also be able to roll the money over into your new employer's plan.

Don't be too cautious. Too many people assume that when saving for something as important as retirement, safety should be the paramount consideration. As a result, a quarter of 401(k) assets are in stable-value funds, money-market funds and other fixed-income options that historically have barely kept pace with inflation. When it comes to retirement investing, however, the real risk is not that you'll lose money—it's that you may not earn enough on your savings to reach your goals. And over the long run, stocks offer the best chance for the big gains you need.

Diversify, but don't go overboard. Even though the average plan offers seven investment choices, the typical participant uses only two. That's not enough to give you risk-reducing diversification. On the other hand, when you're starting out it doesn't make sense to spread a $100 monthly contribution over seven funds, says Mary Rudie Barneby of the National Defined Contribution Council, which represents 401(k) sponsors. For the first few years, direct your contribution into a fund investing in large U.S. stocks and a fund that buys small to mid-size U.S. stocks. As your account grows, Barneby suggests adding two or three options, such as international, real estate or emerging markets funds.

Rebalance your account, but don't try to time markets. Many 401(k)s now allow you to shift your investment mix by phone every day. Having that option may lead you to think you're not being conscientious if you're not moving money around regularly. In fact, constant juggling is the worst thing you can do, because odds are you'll end up buying high and selling low. By rebalancing annually, you'll tend to do the opposite. Set goals for what proportion of your total 401(k) money should be in each type of investment. Then evaluate where you stand when you receive your year-end statement. Say you want to have your money divided equally among five funds. At year-end, you may find that one fund has performed so well that it now represents 30% of your account, while another has been in a cyclical downturn and represents only 10%. To rebalance, lock in gains on your winner by ditching enough shares to bring it down to 20% of your total balance and reinvest that money in the laggard to bring it back up to 20%.

BATTLE FOR A BETTER PLAN

Many 401(k) plans could be a whole lot better. The heart of the problem is that when you enter a 401(k), you give up control of your money. And for a variety of reasons, even well-regarded employers and plan providers fill 401(k)s with decidedly mediocre investment options. Many, if not most, employees are stuck with too few choices and too little information to make the choices they do have. Ultimately, the impact of subpar investment results over, say, a 30-year career can be staggering.

It all starts with the way 401(k)s are designed and administered. Your company, inevitably, is trying to spend as little as possible in sponsoring a plan. Providers of these plans, understandably, are focused on turning a profit. The perspective of the plan participants can get lost in the shuffle. As 401(k) analyst Kathleen Hartman of Chicago investment firm Morningstar explains, "401(k) participants are responsible for their own financial security, but they have no control over the structure of their plans."

Now, it may seem churlish to complain about something as generous as the 401(k), which provides retirement benefits to millions of employees who otherwise might not have any. In fact, says David Godofsky, a Nashville benefits consultant, "except in rare cases, even a bad plan is a lot better than none." We agree. But on the other hand, with so much money being invested in the plans, the shortcoming of a middling 401(k) can prove significant. Last year more than 25 million workers had $1 trillion stashed in their 401(k) accounts, according to Spectrem Group/Access Research, a financial services consulting firm based in Waterbury, Conn. The average balance was a substantial $35,000, and 10% of accounts held $100,000 or more. With numbers that large, the costs of a less than perfect plan become magnified. Say you earn $70,000 a year and stash 8% in a 401(k) that includes a modest employer match. Over 30 years, earning a return of 6% annually rather than 8% could leave you with $936,000 instead of $1.3 million, or 25% less.

We are not alleging that your company or the plan providers are doing anything evil with your 401(k). They are simply approaching these plans as one piece of their business. You have to be just as businesslike to protect your interests. What follows is a hard look at how 401(k) plans may be letting you down, as well as advice on how to persuade your company to upgrade its plan:

Limited choices, poor returns. As a plan participant your needs are pretty simple: a range of top-performing options representing different asset classes and investment styles. Chances are, though, you won't spot that All-Star lineup in your 401(k). "Many companies, especially small and mid-size firms, lack the expertise to evaluate funds," says Peter Starr, a consultant with Cerulli Associates, a Boston market research firm. "So they simply take what the fund company is pushing or what their investment adviser recommends."

Even among large companies, that often means big, brand-name funds from families such as Putnam or T. Rowe Price. But a household name is no guarantee of good performance. Brand-name 401(k) funds often face a special handicap: swelling asset size. When a fund is available in a large number of 401(k) plans, it begins mainlining cash, sometimes millions of dollars a day. Having to put that much money to work all but forces fund managers to load up on the biggest blue-chip stocks. "As 401(k) portfolios grow, they tend to become expensive index funds," says Scott Lummer, chief investment officer at 401(k) Forum, a San Francisco consulting firm. "Inevitably performance gets dragged down."

Won't the people sponsoring your 401(k) plan be quick to dump poor or inconsistent performers? After all, under the law governing retirement plans, the Employment Retirement Income Security Act (ERISA), employers have a fiduciary responsibility to provide sound investments to their employees. But that doesn't mean they have to provide the best investments, which is precisely what you want. Then there are bureaucratic concerns. "Human-resources execs are often hesitant to get rid of funds for fear of upsetting employees who chose them," says Gary Blank, a San Francisco pension consultant. Ted Benna, a pension consultant in Cross Fork, Pa. and inventor of the 401(k) plan, adds that "companies are worried about potential [legal] liability, since there's a fifty-fifty chance that if they drop a fund it may go on to outperform the substitute."

Plan sponsors may also be reluctant to sever ties with a company that provides reliable administrative service. For example, says Jim Klein, a principal with Towers Perrin in New York City, "Fidelity has such a wonderful image and high level of service that sponsors will forgive a lot in terms of performance."

One sign that companies may be putting convenience ahead of performance: Some 40% of plans restrict their offerings to a single fund family. That makes life easy for the administrators but not for you. In many fund families, the managers follow a similar investing style and often hold the same stocks. "There's no way you can have across-the-board, above-average performance if you stick with one family," says Dan Maul, president of Retirement Planning Associates, an investment advisory firm in Kirkland, Wash.

Some company officials contend that having too many choices can be as much a problem as having too few. We're skeptical of that reasoning. Investors seem to have no trouble discriminating among the many fund and bond options outside their 401(k) accounts. And we're convinced that the need for more and better investing vehicles will only increase as plan participants have more money to put to work.

You're in the dark. All the choices in the world won't help you if you don't have the information you need to make sound decisions. As a conscientious investor, you want to know key facts—for example, the background of the fund manager of the specific stocks in the portfolio—before handing over your money. But when you invest via a 401(k), you can find it difficult, if not impossible, to get that data. If your plan offers retail mutual funds, you probably won't automatically get quarterly or annual reports— which are the only documents that provide data on portfolio holdings—but they are usually available on request. If, however, your plan offers institutional funds, which are not open to the general public, things get a lot sketchier. Institutional funds don't issue prospectuses, and you can't track their performance in the newspapers. That is also true with annuities, sold by insurance companies mainly to small-company plans.

Some plan providers now deliver updated returns and portfolio holdings via the Internet. And several firms are gearing up to offer computerized advice programs to 401(k) participants based on the cutting-edge investment information available to professional money managers. But Stacy Schaus, a principal with benefits firm Hewitt Associates, says expense and bureaucratic concerns make companies reluctant to introduce these new programs.

Fees keep climbing. Fees on many 401(k)s are excessive. This fact sparked hearings by the U.S. Department of Labor in 1997 and prompted the agency to make plans to publish a booklet for consumers to alert them to 401(k) fees. And the Labor Department is continuing to study the need for improved fee guidelines for plan sponsors and providers.

Meanwhile, 401(k) expenses continue to rise. In a recent survey, HR Investment Consultants, a Baltimore firm, found that the average total expenses for a 401(k) plan with 100 participants crept up from 1.3% of assets to 1.37% in just a year; average costs for a plan with 1,000 participants edged up to 1.14% from 1.12%. "Employers who have not been paying attention," says Joseph Valletta, a principal with HR Investment Consultants, "may be surprised to find out how much fees have increased."

You get too much company stock. If your 401(k) includes your employer's stock, as do about 40% of plans, you probably don't realize just how big a chunk you own. On average, employees with a company stock option or match in their plans hold a hefty 33% of their account balances in that single investment. That percentage may well be far higher, especially among companies that match in their own stock or when the 401(k) is a converted profit-sharing plan. For example, in Abbott Lab's 401(k), which was combined with a profit-sharing plan, company stock recently accounted for 88% of assets, according to the Institute for Management & Administration, a New York City research firm.

Pension experts and investment advisers urge you to keep no more than 10% of your portfolio in your employer's stock. "By owning company stock in your plan you are tying both your retirement security and your job to your employer," says Shlomo Benartzi, a business professor at the University of California at Los Angeles. Says Roger Smith, a Sacramento financial planner: "At worst, owning too much company stock is courting disaster because if your company goes belly up, you lose both your job and the bulk of your savings. At best, you're taking on totally unnecessary investment risk."

Once again, diversification—the practice of spreading your risk among a variety of securities—has long been recognized as the most effective way to reduce investment risk. Yet out of a misguided loyalty to the company, inertia or overconfidence, many employees are rejecting the principle wholesale. "It scares the bejeebers out of me," says Smith. But rather than urging moderation, some employers have made it more difficult than ever for their work force to avoid overdosing on the home team's stock.

Over long periods of time, holding a well-diversified stock portfolio—say, upwards of 10 blue chips and conservative growth stocks in different industries—helps to ensure you a return close to the market average. The big winners and losers in your portfolio will cancel one another out. With one stock, in contrast, you can't know ahead of time whether the return will be high, average, low or even negative. Of course, some employees have reaped a fortune with company stock. For example, at Coca-Cola Enterprises, where 75% of 401(k) holdings were in stock, participants saw a lofty gain of 120.7% in 1997, according to IOMA. But at Owens-Corning, where employer shares made up 64.6% of 401(k) assets, participants suffered a stock price tumble of 19.4%. And Hanson Industries workers, where company stock accounted for 43.5% of plan assets, watched the share price plunge a stunning 56.8% in 1997. "Participants don't understand how risky their employer's stock can be," says Benartzi. Companies that want to address this problem, he adds, "must actively discourage employees from buying the stock."

But companies have reasons for pushing their stock into 401(k) plans. Employers say, for example, that putting more company stock in staffers' hands aligns their interests with the shareholders' and helps focus the work force on the bottom line. In addition, the companies say that stock options—in lieu of some salary—let them offer employees more generous total compensation than they could otherwise. That's because while businesses must subtract regular compensation from earnings on their books, they don't have to subtract option grants—or the gains that are realized when the options are exercised. As a result, by "paying" employees with options, a company appears to keep salaries low and earnings high.

Benefits experts add that company managements also have more self-serving motives. For one thing, employees are excellent shareholders from a manager's point of view. They're unlikely to make demands of the managers or the board, and in takeover battles, they almost always side with their bosses. All of which may be fine for your company, but not for your 401(k).

To figure out how overloaded you are, start by adding up the value of all your investments, including retirement and nonretirement savings. Determining the value of your stock options is tricky, but one easy way is to figure what you would pocket after exercising the options and immediately selling the shares. For simplicity's sake, leave taxes out of the computation. Say you have an option to buy 100 shares of company stock at $40 a share and the market price of the stock is now $50. If you exercise the options, you'll pocket $1,000 before taxes, so $1,000 is the value you should be using.

If you determine that more than 10% of your overall portfolio is now in company stock, it's time to stop voluntarily picking up more. If the company's shares make up 20% or more of your holdings, you need to take steps to rebalance your portfolio.

You have to wait a year to join. The only thing worse than having a poorly designed 401(k) plan is not being allowed to save in it. Remember, even if your funds are dogs, you still have the benefit of tax deferral on your savings and probably a company matching contribution. Right now some 96% of companies with 401(k)s require you to wait from several months to as long as a year before you can join. With the average employee changing jobs six times during a working lifetime, that can take a toll. Notes Sean Hanna, editor of 401(k) Wire, an online trade publication: "If you miss six years of saving, it's much more difficult to build the nest egg you need."

Here again, companies may simply be trying to avoid paperwork hassles, since many employees end up leaving during their first year. In addition, complicated federal rules have encouraged companies to limit the eligibility of newcomers.

But recent legislation has changed those rules, and waiting periods are starting to shrink. More companies are allowing their workers to sign up for a 401(k) plan when they are hired or at the time they become eligible for health benefits, according to David Wray, president of the Profit-Sharing Council of America, a plan-sponsor trade group based in Chicago. For example, Hewlett-Packard recently began enrolling its new workers automatically, unless they specifically request not to participate in the plan. And last year at NCR, workers were allowed to sign up for the plan and start receiving matching contributions after their first paycheck. Since you may change jobs sooner or later, it's in your interest—even if you're in a plan—to see this trend become widespread.

How to lobby for a better plan. Persuading your company to improve its 401(k) plan may not be as hard as you think. Bear in mind that the top executives in your firm probably have more at stake than you do. And as Ted Benna points out: "A good 401(k) plan has become a powerful recruiting tool in attracting star employees."

Moreover, a better plan doesn't have to cost a lot. Companies with large plans—those with $100 million in assets or more—have the clout to demand more fund choices at little or no additional expense. And even mid-size plans can usually afford to offer funds from several different families.

Clearly, that message is starting to get through. Today, more companies are adding brokerage accounts, which allow participants to invest in a broad range of funds and individual securities. For example, of the $15 billion in 401(k) assets that Charles Schwab & Co. administers, about $1.5 billion is in self-directed brokerage accounts. Says Schwab senior vice-president Benjamin Brigeman: "Over half of new plans are choosing the brokerage option."

The best way to push for plan improvements is to lobby your benefits department—and get your fellow employees to do the same. Most benefits offices and plan administrators routinely log calls and letters from plan participants to monitor quality of service and identify trouble spots. And many companies survey employee opinion to see whether plan modifications are needed. In 1997, for example, Eastman Kodak hiked the number of investment options in its plan from six to 36 after receiving a flood of calls and letters demanding more choices. "What really drove the need for change home for us was when we brought in five of our fund managers to give a talk," says Eastman Kodak savings plan manager George Dascoulias. "We expected a couple of hundred people, but 1,200 showed up on a snowy night asking about fund performance."

Vocal employees also prompted 401(k) reform at Jefferson Smurfit, a St. Louis-based paper manufacturer. "Participants were unhappy and they let us know by every means they could come up with," says benefits director Cynthia Bowers. "I'd get phone calls, letters and complaints in person." The company increased its investment menu from four funds from one family to 15 chosen from three fund families. Since then, says Bower, "I've received only one complaint—why haven't you done this sooner?" That's a question more 401(k) investors wish they could ask.

DON'T LET ERRORS ERODE EARNINGS

As a result of accidental errors, many employers don't give plan participants all the matching money they expect. Bill Karbon, a consulting actuary at National Retirement Planning, a 401(k) administrator in Jamison, Pa., has estimated that nearly 10% of participants could get as much as a third less than they deserve.

The majority of 401(k) plans require that any employer match be a set percentage of the employee's total annual plan contribution. But the administrators of 401(k) plans often calculate each matching amount by looking at how much you've contributed for only that pay period. So if you alter or suspend your contributions during the year, you might get a mismatch. Say you plan to contribute 8% of your $100,000 salary to your 401(k) and your employer promises to match you dollar for dollar up to 6%. However, after six months you stop contributing; then, so does your employer. Sounds fair, but you've been shortchanged. For the full year, you'll have contributed 4% of your salary ($4,000), but your employer will have kicked in only 3% ($3,000). The company owes you $1,000.

To check whether your 1998 match was too small, first look at your W-2 form to see how much was withheld from your gross pay for 401(k) contributions—and look at your 401(k) statements to make sure your company put that amount into your plan. Then, if the amount your employer gave as a match does not equal the promised percentage of your contribution, point out the problem to your employee-benefits office.

WATCH OUT FOR THESE WARNING SIGNS

Unlike a traditional pension plan, a 401(k) carries no federal insurance to protect employees against theft or mismanagement. And it can happen. When something does go wrong, it's usually at a smaller company. Since 1995, the Department of Labor (DOL) has investigated more than 3,000 instances of potential federal pension law violations in 401(k) plans, recovering some $38 million for more than 30,000 workers. Here's what you need to know in order to make sure your 401(k) stash stays intact.

How's the company doing? "If you hear things are going poorly with the firm, pay close attention to your plan," says Alan Lebowitz, deputy assistant secretary at the DOL's Pension and Welfare Benefits Administration. That's because the DOL has seen firms use 401(k) deposits to cover other company expenses. If you have questions, first get in touch with your plan administrator. If you still aren't satisfied, call a pension adviser at the Department of Labor's Pension and Welfare Benefits Administration.

The statement is your friend. Consistently late statements; contributions that aren't deposited into your 401(k) within 90 days of the money's being withheld from your paycheck; balances that don't add up: These are all signs that something may be amiss with your plan. Don't ignore the statement or blithely chalk up problems to run-of-the-mill bureaucratic hassles.

Beware of vaguely described investments. Most 401(k) plans offer you some choice in how your money is invested, but about 10% don't.

If yours is one of those, make sure you understand where your money is going. Get it in writing from the plan administrator. You should receive a summary plan description—which lists your rights under ERISA—within 90 days of joining. If you ask for a listing of your plan's investments, the company is required by law to give it to you within 30 days. You can also ask the Department of Labor for a copy of your plan's Form 5500 and the accompanying schedules that list its investments. But be aware that at big companies this information can be nearly a year old, and plans with fewer than 100 participants are required to list investments only every three years.

CHAPTER 5

RETIRE RICH WITH THESE NEW RULES

When it comes to retirement planning, change is truly a rare occurrence. There is little debate, in fact, about what the key components of investing for retirement are: Save as much as you can, start as early as you can, and take full advantage of tax-deferred accounts such as 401(k)s and IRAs. That has been the basic advice for many years and will likely remain so for many more years to come.

But every now and then, we hit a turning point—a moment when going beyond those basics can make a significant difference. One point before we get to specifics: Most of the investments we are going to discuss are stock-oriented. That's because, historically, stocks have delivered the best returns over the long term. But as we've emphasized throughout this book, over the short term, stocks can be volatile. Investors who are within a few years of retirement should take care before plunging into new equities. For those with longer time horizons, however, equities still represent your best bet for achieving the most comfortable retirement possible.

RETIRE ON YOUR TERMS

For a while, a chorus of doomsayers have been warning that vast numbers of us are headed for a retirement disaster. According to the Merrill Lynch baby-boom retirement index, for example, free-spending baby boomers must virtually double their savings to avoid steep declines in their standard of living. That's the *optimistic* outlook. Under the index's pessimistic scenarios, boomers should ratchet up savings four to 10 times.

Time for a reality check. Sure, plenty of people should boost their savings. But a retirement crisis with hordes of boomers headed for the dole? No way.

What's really driving these dire prognostications isn't our unwillingness to save. (Indeed, a 1993 Congressional Budget Office study concluded that 35- to 44-year-old boomers had already accumulated nearly twice as much wealth as their parents had at the same age.) The problem is that many researchers and financial planners are factoring 1950s and 1960s notions of retirement into their spreadsheets. They assume that we'll leave work, head for the front porch or back nine and mindlessly draw payments from our pensions and IRA rollovers. Then it's just a matter of which expires first, us or our paltry savings.

Hey, guys, this is the '90s. *Perry Mason* has been replaced by *The Practice.* Retirement is a whole new gig. It's changed so much that the word "retire" itself may be a misnomer; "rehire" may be more like it. Today's retirees are healthier and more active than their parents were—and they won't go gently into geezerhood. In fact, when the American Association of Retired Persons (AARP) polled 2,001 baby boomers last year, fully 80% said they plan to work full or part time after retiring, and about a quarter of this group envisioned starting an entirely new career or launching their own business. And they're not doing it just for the bucks. More often than not, those who planned to work said they'll do it because of the interest and enjoyment they get from working.

There are a variety of roads that can lead to a secure retirement. Indeed, the future is much likely to be brighter than you've been led to believe. Here are some reasons why.

You can catch up. Save as much as you can, as early as you can. As we've said numerous times in this book, that strategy is the primary path to a comfy retirement. But for many people, life gets in the way. Just when we should be putting away money for our future, kids need orthodontics, cars have to be replaced, wedding bills and divorces drain our savings. Before you know it, you're approaching the big five-oh and your 401(k) isn't close to seven figures.

A hopeless situation? Not if you're willing to embark on a bold, creative catch-up plan. Consider the position Robert Douglas, owner of the Chicago executive search firm Chase Hunter Group, found himself in five years ago. Douglas awoke on his 50th birthday and realized he had nothing saved for retirement. "I thought to myself, 'I only have 15 years or so left to work. How am I going to do this?'" Even after that insight, it took another three years before Douglas finally sat down with Chicago financial planner Greg Hilton and came up with a three-step retirement plan to make up for lost time.

The first step was to incorporate Douglas' three-year-old executive search business, which specializes in placing medical professionals. That move allowed him to take advantage of a variety of tax deductions, including tax-deferred savings programs. Douglas has since launched a Simple IRA, a tax-deferred plan that lets him stash away $6,000 a year. His firm can contribute another 3% of his $100,000 salary, boosting his $6,000 to $9,000. The second step of the strategy went into place last August. Douglas sold his condo and bought a two-story house that's large enough for him to live in, run his business from and rent out space. The real estate will provide depreciation deductions, plus throw off rental income—nearly $20,000 a year at the moment. The third step: heavy-duty saving. Hilton and Douglas put together a stringent budget that required Douglas to pay off some $25,000 in credit-card debt and rein in his spending. Those moves will allow him to stick an additional $21,000 a year into no-load stock mutual funds.

Hilton projects that by the time Douglas hits 65, the combination of income from the rental property, Social Security and investments (assuming a conservative 7% rate of return) will provide Douglas, who is single, with an income of about $66,000 a year in today's dollars. At that point, he would have the option of selling his business or continuing to run it part time. The entire plan hinges, of course, on the success of Douglas' business—and his ability to stick to the savings targets. Both seem assured so far. Douglas has expanded his recruiting staff to five people, including a physician he hired last year to recruit and place doctors. "The business is ahead of track," says Douglas, noting that he expects his revenues to at least triple this year and he is aiming to boost his savings. He's living proof that even with a very late start, it is possible to catch up.

You need less than they say. One of the most frequently invoked rules of thumb is that you'll need 70% of your salary to retire comfortably. This rule is based on the "income replacement ratios" that Bruce Palmer of the Georgia State University RETIRE project compiles by massaging Department of Labor spending stats. But, like all averages, this one doesn't reflect the huge amount of wiggle room most of us have for adjusting what we spend. If you've been raising a family, you may be surprised to find out how many expenses just disappear once the kids leave home. That may be why many retirees discover they can live just fine on half or less of their pre-retirement earnings.

Take Bill Barr, a 57-year-old retired commercial litigator who now runs La Belle Vie Farms, a 323-acre farm in College Grove, Tenn. Barr has lived on the farm since the early 1970s, but it wasn't until two years ago that he began growing and selling about 75 varieties of herbs, including French tarragon, oregano and thyme. At the height of his legal career, Barr earned upwards of $250,000, which, using the 70% rule, suggests that he would need an annual retirement income of $175,000.

But Barr says he and his wife Wanda live quite comfortably on $50,000 to $60,000 a year. "There's a whole category of expenses I don't have now," says Barr, who retired in 1994. "I had a round-trip 60-mile commute to work by car; there were business lunches, clothing, a cellular phone. It was very important to be a member of at least one of the two luncheon clubs in the city, the Nashville City Club and the Cumberland Club, and I was a member of both." He estimates that work-related expenses alone ate up at least $25,000 a year. The Barrs are also spending a lot less because their four kids are grown and out of school. "At one point we had six cars—one for everybody in the family," says Barr. Plus, of course, taxes now take a much smaller bite of his income—and he's no longer saving for retirement.

Farm life also has its cost advantages. "We have two refrigerators and two freezers full of food that we grow here, and we're too far away from fast-food delivery to have that haunting us. You don't have that feeling, 'Hey, I'm making a lot of money, so I can spend it.'"

The herb farm has yet to turn a profit, so Barr has drawn most of his income from investments, including a lump-sum pension payment he rolled over into an IRA. But Barr expects his business to blossom. Long term, he believes the operation will provide him with $50,000 or more a year, in part because the profit margins are so high.

Not everyone can live off the land like Bill Barr. But stretching the purchasing power of your income by 15% to 20% just by relocating certainly is a lucrative option. Some retirement specialists dismiss this solution, pointing to a 1996 AARP survey in which eight out of 10 older Americans said they prefer to stay in their own home and never move. But tomorrow's retirees appear to be much more willing to pull up stakes. For example, 45% of the 1,836 people 45 or older with incomes of $75,000 or more surveyed online by *Business Week* and America Online last June said they would consider moving to another region of the country after retiring.

That doesn't really surprise David Savageau, author of *Retirement Places Rated*. "Creative and adventurous boomers are thinking about relocating much more than previous generations did," he says. "They're looking for lower living costs, as well as places that are thriving economically because they want to continue a vocation or avocation."

To get an idea of just how much further relocating can make your income go, check out the Homebuyer's Fair site's Salary Calculator (www.homefair.com), which lets you compare living costs in 700 U.S. cities. A homeowner in, say, Philadelphia with income of $75,000 a year would need about $63,000 annually to maintain a similar standard of living in Bradenton, Fla. or just over $58,000 in Savannah.

You can take a "bridge job." For much of the past 50 years, the goal for most working Americans had been to unshackle themselves from the workaday drudgery and escape to a life of unfettered leisure, the sooner the better. But in the mid-'80s, two curious things began to happen. First, the labor-force participation rates of people 65 and older, which had been on a steady downward trajectory since World War II, leveled off and began slowly inching up, climbing from 10.8% in 1985 to 12.2% in 1997. Second, labor economists noticed that the lines between work and retirement have become increasingly blurred. Instead of abruptly retiring, more and more people today take a "bridge job," a sort of transitional position that eases them out of their career and into retirement.

Besides the lifestyle ramifications, the idea of slouching toward retirement can alleviate some of the pressure to save large sums now. Here's a quick example. Let's say you're 45, earn $60,000 a year and have saved nothing—but you would like to retire at age 60 on an inflation-adjusted annual income, including Social Security, of $42,000. To pull off that feat, you would have to set aside 30% of your salary each year until you hit 60, assuming you earn an ambitious 11% average annual return on your savings. But look what happens if you retire at 60 and work part time for 10 years, making just a quarter of your pre-retirement salary: Your savings burden drops to just over 20% of your present earnings. Put off retirement till age 65 and then work part time for the next 10 years, and your savings hurdle falls to 10% or so a year.

Whether you decide to work for financial reasons or as a way to maintain social ties and stay mentally fit, you'll increase your odds of success by laying the groundwork for your retirement job before you leave your current one. Start by making sure your computer skills are state of the art. "Being computer literate will be an asset no matter what kind of job you look for," says Mary McDougall, a career counselor at the Operation ABLE of Southfield, Mich., a nonprofit organization that assists job seekers age 40 and older. "If your skills aren't up to date, consider enrolling in computer or software courses offered at local community colleges."

Similarly, while you're at your current job, go for any training, licensing or certification from a professional organization that you may need to launch a retirement career. Your tuition-reimbursement plan at work might cover your fees. And if you plan to work as a consultant, as many retirees do, think of special projects you could do for your current employer that can get you started in your new venture.

To get advice on navigating the transition to a new career, try organizations that provide career counseling and skill assessments for older workers, as Operation ABLE does in seven cities around the country. Several Websites can help too. At the Work Section of the Third Age site (www.thirdage.com/work), for example, you'll find a forum where older workers share their job experiences, information on starting a business and links to job-listing sites.

Pat Yauch provides a masterful example of how to use your current job as a springboard to a new retirement career. In 1994, Yauch was already contemplating an early retirement from her six-figure sales support job at Ameritech when she read an article about Anna Navarro, a successful career strategist based in St. Louis. She felt an immediate connection. "I had been coaching people informally for years," says Yauch, 53. "It was the part of my job that I loved." She visited Navarro and underwent a 10-hour self-assessment that concluded Yauch would make an excellent career strategist. Navarro refused to take her on as a student, however, until Yauch got her prodigious spending under control. "I kept telling her, 'Pat, you're going to go through a period where you won't be making the kind of income you did at Ameritech,'" says Navarro. "I didn't want her to fall flat on her face because of that start-up time."

Over the next few months, with the help of her husband Gail and a financial planner, Yauch rid herself of $15,000 in credit-card debt and cut back her spending. In the fall of 1995, she and Navarro began a 60-hour training program, during which Yauch provided career guidance for friends. That November, Ameritech announced a restructuring that would spell job losses for 30 people in Yauch's division. Aware of her coaching experience, a vice president asked if she could offer career assistance to departing employees. Seeing this opportunity as a step toward her new career, Yauch accepted, and decided to retire early.

"I was doing career guidance my last six months at Ameritech for about 30 people," says Yauch. "I was building skills, gaining a reputation and being paid by Ameritech to practice my skills before I had to depend on them to feed me." By the time she retired from the telecommunications giant in June 1996 and started WorkTransitions Partners, Yauch already had a solid client base of Ameritech employees and referrals.

Within two years Yauch doubled her client list to 70 and expanded her services to include career workshops and seminars. Although the company is now making a profit, she and her husband still draw most of their incomes from retirement assets they accumulated at their earlier jobs, as well as another $40,000 or so a year that Gail earns consulting part time for his former employers. Within a few years, Yauch expects her business will be profitable enough for Gail to retire completely so he can devote his time to his avocation, photography.

In the meantime, Yauch is living a far more satisfying life. She and Gail sold their huge home and bought a smaller place that sits on three acres and has a horse barn. "I'm now able to ride my horse Freddie and keep him at home rather than just have him boarded somewhere," says Yauch. Finally, she has found more time to get involved with several charities, including Cabrini Allies!, a group that helps children in Chicago's poverty-ridden Cabrini Green housing project.

Clearly, the chance to offer career guidance while still being paid by Ameritech was a lucky break. On the other hand, Yauch wouldn't have had the opportunity at all if she hadn't started training for her new job while still in her old one. "If you plan," says Yauch, "you're prepared to take advantage of the serendipity that occurs in your life."

TAX STRATEGIES TODAY AND TOMORROW

It would be nice if filling up a 401(k) or an IRA were enough to guarantee an early, luxurious retirement, but for most of us that's just not true. Many savvy investors have recognized this, and in addition to putting the maximum into 401(k)s and IRAs, they have been building a retirement portfolio of stocks and mutual funds outside of their tax-deferred accounts. If you are among the people who are supplementing basic retirement accounts with additional savings, the tax laws passed in 1997 and 1998 are starting to kick in with extra help for you. That's because of the widened gap between federal taxes on capitals gains—now as low as 20% for investments held at least 12 months—and taxes on ordinary income, which run as high as 39.6%. Tax-deferred accounts such as 401(k)s and IRAs are ultimately subject to ordinary income tax rates when the money is withdrawn—even if the growth in those accounts has come from capital gains. That means you may be better off putting stocks in taxable accounts, where they face only the capital-gains tax.

Joel Dickson, an analyst with the Vanguard fund group in Valley Forge, Pa., offers this example: Let's say you invest $5,000 in bonds and $5,000 in stocks, and put the bonds in a taxable account and the stocks in a tax-sheltered 401(k). Over a 20-year period, assuming the bonds return 7% a year and the stocks gain an average of 12%, you would end up with $40,600 to spend after all taxes. Now let's say you apply all the same assumptions but instead you put the bonds in the 401(k) and the stocks in the taxable account. According to Dickson's calculations, you would come away with $45,6000—12% more.

The lesson is clear: When investing for retirement, it pays to play the tax angles. "If you don't update your tax strategy, you are going to give away a big portion of your nest egg to Uncle Sam," says financial planner Michael Chasnoff of Advanced Capital Strategies in Cincinnati. Of course, for investors in a lower tax bracket, the impact of this tax shifting will be somewhat smaller. Still, the strategy works for anyone in the 28% bracket or higher.

So which assets go where?

Blue-chip stocks and stock funds. These are precisely the kind of core holdings that until now were instinctively stashed in 401(k)s, IRAs and the like. But because these are the holdings you are least likely to sell until you're in retirement, they are ideal for taxable accounts. If you're not going to face much in the way of taxes until you cash them in, those taxes might as well be at the capital-gains rate, not the ordinary income rate. With mutual funds, as financial planner Malcom Makin of Westerly, R.I., points out, you should favor ones that make a point of keeping annual taxable distributions to a minimum.

Riskier stocks and funds. The more likely you are to be trading your stockholdings—selling them before you reach retirement—the more appropriate they are for tax-deferred accounts. That way you won't have to worry about paying taxes on every profitable trade. The one downside: You won't be able to deduct any losses on your tax returns, as you could if they were in taxable accounts.

Income investments. Whether you're talking bonds, bond funds, money-market funds or income-producing stocks, a tax-sheltered account will have obvious advantages. The income generated each year will compound tax-free. And, in fact, many 401(k)s offer stable-value funds that pay 6% or 7%, says David Bugen, an investment adviser in Chatham, N.J. If your plan has such an option, says Bugen, "consider keeping all of your fixed-income allocation there."

General strategy. How should you go about making these tax-saving moves? Carefully. Hasty shifts could run up a costly tax bill today, offsetting whatever future advantages might be in store. One other caution: This strategy is designed for investors who are putting retirement assets outside 401(k) and other tax-deferred accounts because they have already maxed out those accounts. We're not suggesting that you turn away from your 401(k). Nor are we suggesting that you place liquid emergency funds in a restricted retirement account.

THE CHANGING WORLD OF MUTUAL FUNDS

It's a natural impulse, when investing for retirement, to be drawn to big, brand-name funds. After all, you want your future riding on something solid, reliable, a name you know. But some of the biggest brand names in the mutual fund business have performed disappointingly. The problem, ironically, is that the funds were too successful, attracting billions of dollars from investors and ballooning in size. And bigger funds, nearly all experts agree, are more difficult to manage than smaller ones.

Big brand-name funds are prevalent in many 401(k) plans, and they are hardly unwise investments in that environment. But if you have the freedom to choose from a wider menu—particularly for assets outside of specific retirement account setups—there are other criteria on which to judge a fund than the familiarity of its name. Here are some tips on finding funds appropriate for retirement-oriented investors—funds that are more likely to lead the pack over the long haul.

Stay lean and mean. Size, as we've noted, is often the enemy of performance. Managers who excel with millions of dollars to invest can be overwhelmed by billions. That is especially true for funds that invest in smaller stocks. Thus, says John Rekenthaler, investment strategist at John Nuveen & Co.: "It makes sense to favor funds that will shut their doors if they grow too large." Small manager-owned fund families are often more willing to turn away money than major fund groups are. And some fund companies state clearly that they will close their doors when assets hit a certain a level.

Cheaper is better. The one certainty in choosing a fund is the expense ratio you will pay. And all other things being equal, a high-cost fund will return less than one that keeps costs low. When it comes to bargain-priced funds, it's impossible to ignore the Vanguard fund group and its stable of low-cost index funds. Vanguard is unique among major fund complexes because it is, in effect, owned by the investors in its funds. That means fees that generate profits at other firms simply don't exist here. And costs are especially crucial for bond funds, where returns are generally lower than stock funds.

Stick with a smooth ride. Something you can learn from studying a fund's past returns is how smooth a ride it delivers. Some funds swing wildly from one year to the next. "A volatile fund is likely to remain a volatile fund," says Don Phillips, chairman of Chicago fund research firm Morningstar. What's wrong with that? All too often, says Phillips, investors will bail out of such bouncy portfolios right at the bottom. If you think you might be spooked by a sudden slide in your fund's value, search out steadier performers.

Look for committed management. Particularly if you're planning to hold a fund until you retire, you want a manager who's going to hang around as long as you do. You also wouldn't mind if the manager has a stake in the success of the portfolio. These two things often go hand in hand. "The managers most likely to stay put are those who own their own fund company or hold a sizable equity stake," says Ken Gregory, editor of the *No Load Fund Analyst* newsletter.

A LITTLE EXTRA SAVING ADDS UP TO A LOT

Perhaps your nest egg is not on target for your personal retirement goal. As we said early in this chapter, if you're behind, don't despair. Even a little extra saving can help you make up lost ground. For example, stashing an extra $100 a month in a taxable account earning 10% annually for 30 years adds up to more than $226,000. If your earnings slip to 8%, you still get almost $150,000. That's not bad for saving only an extra three bucks a day.

Here are some more details about how far that $100 a month can go: If you invest $100 a month at even a modest 6% annual return, you'll have

$7,000 after five years, $16,400 after 10, $29,100 after 15, $46,200 after 20 and $100,500 after 30 years. Invest it at an 8% annual return, and the $100 a month grows to $7,300 after five years, $18,300 after 10, $34,600 after 15, $58,900 after 20 and $149,000 after 30. At a 10% annual return, the $100 is pumped to $7,700 in five years, $20,500 in 10, $41,400 in 15, $75,900 in 20 and that super total of $226,000 in 30 years.

CUTTING THROUGH THE IRA CONFUSION

When Congress created the Roth Individual Retirement Account (IRA) in 1997, who knew what lawmakers had unleashed? For all the stories in the financial press, online calculators, industry ads and educational pamphlets, people are still confused. Fund company Fidelity attributes a 120% increase in customer service calls to Roth confusion. Accountants and financial planners are encountering the same puzzlement. And, yes, even the IRA's eponymous champion, Sen. William Roth, Republican from Delaware, reports that constituents stop him on the street to pose questions.

To cut some of the confusion, let's start with a brief refresher course on where you can invest the up to $2,000 a year that the government allows you to put into an IRA. There are three types of IRAs. The traditional deductible IRA gives you a tax benefit right away. If you're eligible for one, you deduct contributions from your taxable income in the tax year that you make them, and the earnings grow tax-deferred until you take out the money and pay taxes on the withdrawal. A nondeductible IRA is funded with after-tax dollars. It gives you tax-deferred earnings, but you pay taxes when you make withdrawals. The third type, the Roth IRA, is also funded with after-tax dollars and also grows tax-free. But if you wait until age 59 1/2 to tap the account, you pay no taxes on the earnings.

You can contribute up to $2,000 a year ($4,000 for couples) to a Roth if your modified adjusted gross income (AGI) is $95,000 or less for singles, $150,000 or less for married couples filing jointly. Singles with an AGI up to $110,000 and couples with an AGI up to $160,000 qualify for a smaller partial contribution. Unlike other IRAs, Roths do not require that you start withdrawals from your account at age 70 1/2, and you can keep contributing as long as you have earned income.

Which IRA should you choose? A Roth IRA always beats a nondeductible IRA because, as we just noted, with a Roth, you can escape taxes entirely on the earnings of your after-tax contributions. If you're not eligible for a deductible IRA, the Roth is your best deal.

A Roth beats a deductible IRA if your tax bracket will stay the same or rise after you retire. Because the decision between a Roth IRA and a deductible IRA boils down to taxes now vs. taxes later, one big factor in choosing between the two is how your tax bracket will change over time. Most people find their tax bracket declines in retirement because their pension, Social Security savings and portfolio income fall short of their former paychecks. If you expect your tax bracket will fall, a deductible IRA will most likely put you ahead. But if you think you have a good chance of maintaining or even boosting your income in retirement, then the Roth wins.

The longer you can wait to tap your IRA after you retire, the more attractive a Roth becomes. Since you needn't begin taking distributions from a Roth IRA at age 70 1/2, you can get a huge financial lift by keeping your retirement stash tucked away in a Roth into your 70s and beyond. If you're age 70 and earn a modest 7% a year in a Roth IRA, you can literally double your money by age 80 by leaving it there instead of withdrawing it and spending it.

What if you're over 70 1/2 and want to keep saving? A Roth IRA is your only option. With a deductible or nondeductible IRA, once you hit 70 1/2, you have to start taking money out of your account and you must stop contributing. But just as you can keep your money in a Roth for as long as you like, you can keep adding to it each year too, so long as you have earned income. Those attributes make the Roth IRA a powerful estate-planning tool for people who will continue to work part time in retirement. When you die, the Roth IRA will go to your beneficiary and no one will have to pay income tax on the money. (However, your estate might owe taxes on the IRA just as it might on any other asset you own.)

Should you convert to a Roth? You can convert an existing IRA to a Roth. If you do that, you'll owe income taxes on your earnings and (if the IRA was deductible) the original contribution. Much of the recent IRA confusion has centered on conversions from old IRAs to Roths. The terrain has been tricky, but with help from some clarification by Congress last summer, the ground rules for conversion are now more flexible.

For starters, your modified adjusted growth income must fall below $100,000 (single or married) to qualify for a conversion from a deductible IRA. If you make a conversion during the year and your AGI jumps above the limit for the year, you're subject to severe tax penalties. However, regulations passed by Congress last summer give you the freedom to change your mind. Now you can convert even if your AGI is dangerously close to the $100,000 cap. Under the new law, if, say, a bonus puts you over the limit, the IRS will let you annul the Roth and switch the funds back to your old IRA penalty-free. For 1998 conversions, you have until April 15, 1999 (or later, if you file an extension) to do so.

Because you can change your mind for any reason, this new rule can save you from more than goofs, says Joan Vines, a partner at the accounting firm of Grant Thornton in Washington, D.C. Say you roll over $60,000 from a deductible IRA into a Roth. You'll owe $18,600 in income taxes if you're in the 31% bracket. But if a subsequent market drop cuts the value of your Roth to $40,000 before you file your tax return, you can avoid paying taxes on money you've already lost. Just reverse the conversion and then roll the money into a new Roth. You'll owe taxes on $40,000, a $6,200 saving.

Congress also clarified when you can take money out of a converted Roth. You can't tap converted funds tax-penalty-free in the first five years unless you're over 59 1/2 or you're using the money for medical or college expenses or a first home. However, you can tap nonrollover Roth contributions penalty-free at any time and for any reason. So if you put your annual Roth contributions in the same account with your converted Roth, those contributions will not be subject to any five-year waiting period.

If your AGI is less than $100,000 and you're eligible to convert an existing IRA to a Roth, under what circumstances should you do so? Converting a conventional IRA to a Roth lets you make tax-free withdrawals later but gives you a big tax bill today. Remember, you'll owe income taxes on all deductible contributions you made to your IRA and on all its investment earnings. For some rules of thumb, answer the following questions:

♦ Do you expect to fall into a lower tax bracket when you retire? (When estimating your retirement income, remember to include your annual pension, projected investment income and taxable Social Security benefits.)
♦ Will you need the money within five years of opening the account?
♦ Would you have to tap the IRA to pay for the taxes you would owe by converting?
♦ To pay the conversion taxes, would you be forced to sell investments and incur substantial capital-gains taxes?
♦ Will the extra income tax liability you incur by converting your IRA end up pushing you into a substantially higher tax bracket or cause you to forfeit any significant tax deductions, credits or exemptions?

If you answered yes to any of the questions, do not convert to a Roth. If you answered no to all of the questions, it makes sense to convert to a Roth.

Additional IRA concerns. "We're getting a lot of people saying, "What exactly does the Roth mean to me?'" says Robert Viceonte, a tax partner at the New York City accounting firm M.R. Weiser. Five of the most frequently raised concerns are essentially these:

Can I convert my 401(k), profit–sharing account or employee stock–purchase plan to a Roth?

No. You can convert only a deductible or nondeductible IRA. You can, however, roll your 401(k) into a deductible IRA when you leave your job and then flip that IRA into a Roth. But you'll owe taxes on the entire amount.

I've invested $10,000 in a nondeductible IRA, which has grown to $30,000. Can I convert just the $10,000 contribution to a Roth and avoid income taxes?

Again, no, because the IRS will prorate your withdrawal to match your IRA's rate of contributions to earnings. In this case, if you convert just $10,000, two-thirds will be considered taxable earnings.

Can I contribute to both a Roth and a deductible IRA? What about a nondeductible IRA?

Yes, in both cases. In any one year, you can contribute a total of $2,000 ($4,000 for married couples) to any number of IRAs. For instance, you might want to fund a Roth and a deductible IRA if you only partially qualify for one of them. But if you can fund a Roth, there's no reason to contribute to a nondeductible IRA.

How can I use a Roth to buy a home?

Five years after you open a Roth, you can withdraw up to $10,000, free of penalties and taxes, to buy your first home. But there's a way to take out even more, says David Wasserstrum, a tax partner at the New York City accounting firm Richard A. Eisner & Co.: At any time after you open a Roth (or after five years if you convert), you can withdraw your after-tax contributions penalty-free, for any reason. And Roths let you withdraw contributions before you tap earnings. So if you fund a Roth with $20,000 and earn $15,000 on that investment, you should be able to pull out the $20,000 first and then use the first-time-home-buying provision to withdraw $10,000 in earnings.

I have an old IRA and a Roth. Can I tap the money in my deductible IRA for school without paying a penalty?

Yes. Thanks to the law that created the Roth, you can pull money out of any IRA—including that deductible one—for college expenses without penalty. But you will owe income taxes.

HOW TO GIVE AND GET BACK

In the months ahead, you're likely to hear more from charities about gift annuities—an investment-donation hybrid that pays you a steady income for life *and* supports charitable works. A June court ruling ended four years of wrangling over the legality of the rates paid on gift annuities, which are sold by 3,000 or so charities. "Many charities had put their gift annuity programs on hold," says Frank Minton, president of the Seattle-based consulting firm Planned Giving Services. "Now they have the confidence to start promoting them more actively."

Should you consider a gift annuity? Yes, but first, here's how they work. Once you buy a gift annuity—which you can generally do for as little as $5,000—you collect payments for life from the charity, at a rate based on your age. Nearly all charities follow rates set by the American Council on Gift Annuities; they recently ranged from 5.5% for a single 20-year-old to 12% for a 90-plus single. Because the charity doesn't get full use of your donation, you can deduct only a portion of the gift, depending on your age. (In general, the older you are, the more you can deduct.) Yet since you earn money on what you donate, an annuity lets you give more than you might otherwise be able to afford.

As another option, use a deferred gift annuity to save money tax-free for retirement. Say you're contributing the maximum to your retirement plans. With a deferred gift annuity, you can make a charitable gift when you're 50, let the money grow tax-free with the charity, and then collect payments when you retire at 65.

YOUR HOUSE CAN BE A CASH COW

Reverse mortgages are an enticing way for older homeowners to cash in on the equity in their residences without having to move out. A reverse mortgage lets you borrow against the value of your home. But instead of you making payments to the bank, the lender pays you. The amount you qualify for depends on factors such as your age, prevailing interest rates, the amount of equity you have in your home and borrowing ceilings set by lenders. For example, the two biggest reverse-mortgage lenders—the FHA, through its Home Equity Conversion Mortgage program, and the Federal National Mortgage Association, with its HomeKeeper plan—have loan maximums of $170,362 and $227,150 respectively.

You must be at least 62 to take out a reverse mortgage; the older you are, the more you can borrow. Under the FHA's program, for example, a 62-year-old Los Angeles resident who owns a house, free and clear, worth $170,000 or more could qualify for a loan of just under $77,000. He could take the money in a lump sum, a line of credit or monthly payments of roughly $474 for the rest of his life. A 75-year-old person who owns the same home would qualify for a lump sum of nearly $101,000 and monthly payments of about $700.

The cash isn't taxed, by the way, since the money isn't earnings but the proceeds from a loan. Typically, the loan doesn't come due until you die, sell your residence or stop living in your home for 12 months or longer (if, for example, you've entered a nursing home). You or your heirs eventually pay back the amount you borrowed plus interest. But the amount you must repay can never exceed the home's value, even if home prices sag after you sign the deal. Repaying the reverse-mortgage debt, however, could deplete all the equity in your home, leaving nothing for heirs. If that prospect bothers you, a reverse mortgage may not be an option for you.

That "borrow now, pay later" strategy proved to be an ideal way for Wilbur Henry, a 78-year-old former public relations executive, and his wife Anne, 72, a retired archivist for the federal government, to boost their retirement income. The couple had been getting along comfortably on the $60,000 a year they receive from pension and income from their $250,000 investment portfolio. But with their expenses rising, says Wilbur: "We needed a margin of safety."

Based on their ages and an estimated value of $310,000 for their Bethesda, Md. home, the Henrys qualified for a $76,000 reverse mortgage, which they decided to take in monthly payments of $678 for the rest of their lives. They've already used some of the proceeds to replace their furnace and an air conditioner, and they figure the checks will also come in handy for the trip to the Scottish Highlands they're now considering. "This was our savior," Wilbur says. "It was like money from home."

Reverse mortgages are certainly a convenient source of cash, but they have one major drawback: The closing costs and other fees on reverse mortgages can total upwards of $8,000, which can push the effective interest rate up to 40% or more if you have the loan only a few years. "Generally, you should consider a reverse mortgage only if you plan to stay in your house as long as you can," advises Ken Scholen, director of the nonprofit National Center for Home Equity Conversion (NCHEC). You can do a quick comparison of the cost of the various reverse-mortgage options by trying the calculator at NCHEC's Website (www.reverse.org) or by talking to one of the home-equity counselors or reverse-mortgage lenders whose phone numbers are listed on the site.

SACRIFICING FOR YOUR KIDS

There's no doubt that an uber-parenting style costs serious money. According to the U.S. Department of Agriculture, Americans will spend an average of $150,000 over 17 years to raise a child born in 1996. Then college costs kick in. Certified financial planners Jane King of Wellesley, Mass. and Robert Steffen of Minneapolis say that the most important piece of advice they can give to us is this: Don't sacrifice your retirement savings for your kids' education. One of the cardinal rules of financial planning is that you must not put college spending ahead of retirement saving. "Students can always borrow or work to pay for college, but no one is going to loan you money to live on when you're 65," says Steffen.

CHAPTER 6

REAL ESTATE STRATEGY TO USE TODAY

he National Association of Realtors predicts home prices will rise
4.5% this year, and a survey of appraisers by the Chicago-based
Appraisal Institute concludes that home values will go up an average of 4.4% nationwide in 1999. What do these twin forecasts mean for homeowners? Experts say the real estate market should still favor sellers. Buyers, on the other hand, shouldn't put off shopping, especially with mortgage rates well below 7% recently. Current mortgageholders should check out the rates and see if it makes sense to refinance.

For remodelers, a higher home value means more equity to borrow against for construction. If you're paying private mortgage insurance (PMI), you could find that after a new appraisal you'll have enough equity in your home to drop PMI.

SAVE MONEY ON YOUR MORTGAGE

With the late-'90s run of favorable inflation and long-term interest rates, half of today's mortgage holders—some 22 million—could benefit from trading in their current loan for a new one, says Mark Zandi, chief economist at Regional Financial Associates, a West Chester, Pa. economic consulting firm. Are you among them? If you have an adjustable-rate mortgage (ARM) or if you're paying 7.5% or more on a fixed-rate loan, the answer is probably yes.

When you're making your decision, keep these three things in mind. First, even a small rate cut can pay off quickly. That's because you can easily find lenders willing to waive routine refinancing charges such as application, appraisal and legal fees (which can add up to $1,500 to $3,000). Of course, in exchange for low or no up-front costs, you'll have to be willing to accept a rate that's somewhat higher than the prevailing rock bottom. But as Keith Gumbinger, vice president of HSH Associates, a mortgage research firm in Butler, N.J. points out, if you can refinance for a percentage point less, with no costs, why not do it?

Second, if you are planning to stay in your home for at least three to five years, it may make sense to pay "points" (a point equals 1% of the loan amount) and closing costs to get the lowest available rate.

And third, you can avoid laying out cash and still get a low rate by adding the points and closing costs to your new mortgage. Does that mean shouldering a lot of extra debt? Not necessarily. If you've had your current mortgage for at least three years, you've probably reduced your balance by several thousand dollars. So you may be able to tack your closing costs onto your new loan and still end up with a mortgage that's smaller than your original one—plus, of course, a lower rate and lower monthly payment.

Thanks to heavy competition among lenders and increased automation, the refinancing process itself is relatively painless. You can apply over the phone or via the Internet and stop by the bank or title company for the closing. In most cases, you'll need a new appraisal, credit check and title search. Still, you'll generally be able to close on your new loan in three to four weeks. "I don't think the whole process ate half a day of our time," recalls Jim Neill, a recent refinancer in Carrboro, N.C.

Here are strategies for cashing in on lower rates.

Trade your ARM for a fixed-rate loan. By switching from an adjustable-rate mortgage to a fixed-rate loan today, you can not only reduce your payment, but you will also lock in an attractive rate for as long as you own your home. While one-year ARMs offer tempting introductory rates, most experts recommend avoiding them, because you could easily find yourself facing sharply higher payments in the near future—even if interest rates don't rise. Here's why: After the introductory rate expires, ARMs are typically pegged to the one-year Treasury rate, plus 2.75 percentage points, with increases of as much as two points per year. So if you took out the ARM at an introductory rate of 5.59% when the one-year Treasury was 5.25%, even if interest rates didn't change, you would pay 7.59% in the second year (the full two-point increase) and 8% the third year.

There are certain cases, however, where an ARM makes sense. If you are fairly certain you'll be moving within five years, you can save some money—and avoid rising payments—with a five-year ARM. Such loans offer a fixed rate for five years and adjust annually thereafter.

Get your hands on some cash. Another way to make low interest rates work for you is to refinance for more than the balance remaining on your old mortgage—in effect, tapping your home equity or "cashing out," in lenderspeak. Thanks to favorable rates, you may be able to do so without boosting your monthly outlay. For example, at 8.5%, the payment on a $200,000, 30-year fixed-rate mortgage is $1,538. But at 7.5%, that same payment lets you borrow nearly $20,000 more.

The best use for the extra cash is to pay off any higher-rate loans you may have. Let's say that you are making minimum payments on a $10,000 credit-card balance at 17% and on a $15,000 credit-card balance at 10%. Your monthly payments of those debts would total $680. Then assume you refinanced your mortgage, taking out an additional $25,000 to pay off your credit-card loans. Rather than having to pay $680 each month, at 7.5%, your additional monthly mortgage payment would total only $175, so you would come out $505 ahead.

One warning: When you decide to increase the size of your mortgage significantly, remember that if you default on that loan you can lose your home. So be sure you don't spend the money frivolously or increase your overall debt load by running up your credit-card balances again.

Build home equity faster. The opposite of cashing out is to use a refinancing to shorten your mortgage's term. And brace yourself: Even at today's low rates, a shorter term means a higher monthly payment. The benefit is that you'll build up equity faster and pay far less in total interest over the lifetime of the loan.

Consider Jim Neill, 48, a real estate broker, and his wife Merrily, 55, a psychotherapist. Last year, the couple took out a 15-year fixed-rate loan at 6.75% to replace an 8.13% ARM with a 30-year term. Their monthly payment jumped by $200, but now they will own their own home outright by the time they retire. In addition, the total interest on the 15-year loan will come to $95,447, vs. $222,234 on the remaining life of the ARM—and that assumes their adjustable rate would have held steady at the 8.13% it was charging when they refinanced. "This is forced savings," says Jim. "When we retire, we can scale down and take equity out of the house."

If you can't afford the payments on a 15-year mortgage, your next best means of building equity is to refinance for less than 30 years. To do so, ask your lender to customize your new loan's term to match the years that are left on your old loan—if you are five years into a 30-year mortgage, for example, ask for a 25-year loan. According to HSH's Gumbinger, a large lender, such as Norwest or Countrywide Home Loans, may be the most amenable to tailoring a loan to your specifications.

Refinance once, then do it again. When rates have fallen steadily, refinancing may make sense even if you have done so once already. Bob and Michelle Barbo of Kirkland, Wash. refinanced twice within three months. In October 1997 they trimmed the rate on their 30-year fixed mortgage by a full point (from 9.13% to 8.13%) for a monthly savings of $63. Plus, because home prices in their area had boosted their home equity, they were able to stop paying private mortgage insurance that cost them $120 a month.

To exploit the continued decline in rates, the Barbos refinanced again in December. The new 30-year fixed mortgage was at 7.37%, lopping another $55 off their monthly bill. Since the couple had chosen a no-cost refinancing each time, their total out-of-pocket expenses came to just $400 in appraisal fees. Within months they recouped their up-front costs. "And now we can use the savings to build up a cash emergency fund," says Bob.

If you are considering a second refinancing, don't overlook this potential tax write-off: When you pay points to refinance, you must deduct the amount over the life of the loan, usually 30 years. But when you refinance a second time, all of the points that have not yet been deducted from the first refinancing can be written off in a lump sum. Say you refinanced to a 30-year mortgage in 1994 and paid $3,000 in points. By 1998, you would have written off roughly $500. If you refinanced again last year, you could deduct the remaining $2,500 on your 1999 tax return. For a homeowner in the 28% tax bracket, that works out to a saving of $700—enough to offset some or all of your costs.

When you're ready, move fast—and lock in. David Lereah was looking to take advantage of mortgage rates as they scraped the bottom of the barrel. On Tuesday, Oct. 6, 1998, the 30-year rate dropped to 6.58%, according to HSH—its lowest point since the 1960s. Lereah had a 15-year loan at 7.5%, while new rates had plunged to a thrifty 6.5%. But he got sidetracked—his phone started to ring—and he waited until the next day. By then, it was too late. Rates were headed back up; on Thursday, they jumped a full 50 basis points. The last time that had happened was 12 years earlier. "I missed it," admits Lereah.

That's a tough admission, considering it comes from the chief economist of the Mortgage Bankers Association—a man who spends his days watching rates. "If it happened to me," Lereah notes, "it can happen to anyone."

Even when there's havoc in the mortgage market, says Zandi, "the good news is that there will be brief periods [as in early October] when there will be tremendous bargains—if you're quick enough to take advantage of them."

And as soon as it makes financial sense for you to do the deal, lock it in. That can be at the time of application or at any point in the process. Just make sure that when you pull the trigger, you get it in writing, extend it far enough and have all the pertinent dates and rates clearly specified. "A lock-in is really a legal side agreement between you and the lender; it's not part of the loan itself," says Earl Peattie, president of Mortgage News Co. "And a verbal agreement is no agreement at all."

In order to lock, you may have to put down a deposit of a quarter of a point or so. Generally that amount is applied to the loan or refunded at closing. But some lenders are charging an actual fee: The longer you lock your rate, the more you pay. "In this environment," Gumbinger advises, "it can be worth paying." It's also worth figuring out how much waiting will cost you. Each month you let go by, hoping for even lower rates, is another month you'll forgo saving a few hundred dollars on your existing loan. Do the math on the rates currently available to make sure you aren't passing up substantial savings while you're waiting on the sidelines.

What if you expect rates to fall? Ask your lender about a "float-down" that gives you the opportunity to take advantage of a drop in rates. If rates do drop, you can re-lock, typically 10 days before closing. Some lenders will give you this gratis, but others charge. It's okay to pay a small sum. Just be sure there are no unreasonable caveats and that you consider how much you're paying in relation to how quickly you expect to get it back. If you don't get a float-down and rates fall, try to renegotiate. On a refinance where you haven't put up a lot of cash, lenders will often capitulate, knowing that they will lose you otherwise.

Be a smart shopper. The Internet is a powerful research and shopping tool. Perhaps too powerful, contends Doug Naidus, president of IPI Financial Services, the Northeast's largest mortgage brokerage, which also runs a mortgage site, NYFinance.com. Consumers, he says, are "blind to the fact that every day mortgage brokers get rate sheets from 100 to 150 different lenders listing thousands of different types of loans. And that the next day those rates are completely reshuffled." Consumers now get that information from the Web. "That's a good thing," says Naidus. "But it can be a little hard to decipher."

As a result, you'll be best off if you shop using all three channels—banks, mortgage brokers, the Internet—and play them off against one another. According to HSH, which publishes lists of mortgage rates throughout the country on its Website, www.hsh.com, spreads on mortgages can vary as much as two percentage points in individual markets. That can easily cost you hundreds of thousands of dollars over the life of a large loan if you don't shop carefully.

What about mortgage brokers? They now make more than 50% of all loans, up from 20% in 1987. Why the surge? They're easy. These days, brokers are simply another storefront for mortgage banks, a way to access a lot of lenders at one time. How do you find a good one? A reference check is a must. Size is another consideration. Brokers buy loans from banks at wholesale and pass them on to you at retail. The price they pay depends somewhat on the volume they do and the quality of the loan packages they present. You're generally better off with a large operator who runs a professional-looking outfit.

But even if you have a broker shopping for you, you should also shop for yourself. The higher the rate a mortgage broker gets you to pay, the more money he puts in his pocket. One way to keep a broker competitive is to play him or her against another broker. That's what Connecticut C.P.A. Sean Murphy did. He told two mortgage brokers they were going head to head to refinance his 7.5%, $160,000 loan in late September. "I laid it on the line—whoever has the best pricing wins," Murphy recalls. In the end, he locked in at 6.25% with one point, saving a half-point worth $800 from the broker's original quote.

Most Internet loan sites can give you a snapshot of the best rates in your area. And the Web is also blindingly fast in getting answers. Ellen Hampshire, a travel consultant in New York City, got a response from E-Loan the day she visited the site: an offer for a 6.625%, 30-year fixed mortgage. "The next day I had a FedEx [package] on my doorstep, including my case number," she says. "Plus they were running a special, so I'm getting back $900 in closing costs."

That's not to say consumers don't have issues with applying for loans via the Internet. One big fear is that shoppers are inviting a slew of junk mail; in fact, all of the national mortgage sites say they don't sell your personal information to others. Another concern is that by applying to a number of sites, you could hurt your credit score. That's largely unfounded. Recent changes to credit reporting laws say that an unlimited number of inquiries for the same purpose (like getting a mortgage) within a 30-day period count as only one query. The bottom line: Internet sites are grabbing an increasing share of the mortgage market, thus driving down costs and increasing competition.

How to Win in a Hot Housing Market

Here's a story that became all too familiar last year. On a rainy Sunday in San Mateo, Calif., Sandy Justman, 36, and her husband Alex, 37, set out to shop for a new home, hoping to encounter few other buyers. A two-bedroom condominium they liked had an asking price of $230,000. "We had just seen a couple of crackerboxes for $300,000 or more," recalls Sandy, "so I thought we should jump on it. But Alex wanted to mull it over." You know what happened next. The condo sold later that day, and when Sandy and Alex saw a nearly identical version in the same apartment complex two weeks later, the asking price was $247,000, a 7% jump.

There are many lessons to be learned from the hot housing market of 1998. First, don't let stories like Sandy and Alex's discourage you. Check out these rules for keeping a cool head in a crazy market—and for getting the house you want without resorting to desperate measures.

Speed is power. There's no way around it: In a hot housing market, the overly cautious, unprepared bidder will lose out every time. We're not suggesting that your response should be to overbid or to bid for something you haven't seen, but there are a few steps you can take to make sure you're ready to make your best offer the minute you see what you want.

For starters, before you even begin to shop, get a clear gauge on how much spending power you have by getting pre-approved for a mortgage. To do that, have a lender analyze your credit history, income and assets and then guarantee a mortgage up to a certain size, pending the home's appraisal. (Don't confuse pre-approval with pre-qualification, which is just a cursory look at your finances and a ballpark estimate of how much you can borrow.)

On top of giving you a budget, pre-approval makes you a virtual cash buyer who can close fast. "It's a strong position you can't afford not to have in this kind of market," says Ray Llosa, president of the National Association of Real Estate Buyer's Brokers.

Once you have a mortgage in hand, keep up the momentum. "Make your bid quickly," says Joseph Eamon Cummins, author of *Not One Dollar More*, "and don't wait to talk to your friends and parents." Cummins also suggests turning the tables by setting a deadline on your bid. If your offer expires in a day, that discourages the seller from waiting for a higher bid before accepting yours.

Another way to make your bid stand out is to make it clear that you'll accommodate some of the seller's (reasonable) wishes besides the price—or that you'll at least alleviate their annoyances. For instance, agree to have the house inspected within a short time frame—say, 48 hours—so the seller won't have to wait a week or so before knowing whether the deal will go through.

Another possible concession you can offer: Say when you bid that you're willing to take care of mandatory local certificates, such as ones for smoke detectors or water safety. That shouldn't be too onerous.

Don't always say yes. Now, that doesn't mean you should go over-board—getting the house at all costs shouldn't be your goal in a bidding war. Obviously, you don't want to needlessly compromise your finances (or your dignity).

Be wary of some seller demands. Waiving a contingency clause in the contract, for example, is a concession that could leave you broke. Waivers are becomingly increasingly common in competitive markets as desperate buyers try to differentiate themselves, says Jacelyn Botti, an agent with Weichart Realty in Morris Plains, N.J. Waiving the home-inspection clause may not sound terribly unsafe until you see rain indoors or evidence of termites.

You'd be making a mistake, too, if you waive the mortgage contingency, which lets you back out of buying the house if your financing falls through. Even if you're pre-approved, your mortgage still hinges on the value of the house, and a lower than expected appraisal could mean finding another mortgage, perhaps at a higher rate. Or you could theoretically forfeit your down payment.

Get the market's true temperature. Even when most markets are hot, you may be buying in a neighborhood or city that's not. So before you let agents or sellers convince you that a place is the next big thing, get a handle on how hot that market really is and what a property in the area is really worth.

To see if a market is overhyped, ask local agents the typical difference between asking and selling prices and how many days similar homes have spent on the market. If homes sell in less than 30 days for within 5% of the asking price, the heat is on, says author Cummins. In a normal market, you can bid 12% to 15% below the asking price and bargain up. In a strong one, bid what's asked or just below, and be prepared to go up.

Figuring out a fair top price for a home is somewhat time consuming and imprecise. With a little legwork, you can find out from local agents or in the newspapers about recent sales. If you have the time, you can get an official opinion on a particular home from your local tax assessor's office, which regularly takes old property assessments and applies an equalization ratio to approximate a fair market value. "In a really hot market, an assessment may be slightly off," says Botti, "but you won't grossly overpay."

Of course, brokers have all this information in local databases, including more up-to-date details about the deals still under contract. So to save yourself time and effort, you can hire a buyer's broker, who, unlike a traditional seller's agent, works for your best interests—and will sign a contract saying so. Buyer's brokers negotiate with the seller's agent and split the sales commission.

When buying, think about selling. A booming market can fool you into thinking that you'll make money no matter when you sell. But real estate markets are cyclical, and when sales inevitably slow, your home's value could drop 3% to 5% or more before rebounding. "The good times aren't going to last forever," warns Keith Gumbinger.

So don't convince yourself that you can simply overpay because you'll make it up when you sell. Those defects you were willing to overlook—a high school parking lot right next door, a lousy school district or a home perched on a steep slope—could seriously erode your home's resale value in a less frisky market. And you'll take the hit.

When debt gets dangerous. Buying a home most often involves taking on debt, which is fine as long as you can afford the payments. Still, some increasingly common borrowing strategies look downright dicey to us. For example, in recent years, lenders have dropped the minimum down payment to as little as 3% of the purchase price. In late April 1998, Fannie Mae rolled out a mortgage that lets you borrow the entire amount by financing that 3% down payment with a loan from a family member or one secured by an asset such as your 401(k). Previously, the money for a down payment had to be cash, not a loan or a gift.

What's good about low- or no-down-payment loans is that you can keep money aside for renovations, a cash reserve or investments. But again, there's a big risk here if you're buying in an area where home prices have risen quickly. Let's say you buy a home today for $200,000 with no money down. Sell it three years later, and you could owe $194,000 on your mortgage and—if the market has cooled off—find you can get only $192,000 for your house. Subtract a $10,000 realtor commission and $1,000 in other fees, and you'll have to pony up $13,000 before you walk away.

Similarly, lenders may pre-approve you for a much larger mortgage than you might have imagined. But before you take everything the bank offers (after all, the bank said it was okay), remember that overspending in a hot market can come back to haunt you.

AVOID ANY ESCROW SHOCKS

When you work up your financial plans for buying a house, don't forget to figure in the escrow account that lenders make you fund to cover property taxes and certain insurance premiums for one year or more. Calculating how much to set aside is getting trickier.

Several years ago, the U.S. Department of Housing and Urban Development (HUD) limited how much mortgage lenders could force homeowners to tie up in escrow. The motive was to lighten the burden on home buyers, but it's had an unfortunate side effect: "payment shock," when the assessed value of your property—and hence your property tax—turns out to be much higher than what you put away in escrow.

How can that happen? Your property's value can rise quickly if you've bought in a real estate market that suddenly heats up. And if you've moved into a newly built home, your property may last have been assessed while it was vacant land: A house will obviously boost the value soon.

In late January 1998, HUD fine-tuned its escrow calculation guidelines, recommending (but not requiring) that lenders collect escrow funds in monthly installments, not one annual payment. And HUD gave borrowers the option to overpay their escrow.

David Ginsberg, president of Baltimore mortgage consulting company Loantech, advises paying your escrow monthly, even if that means a fee of up to 0.5% of your escrow balance. "Keep tabs on your monthly escrow analysis," he adds. If you have doubts about whether the account is big enough, check with your lender.

HOW VALUABLE IS A WARRANTY?

If you want to purchase some peace of mind to go with those aging appliances in the house you're buying, an increasing number of sellers will oblige. In 1997, for example, a quarter of the existing homes that were sold came with a warranty. These policies typically cover major built-in appliances and mechanical systems in case of breakdown; sales of such warranties have almost doubled over the past five or so years, according to the National Home Warranty Association (NHWA).

But are these policies worth the price, or are they just an empty gimmick? That depends on who's asking. While a warranty can add value to your home when you sell, buyers may find that the policy loses its luster once the dishwasher breaks.

The seller's perspective. Whether a warranty can help sell your house hinges on where you live. In some areas home warranties aren't an important marketing tool. But in California, for example, eight out of 10 listings carry warranties, and agents agree that sellers who don't purchase them lose an edge. "In markets where they're common," says Forrest Pasenberg, director of real estate finance research at the National Association of Realtors, "home warranties can significantly speed up sales." In fact, a survey two years ago by the real estate firm ERA found that homes with a warranty sold 27 days faster and for 2.7% more money than those without one.

To see if warranties are the norm in your market, check the real estate ads or ask local agents. You can buy a one-year warranty, which typically costs $350 to $450, from your real estate agent or directly from a contractor. Brokers may collect a small fee for their help, but they often get bulk discounts that make your end price about what it would be if you bought on your own.

The buyer's perspective. If you're buying, should you pay more for a house with a warranty? The truth is, these policies can be a lot less impressive once you read the fine print. They usually cover built-in appliances and heating, plumbing and wiring systems, yet "warranties won't cover some major things that could cost you your checkbook," warns Bruce Hahn, president of the American Homeowners' Foundation, a Virginia-based consumer advocate. Structural items such as roofs and foundations are typically excluded. So are any breakdowns traceable to inadequate wiring or other pre-existing conditions. And covered repairs aren't free, just capped, so you'll pay anywhere from $35 to $200 for each breakdown. Some warranties can shortchange you if a part isn't available anymore; others don't cover replacement at all, just repairs.

What about paying for one of these policies after you buy a house? Consider such a move only if your appliances are approaching a double-digit birthday or are high-end. "If your house is full of upscale appliances—

a Sub-Zero refrigerator, for instance—repairs are expensive and parts hard to get," says Jim Hodl, contributing editor of *Appliance Service News*. In that case, a warranty can save you from the unforeseen expense of replacing a pricey fixture right after you've depleted your savings to buy a home.

WILL YOUR POLICY REBUILD YOUR HOUSE?

Chances are slim that your house will burn to the ground. But if the unlikely happens, at least you know your insurance company will make you whole no matter the cost, right? Don't bet on it. Until recently, as long as you had a guaranteed replacement clause in your policy, your insurance would cover rebuilding even if rising construction costs meant the price tag exceeded the value of the policy. But the three largest home insurers—State Farm, Allstate and Farmers Group—are now capping the payout for replacing your home at 120% to 125% of the policy's value.

The change means you must get your coverage correct from the start. "You definitely don't want to be underinsured," says Robert Hunter, director of insurance for the Consumer's Federation of America. Don't rely on an insurer's estimate, which may be based on average building costs in your area. Instead, have an insurance adjuster estimate the actual cost to rebuild, or pay a builder about $200 for an appraisal.

REDUCE THE STRESS OF RELOCATION

Few things in life have the power to roil the tranquil waters of domestic life as much as a relocation. But moving your family doesn't have to be a nightmare. We talked to corporate relocators, moving experts and work/family consultants to find out what you can do to smoothly make a fresh start in a new place. Here are four steps you can take.

1. Talk to your family about what relocation will mean to everyone before you accept a job-transfer offer or make any other commitment to move. Laying the groundwork for a smooth switch requires lots of discussions, says Jean Snyder, a work/family consultant with the Impact Group in St. Louis. "Couples need to list the pros and cons of a relocation before making any decisions that could be disruptive to your family. Talking about your short- and long-term goals honestly will make everyone feel better."

2. Find the supermarket and check out the schools before settling on a neighborhood. "When you're forced to make a lot of decisions in a very short time frame, the more you know about the place you're headed for, the better," explains Tom Peiffer, a Portsmouth, N.H. consultant for the relocation research firm Runzheimer International. Everyone checks real estate prices and makes cost-of-living comparisons, but it's often the small things about a community that make it a good place to live. Peiffer encourages you to check the proximity to schools, supermarkets and hardware stores, and to determine how long the commute to work will be before settling on a place to live. If possible, schedule a few house-hunting trips to explore several neighborhoods.

3. Try to move school-age children during the school year. It's counter-intuitive, but just about all the experts recommend moving your kids while school is in session. "Kids—whether they think so or not—are sure to make friends in the new school," explains Dennis Taylor, another Runzheimer consultant. "Besides, schoolteachers are trained to help a new student acclimate." If you wait until summer, you take the chance that the kids in the neighborhood will be off to summer camp and away on vacation.

4. Be patient; settling in takes time. "Relocating is about managing change and uncertainty effectively," says Jane Holston, author of *Smart Moves for the Relocating Family*. "We all want to feel settled the minute the boxes are unpacked, but it usually takes at least six months to two years to fully adjust to a new town." And just when you think the drudgery of moving is over, something will come up—such as trying to find the electric lights for the Christmas tree—to remind you that you're not in your old home anymore. That's why the bottom line to making any move work, adds Holston, is to "keep your sense of humor."

THE TIME IS RIGHT FOR A SECOND HOME

For years, Dan McElhatton and his family spent summers in Avalon, on the Jersey Shore. In the beginning they rented. But in 1979, noticing that real estate values were climbing, they bought a three-bedroom bungalow, just a block from the beach, for $85,000. "We figured we'd sell a decade later and have a nice nest egg for college tuition," remembers McElhatton. Very nice, indeed. The Philadelphia attorney sold the house in 1990 for $325,000.

Paying for college may not be your goal, but chances are you've considered buying a second home. What you may not have considered is that—despite high prices—the recent tax-law changes and free-flowing mortgage money make this a good time to buy.

According to HSH Associates' Keith Gumbinger, many banks are now willing to let you take on housing debt of up to 33% of your income, a steep increase from 28% a few years back. That, plus today's low interest rates, means a family earning $75,000 with a $1,250-a-month first mortgage can qualify for a $100,000 loan—$30,000 more than in 1994.

But buying and buying smart are very different. It's important to decide what you want from a second home *before* you start shopping. These strategies can help:

The pre-retirement home. Before the tax rules changed, most people didn't purchase a retirement home until they had sold their primary home. That way they could roll over any gains and avoid a hefty tax bill. But there's no need to wait, now that couples can pocket a tax-free $500,000 (singles, $250,000) on that primary home whenever they sell. If you want a place to vacation in now and move to later, look for a well-populated area with good health care and a solid job market. Remember, an income-tax-free state can put 10% of your paycheck or taxable retirement payout back in your pocket once you move. And if you live full time in the new home for two years or more after you retire, you'll get the same capital-gains break when you sell.

The weekend getaway. Come the off-season, when tourists vanish, weekend homeowners tend to get nervous about being able to sell. And that's to your advantage as a buyer because prices dip.

Of course, when it's your turn to sell, you won't want to wait until the tourists creep back into town. So buy in a place where tourism is growing. Hotel occupancy and new construction rates are good barometers. Also, look for a vacation home with the conveniences of a primary residence. Thanks to faxes and high-speed modems, more people are telecommuting and stretching their weekends into full weeks or even months.

The rental property. Every six weeks, Baltimore's Robin and David Mattheiss head to their place on the Outer Banks of North Carolina. They relax in the hot tub, dip into the pool and revel in the fact that their place is essentially free. Their renters, who pay $2,500 a week during the season, cover the mortgage.

The IRS rules in this area are complicated, says Manhattan accountant Nick Morrow, but here are the basics: Use the house yourself more than 14 days a year or 10% of the time it's rented, and it's considered a residence. That means your deductible expenses can't exceed your rental income. Use the house for 14 or fewer days a year or less than 10% of the rental period, and it's a rental property, with no expense cap. Finally, rent fewer than 15 days a year and you don't have to report the income.

Be aware that what renters want in a vacation property may differ from what you want. Water for swimming and boating is a plus, as is proximity to town. And amenities like cable, VCRs and gas grills can make or break a deal.

The time-share. The American Resort Development Association says most of us vacation just two weeks a year. If that's all the time you get, a second home may seem like a waste

No question, time-shares have a bad rep. High sales and marketing costs mean you buy, on average, for $10,000 and sell for 40% less. But time-shares are convenient, and the IRS thinks of them as second homes, meaning you can deduct mortgage interest and taxes of as much as $1.1 million on your first residence and time-share combined. And if you pay up for the high season, you'll get a place that's not only swappable but rentable as well.

A HOME LOAN THAT CAN BRING BIG TROUBLE

Adam Gordon of Arlington, Va. had a dilemma: A family member was willing to give him a loan secured by Adam's house. But Adam was worried that he wouldn't be able to take a tax deduction for the interest unless he went to a bank or a mortgage company. "Does the Internal Revenue Service require that a home-equity loan come from a financial institution to qualify for a tax deduction?" he asked.

Adam was right to worry, but not for that reason. In general, you can write off the interest as long as your house is the collateral for the loan. But borrowing from a bank can save you a lot of fiscal—and familial—hassle. Unlike a deal you cut with, say, Behemoth Guaranty & Trust, you and your relative will have to convince the IRS that the loan is legit, not a covert gift. To make sure the deal holds up to tax scrutiny, your relative must charge a fair interest rate, roughly 6% or more by recent IRS standards. The two of you must draw up a formal agreement specifying payback terms. Ideally, you should also include an amortization schedule showing exactly what portion of each payment is interest. Your lender must then register a mortgage against your property with the county clerk and, in some states, pay a tax of 10 cents to 26 cents per $100 of loan. Not too bad so far.

Naturally, when you deduct the interest on your tax return, your relative must report the interest as income on her return—but here's where it can get tricky. Each of you will be dealing with a loved one, so you each might get a little lax. If you don't pay what you promised and your relative forgives a few missing installments, you both could run into problems with the IRS that are too complex—and horrible—to explain in detail here. Suffice it to say you could be stripped of all the interest deductions you claimed on that loan in the past three years and lose the right to deduct any payments on it in the future. And, of course, if you don't make your loan payments and your relative forgives nothing, you'll definitely run into troubles at home. On top of all that, if one of you dies, there could be an estate complication.

CRIME PROTECTION AT THE RIGHT PRICE

Even as burglary rates have dropped to their lowest level in 30 years, Americans continue to spend more than ever on home-security systems. And after all, for the typical homeowner, it seems a simple equation: A sign in front plus contacts on windows plus motion sensors throughout equals a secure house. Besides, with the insurance breaks, many buyers figure such a system will practically pay for itself.

Unfortunately, nothing about these security systems is as simple as you might assume. They can be expensive to install and to maintain—generally much more expensive than any reductions in your insurance premiums. And even when used properly, security systems are not fail-safe deterrents. There may be cheaper and more effective ways to ward off or trip up criminals. We arrived at this conclusion after taking a hard look at security—a look that included seeking out a perspective generally excluded: that of burglars.

The perp's-eye view. Enter Scott Decker and Dietrich Smith. Decker is the department chair of criminology at the University of Missouri-St.Louis and the co-author of *Burglars on the Job: Streetlife and Residential Break-Ins.*

Seven years ago, after a lecture on the miscreant mind-set, a colleague of Decker's was approached by a wheelchair-bound student who said, "That's not exactly accurate." That student was Dietrich Smith, who had grown up in one of St. Louis' roughest neighborhoods and now helps Decker supplement academic theory with street-level reality. Specifically, they study "active" residential burglars.

Their research takes them all over the city, from low-income neighborhoods teeming with security signs, past storefront churches sprinkled among row houses of red brick fired from Mississippi River clay and to some of the finest homes that suburban St. Louis has to offer. They tell colorful stories, like the one about the burglar who used a narrow gangway to "Spiderman" his way up the sides of two closely built homes, and the one about the neighborhood barbecue where a guest took leave and proceeded to clean out everyone else's house. But Decker's and Smith's commentary is more than just colorful anecdotes. They have learned a thing or two that a home-security salesman might leave out. To be sure, Decker concedes, "home-security devices will work against some types of people." They are not universal deterrents, however. "Based on our research with residential burglars, these devices are of less consequence," Decker says. That's because burglars have told him that even if there's an alarm, they figure they have three to five minutes before the police arrive—and that may be all the time the burglars need.

Moreover, burglars may look to other cues to conclude that you aren't home, and they may know from experience that a sign in the yard might mean the owner has been lulled into a false sense of security and might not even have activated the alarm that day. In fact, a 1994-95 study by Temple University economist Simon Hakim found that in burglarized homes with alarm systems, 41% were not activated. Obviously, notes Decker, "the best system doesn't do any good if you don't use it."

Finally, he says, there's one more thing that the sign in front may be saying to a burglar about your house: "It must have something in it worth stealing."

Your moves. Again, all of this doesn't mean that a home-security system can't help, just that it isn't a panacea. And any number of smart—and cheap—measures may be equally effective. So think about the question from the burglar's point of view. "Often," says Decker, "little things tip the balance for someone who's looking for a place to rob."

First, you should utilize "keep-away" tactics. Probably the key issue for a robber is figuring out whether you're home or not. So if you're leaving town, stop newspaper delivery, ask a neighbor or friend to pick up mail, and arrange to have someone take care of your lawn. That's pretty straight-forward stuff.

But remember, a burglar doesn't need you to be gone for a week—a few minutes will do. In fact, most burglaries take place during daylight hours, when residents are likely to be at work. Decker says that open garage doors are a particularly obvious sign that a homeowner has stepped out. Drawn blinds on a quiet unlit house can also be a giveaway. He recommends using timers for lights and maybe even the stereo; lights that never go off spell an empty house.

Your home is even more likely to be targeted if you leave tools around that will make a burglar's life easier: Ladders, for instance (yours or a neigh-bor's), can offer easy access to the second floor, where windows may not be secured or the alarm may not be wired. High shrubs can also catch a bur-glar's attention. They are an easy hiding place if someone comes home.

Once a burglar is inside, says Decker, "The bedroom is usually the first place they go. Because that's where jewelry and other valuables are most often kept." So Decker recommends that they be stored in bathrooms, kitchens (not the cookie jar) or kids' rooms instead. Basically, anything that prolongs a burglar's search is in your favor. "The more obstacles, the more you'll put them off," Decker notes. Dogs, he adds, are particularly effective.

With or without a security system, there are ways that you can fortify your house for relatively little expense. For starters, replace locks when moving into a home that's been occupied. Install dead bolts on all exterior doors, and make sure lock receptacles (held in place with two-inch screws) were not hastily repaired after a previous break-in.

Next, consider double-pane windows (which make burglars work twice as hard) and solid-core doors (which are more difficult to kick in or other-wise break through). Finally, motion-sensing outdoor lights that turn on when approached can fool a burglar into thinking he's been spotted.

Working the systems. Decker has no alarm system at his home. He's comfortable with dead bolts on all the outer doors, double-pane win-dows and a solid-steel door to his walk-in basement. But he concedes that, for some, security systems supply a feeling of extra safety and peace of mind. "If they get that," he says, "they aren't wasting money."

Unfortunately, this can make a buyer vulnerable to overpayments. So before you opt for the fanciest system available, security experts say, make sure you're getting one that's consistent with your lifestyle. Complicated motion sensors that have to be turned on and off every time someone leaves the house can be a nightmare if you have kids coming in and out, for example. Supersensitive systems are also prone to false alarms—which make up 94% of all security-system activations. (That shockingly high figure causes other problems: Many cities now levy fines for false alarms.)

It's also critical to select the right alarm company. Many of these businesses, says Temple economist Hakim, are "fly-by-night installers just looking to get a monthly check." For recommendations, talk to your insurance agent or friends who have systems. Companies registered with the National Burglar and Fire Alarm Association (NBFAA) are required to conform to an industry service code. "You really want to have detailed conversations with the company you choose," adds the NBFAA's Dave Saddler.

DON'T GET HAMMERED DURING HOME REPAIR

Everybody has at least one outrageous home renovation story to tell, but the one that remodeling consultant Richard Connolly relates may top them all. "I once met a guy who wanted to save a few thousand bucks on a whole-house renovation by doing all of the demolition work himself, including hauling the debris," says Connolly of Weymouth, Mass. "It was tough going, but I must say that for a do-it-yourselfer, he did a terrific job. The only thing left was the wiring, the heating systems and the shell of his house. The problem," continues the veteran contractor, "was that because the guy didn't know the renovation business, he forgot to secure a home-equity loan to pay for the remodeling before he began tearing up the house. So you can imagine how shocked he was when the bank denied his request. In their view, the equity for the loan was in his Dumpster."

What is it about remodeling that turns the best intentions into the worst nightmares? Maybe it's the proliferation of home improvement television shows that make it all look so easy.

In 1997, Americans spent an estimated $118.5 billion on home improvement, reports the National Association of Home Builders (NAHB). This exceeded—for the first time—the amount they spent on new-home construction. But are people generally satisfied with their renovation experience? Not really. According to the Better Business Bureau, complaints against home repair firms always rank in the top 10 of the more than 300 types of businesses it monitors.

That may be because people don't spend enough time planning their renovation, says Susan Maney, director of marketing for the National

Association of the Remodeling Industry. "People will research new cars for months before they buy one, but they only spend a few days when it comes to checking out remodelers."

To help you avoid contractor catastrophe, we talked to home inspectors, homeowners and professionals in the business. While there are an unlimited number of things that can go wrong on any given job—and one or two certainly will—the following misperceptions lead the pack when it comes to sandbagging your renovation.

My friends loved the contractor, so he must be good.

Getting references is always the best way to start a search, but before you whip out your checkbook, think back to the last time someone set you up on a blind date. So what makes you think a friend's contractor will be any more successful?

Take the case of Sally Yates, an administrative assistant for a school district in San Juan, Calif. who wanted to remodel her kitchen and bath. After receiving three glowing endorsements from co-workers for the same contractor, Yates figured she had found Mr. Right. To make sure, she even went to the home of one of her friends to inspect the work. But Yates still got burned.

"Everything went wrong," she laments. "He charged by the day and wouldn't show up until noon. He never got a permit for the work. He'd disappear for days at a time and, now, the toilet he installed won't even flush. My one-week $4,000 job has turned into a four-month $12,000 ordeal, and it's still not finished."

Developing a sound working relationship with your contractor obviously requires more than a few reference checks. Here's what else you should do:

Drop in on your contractor's crew in the middle of a renovation. See how disruptive they are to the daily lives of the family to determine if you can tolerate their work style.

Request a copy of your contractor's workers' compensation or liability insurance policies. If he isn't fully covered, you will be responsible if one of his workers gets injured on your property.

Find out if the contractor's business is financially sound. Call his banker and suppliers. You can also check with the Better Business Bureau or your local building department to see if any complaints have been lodged against him.

Determine who will actually perform your work. It's important to meet everyone—employees and independent contractors—who will be assigned to the project. Find out how long and how well they have worked together. Plus, you should know who is going to be in your home.

Get everything in writing, including bids. Make sure your written contract includes cost estimates, start and end dates, an itemized list of materials, a cancellation clause and a daily cleanup agreement. The design plans—upon which these details are based—should also be attached.

Arrange a payment schedule. Never pay in cash or pay in full up front. Instead, negotiate a plan that allows you to pay in thirds or as major phases of the job are completed.

Nail down an arbitration process for disagreements. Your options for locating a professional arbitrator include calling your local Better Business Bureau or an organization like the Association of Attorney Mediators.

Request a warranty. Typically, you want it for one year to ensure that the job has been done to your satisfaction.

Doing your own vetting is critical, since we all have different standards. If there's something about a contractor that makes you uncomfortable, no matter how exemplary his recommendations and work, don't hire him. And if you are unhappy with your contractor's work while the job is in progress or if he is unresponsive to your concerns, stop the work. Throwing good money after a bad job may prove more expensive than starting over with a new person.

I'll go with the lowest bidder because contractors pad their bills.
Well, some do, but without comparing detailed bids, the lowest estimate could end up costing you the most. Think of it this way: If the contractor can't make a living off your job, how responsive do you think he's going to be? You'll pay for your frugality with shoddy workmanship or costly additions. You may even have to hire a second contractor to come in and right the wrongs of the first.

Scott Burka, a principal in Delby Home Services of Bethesda, Md., gets several jobs a year redoing botched renovations done on the cheap. Not long ago, one couple hired him to replace a poorly installed skylight that had cracked and caused the roof to leak. "The contractor had attached the skylight directly to the roof," Burka recalls, "which is something you should never do. So what should have been a $500 job replacing the skylight ended up costing these people $2,000 to remove the damaged unit, buy a new one, build a frame to hold it and, finally, repair the roof."

Al Ubell, founder of Accurate Building Inspection of Brooklyn, advises homeowners to get multiple bids in writing. "Take the one in the middle," recommends the 49-year-contracting veteran. "No one is going to give you $100 worth of value for 10 bucks." A contractor who has factored in a fair profit is probably the pro who will give you an honest day's work and a roof you can live under.

Doing the prep work myself will save time and money.

Sounds reasonable, right? It sure did to the man Richard Connolly told us about, and we know where that led him. But what harm could a home-owner do by taking on just a few simple tasks—like removing pipes under a sink—before a contractor begins the real work?

"People really love tearing things down," says Dan Bawden, president of Legal Eagle Construction in Houston. "They think it's fun and a great way to get out their aggression." Plus, adds Charlotte, N.C contractor David Tyson, "who can blame a guy for trying to save a few bucks?"

Scott Kusel, a youth ministry executive, learned the hard way. He tried to shave $1,000 from a bedroom-expansion project he contracted Tyson to build. Armed with crowbars, hammers and Tyson's blessing, Kusel and his crew of local high-schoolers had just started stripping paneling and pulling two-by-four studs in the basement when they heard his wife scream: "The refrigerator is moving. The floor is sinking." When he reached the top of the stairs, Kusel knew he was in trouble. The kitchen floor had dropped several inches below the shoe molding.

Fortunately, his contractor lived in his neighborhood. "Scott and the kids had removed some load-bearing studs," recalls Tyson. The contractor used a car jack and a few pieces of discarded wood to prop up the floor and then finished the job.

For novices like Kusel, botching a demolition can really ratchet up costs unless a professional like Tyson takes pity on them. The do-it-yourselfer even has to dispose of the waste, which can run from $10 to fill a 20-gallon trash bag and leave it on the curb to $2,000 to rent a Dumpster. On the other hand, a contractor like Bawden says he can come in for a couple of hours with two guys, take everything down to the studs, haul it off for $500—and leave your kitchen standing.

He's an experienced pro who knows how I want the job done.

Although your contractor may seem to understand what you want, don't expect him to read your mind. Not surprisingly, every contractor we talked to cited lack of communication as one of the biggest hindrances to a successful renovation.

"Clients often assume that their contractor knows what they want," says Maryland contractor Scott Burka. "For instance, I'll get a client who wants a ventilating system added to an interior bathroom that I'm renovating, but never mentions this when we discuss the project. Halfway through the job he'll realize that the ceiling has been painted and there's no vent." Adding the system when the ceiling was open is simple, explains Burka, but to install it once the ceiling's closed will probably add another $2,000 to the job.

"That's why I set up a communication board—whether it's a chalkboard or legal pad—on every job site, so that my clients and I can leave little 'love notes' to each other," says Bawden. "I can put out small fires if they let me know what they need as soon as possible."

It's just a small job. My contractor will throw it in.

Once a job gets started, some homeowners expect contractors to take on all sorts of unexpected little jobs for free. Don't even think about it. Nothing balloons the cost of a renovation faster than a simple thing called a change order. Even minor fixes, such as replacing cabinet handles, can run up the cost of materials and labor.

Simple additions can also blow your construction deadline. Outside vendors such as cabinetmakers or electricians must be scheduled in advance.

Most renovators really have to be careful not to get caught up in a construction feeding frenzy, explains Jeff Winn, the co-owner of Big Sky Construction & Design in San Jose. "When homeowners begin talking to everyone they know about the work, all of a sudden they just have to have that heated towel rack," laughs Winn.

"Of course, we all want to be accommodating if the while-you're-at-it-job is small," says George Christiansen, a Fairfield, Conn. contractor with 16 years under his tool belt. "But if it's not so small, you should really draw up another contract."

He didn't get permits, but he must know what he's doing.

Don't bet on it. Municipal building departments require contractors to file for permits to ensure that construction—even if you're just replacing a fuse box—complies with local ordinances. Permits also ensure that when you put your home on the market, you won't be in for a rude shock. If your house is not up to code, you won't be able to sell it until all violations are corrected. So if your contractor tells you he doesn't need a permit, call your local building department to make sure. While you're on the phone, check out the contractor too. You may want to find someone else.

As long as I'm paying, I should get exactly what I

want. While that may be true, adding too many personal touches may not be your smartest move if you're thinking about selling your home in the future. Just consider the plight of one diehard do-it-my-way San Marino, Calif. couple who insisted that a contractor build the family room underground, complete with authentic portholes that looked into the pool. "It was too user-specific," says Boyd Smith, an estate director with Coldwell Banker in Pasadena. "Potential buyers said the room felt like a bomb shelter, and the house finally had to be taken off the market."

Even small indulgences can prove costly. Rob Davis, owner of 100% Realty, had a problem selling a waterfront house in Fort Walton Beach, Fla., because the kitchen countertops were purple. "Buyers would just turn around and walk out," says Davis. "That color really turned people off." When the house did finally sell, it was with the understanding that the former owners would pay for the removal and replacement of the purple counters.

If you are going to stay in your house for the long haul and you can afford to indulge a taste no one else shares, go ahead. But if you are like the average homeowner and anticipate moving every three to seven years, consider the resale value of your renovation project. Most common makeovers such as those in the kitchen, bath and master bedroom will return a healthy chunk of their cost if you sell the house within a year of the work. According to *Remodeling* magazine, an additional bathroom will recoup 92% of its cost, and you'll probably get 90% for completely overhauling your kitchen. Replacing old appliances with top brands will also help, says Smith. But if your house is already at the high end of the market relative to other homes in the neighborhood, you will probably never recoup what you paid.

GROW VALUE IN YOUR GARDEN

How do you put a price tag on a barefoot walk in lush green grass? Consider this: Every dollar you spend on landscaping can easily return 100% when you sell your home. But that's just one reason why Americans plow an estimated $25 billion into their yards each year. "Some people are on a mission to enhance their homes," says Joel Albizo of the American

Nursery and Landscape Association in Washington, D.C. "Others feel that neighborhood pressure forces them to keep up their space."

Whatever your motivation, the challenge is putting your money to the best possible use. "Most people spend too much buying supplies and services they don't need," says Doug Fender, director of the Turf Resource Center, a clearinghouse for lawn information in Rolling Meadows, Ill. And despite their diligence, he adds, "many homeowners give their yard the wrong kind of care."

Fender, like most of the landscapers, horticultural experts and pest-control professionals we interviewed, recommends using simple, affordable treatments to care for your lawn and trees. They also encourage homeowners to eschew nationally advertised lawn and pest services and mass-merchandise discount stores in favor of local—often family-run—garden centers. Their reasons: Experienced local professionals can help you keep costs down by tailoring your purchases to your yard's specific needs. Perhaps more important, seasoned local pros can usually render solid advice on soil, grass, trees, flowers and shrubs for your region and can provide the most plausible estimates of the time and costs for upkeep. "My sons and I didn't just move into the 'yard department' two months ago," says Chuck Johnson, whose family has run a garden center in Cookeville, Tenn. for 83 years. "This is our profession."

Your county extension service—a government-funded agency operated through state colleges that employs horticulturalists and master gardeners—is also an excellent source of free or low-cost assistance for most yard concerns. To find one near you, consult the Blue Pages of your telephone book.

Whether you're driven by love or money—or a combination of the two—here are tips on making your yard flourish without going broke. The prices and quantities listed below are for a 10,000-square-foot yard or roughly a quarter of an acre.

Lawns. The biggest risk to your grass—and your wallet—comes from doing too much. Prime offenses: overfertilizing, overkilling of weeds and overwatering. Too much fertilizer or herbicide, for example, can burn your tender blades, forcing you to reseed the damaged areas.

What your lawn really needs to thrive is disarmingly basic: First, choose a type of grass that is appropriate for your part of the country, and then use a nitrogen-based fertilizer three times a year—in early May, early June and mid-August. Combine the May feeding with a "weed-and-feed" herbicide treatment. Total annual cost if you do it yourself: about $50, plus another $30 for a spreader. If one weed treatment isn't enough, you can apply another batch of herbicide—you'll pay about $20 at your nursery for the chemicals you need. In contrast, a lawn-care service will typically charge about $230 a year.

As for water, check with your nursery to see how much your grass typically requires and make up for what nature doesn't provide by following the tips we will offer you shortly. Additionally, to keep your lawn in top shape, use a mulch mower, which finely chops the clippings and distributes them as lawn food. Cost: $200 to $400, depending on horsepower and extras, such as self-cleaning engine.

Trees. The right tree in the right place can greatly enhance the aesthetic and financial value of your property. Conversely, the wrong tree in the wrong place can cost you thousands; a deep-rooted oak that wraps its roots around a utility line is a disaster, no matter how beautiful it may be.

When shopping for trees, opt for disease-resistant, sturdy varieties that are suited to your area. In the Northeast, for example, red maples will generally live for decades, while white paper birches usually last only 15 years. For the best planting results, choose saplings that are five to 10 feet tall and weigh 50 to 75 pounds. Most common types, such as ash, maple and oak, cost from $70 to $100. Smaller trees may get whiplashed by adverse weather; larger ones will run you at least $200 apiece, plus $100 to $150 to hire a pro to transport and plant them.

Check with your nursery about where to place your trees. For instance, deciduous trees generally belong in the southwestern part of your property, where their leaves cast shade in the summer and their bare branches let the sun in during the winter. And never plant a tree before locating all utility lines. To find out where they are, ask your local garden center whom to call: In many states, you need to get in touch with the local One-Call agency listed in the White Pages.

Finally, get written instructions on how to plant and care for saplings, including how often you should water, fertilize and prune them. If you can't prune your trees yourself—because they're too large or precariously situated, for example—you'll need to hire a tree-care expert or arborist. Costs can vary widely, depending on where you live and the types and numbers of trees you have; pruning and thinning one 40-foot ash can cost from $200 to $500. So treat arborists as you would any contractor. Obtain referrals from neighbors who have paid for similar work. Then get several estimates, and make sure that anyone you consider carries adequate liability insurance and workers' compensation and hasn't generated complaints to the local Better Business Bureau.

Pests. All kinds of unexpected guests will buzz and burrow through your yard. For four-legged pests, you'll need a pro, but you can probably cope with flying or crawling pests on your own. Strong grass outgrows most pest problems, so controlling bugs is ideally a subset of the overall lawn care outlined above, with one addition. Once a week, you should cut or pull weeds, since these are hatcheries for pests such as slugs and cutworms. A weed whacker, which costs about $50, will cut down unwanted greenery. You must pull out a weed's roots, however, to keep it from growing back.

Don't assume you have a pest problem just because your lawn, plants or trees exhibit a troubling symptom, such as discolored or perforated blades, or leaves. "People see a spot and want to spray their whole lawn," says Fender. Instead, take a sample, such as a leaf that appears to have been munched, to your local nursery for a consultation. Bring along any suspected perpetrators that you can snare. It may turn out that you've simply overwatered.

You can also eliminate harmful invaders by using "beneficials"—benign bugs that feast on pests. For instance, ladybugs (about $10 per 2,000) eat aphids and mites. Beneficials are sold at some local nurseries or through mail order. If taking the natural route doesn't eliminate your problem, consider low-toxicity treatments. Ultrafine horticultural oil, for example, will often fend off small bugs like aphids or spider mites; insecticidal soap can protect trees and specimen plans from similar critters (cost for each: under $25).

You may need heavier-duty intervention to combat a recurring problem (such as moths) or a real danger (like a wasps' nest). Even then, however, you can minimize the use of poisons by employing a lawn service that offers integrated pest management (IPM). This treatment protocol attempts to rid your property of pests by controlling the root causes of the infestation and by using relatively safe chemicals for spot treatments. For instance, an IPM professional would first locate the breeding grounds of moths (such as a branch that serves as a caterpillar hatchery), remove it and then kill the existing pests. For a single IPM treatment, expect to pay from $25 to $50 per tree. If you need several treatments, check out an annual IPM contract, which will generally cost from $400 to $600.

There is no explicit license for IPM. However, any bug hunter you employ should be certified by your state for outdoor pest control. Then, ensure that he or she is using IPM techniques by examining the treatment plan for your yard. It should emphasize baits and biological means of controlling your problem pests. IPM pros do not use highly toxic chemicals such as chloryrifos and malathon.

You will also need professional assistance if your pest problem consists of major yard beasts. True, you can chase gophers and other interlopers. But catching such creatures is difficult—and what are you going to do with them if you snare them? Also, some animals, such as raccoons, can carry rabies or other dangerous diseases. See if your town or county has a wildlife-control agency that will help you out for free. You can probably get a listing through your county extension service. If you need to hire a private company, expect to pay $50 to $100 for someone to set traps to capture your problem animal alive and cart it away either to distant woods or the big woods in the sky.

Water. For about $25, your local garden center will sell you an impulse sprinkler (the kind that goes tch-tch-tch as it rotates), which will efficiently irrigate an arc of lawn with a radius up to 35 feet. To inexpensively water your trees, shrubs and flowers, you can try a drip irrigation system, which consists of a series of water emitters attached to a hose that you can snake out around your landscaping. (Cost: $75 to $120 for parts that you can easily assemble yourself.) For help in designing a system or purchasing parts, consult your local nursery.

If your yard has many different kinds of trees and plants, or if you're often away from home, you can pay an irrigation contractor to plan and install an automatic sprinkler system that allows you to set one zone of sprinklers to water your grass, say, every morning and another to hydrate your trees twice a week. From start to finish, you'll pay a professional about $2,500, although you can trim the tab by doing some of the assembly work yourself once your pipes are installed.

First you'll need a contractor to design your system, which includes pipes, heads, valves and hydraulics. Cost: about $150. To select a contractor, get names from neighbors or the Associated Landscape Contractors of America (800-395-2522). Then ask for written bids from the contractors you're considering—and reject any that do not explain how much the installation will cost and how long it will take.

Also request a list of items (identified by type and brand name) that the contractor will use to build the system. State-of-the-art materials for a 10,000-square-foot yard will cost you about $1,200, but if you agree to purchase them from the designer, he or she will generally rebate the design fee.

Don't balk at the cost of parts, because skimping can lead to disaster. For example, cheap thermostat wire can disintegrate underground. Your wire should be approved for underground use by Underwriters Laboratories (UL); your pipe by the National Sanitation Foundation (NSF); your heads should be of commercial quality, not from a discount store; and your screws and clamps should be made of stainless steel. "Sprinkler contractors bury their mistakes, so inspect materials and the work before the trenches are covered," says Ed Heckman, president of Lawn Design Irrigation Centers in Littleton, Colo.

The biggest part of installation is "pipe pulling," the process of actually laying sections of pipe under your yard—and is a job for your contractor. You'll need about 70 feet of pipe and two dozen heads (total cost: $350).

Next, the pipes, heads, valves and wires have to be linked and the excavated turf replanted. At this point you can save $1,000 or so by doing the work yourself according to the contractor's plan. Sure, it will probably cost you a week and a half of your life, but what's 10 days of sweat equity compared with the dollar value you'll add to your homestead—plus all the luscious springs and good ole summertimes you'll spend in your perfect yard?

◆ CHAPTER 7

CONSUMER TIPS THAT BOOST YOUR SAVINGS

Day in, day out, the decisions you make shopping for goods and services not only affect your current cash flow but also help shape your financial future. For example, as we'll soon show, if you conduct a lackluster search for health insurance, you can end up paying super-high premiums at 140% to 600% of standard rates. If you fail to keep your credit-card spending in check, you may have to pay 50% to 100% more than otherwise for home and auto insurance. If you don't explore all the options for financial aid, the cost of college can skyrocket. Add up all the dollars you needlessly spend each year, and you can come up with major money that could grow into thousands of dollars if you stashed it instead in stocks and bonds. The following tips on smart spending and aggressive consumer action can fatten your wallet today and your investment portfolio tomorrow.

HOW INSURERS SET YOUR RATES

About a decade ago, after being rejected for a credit card (and not having the slightest idea why), a MONEY editor requested a copy of her credit report. Then she understood. There, among her timely payments, was a lien—an accusation from a contractor that she hadn't paid a bill. Someone else's credit information had seeped onto her report.

It took her weeks of letter writing to clear her name, but as she looks back on the experience, she realizes that she was lucky, because if the same thing happened today, it could cost her hundreds of dollars in insurance premiums.

What does your credit report have to do with your insurance coverage? Plenty, as it turns out. More than 300 auto and home insurers are now consulting credit information when screening applicants. Folks with a blemish or two on their reports—even if it's there by mistake—may be denied coverage or shunted to a second-tier carrier with higher rates, sometimes 50% to 100% higher than what someone with a clean credit history would get.

Insurers put such weight on your credit history because it is believed to be predictive—more predictive than even your driving history. "[Credit reports are] not based on zip codes or geography," explains Marty Abrams of Experian, one of the country's three credit bureaus, "but on your actual behavior."

The silver lining is that a spotless credit report can help you as much as a poor one can hurt you. Consider this example from Allstate: A 34-year-old married man living in downstate Illinois applies for auto insurance with a record of two accidents in the past three years. Clearly, this guy is a risk, and usually the company would offer him coverage with its second-tier carrier, Allstate Indemnity, for $1,600 a year. But a clean credit report makes him acceptable to the top-tier Allstate Insurance Co. His rate: $1,000 a year.

Ironically, many insurers aren't even looking at your actual credit report when making these decisions but rather at a credit score, a concoction that mixes together 30-some different factors from the report, including late payments and the size of your credit line, as well as bankruptcies, liens and foreclosures. Unfortunately—and, consumer advocates say, unfairly—these scores aren't available to the consumer. So the best thing for you to do is focus on keeping your credit report in good shape.

Watch your limits. Take a look at how much credit you have available from all sources. If you're tapping 80% or more, it pays to sign up for another card or ask to get your credit limit raised on your existing cards. As long as you don't tap that larger reservoir, having it should help bring your balance back into the acceptable range.

Close excess accounts. On the other hand, having too many cards can hurt you. Even if you're not using them all—and perhaps haven't for years—insurers and lenders figure you could go on a spending jag at any time. This can be a particular problem with department store cards, which people often forget they have. To cancel a credit card, send a letter, by certified mail, to the issuer. Ask for written verification that your card has been canceled. In a month or so, whether or not you have received that verification, get a copy of your credit report. If the card still shows up, notify the credit bureau; include copies of your certified mail receipt and the verifying letter (if you have one). A law that went into effect in September 1997 says that the problem now becomes the credit bureau's to resolve with the issuer.

Limit inquiries. The more often someone asks a credit bureau about you—which happens whenever you apply for a loan or new card—the lower your credit score will be. It's best not to apply to more than four or five places for credit in any six-month period.

Expect errors. You can't assume that credit bureaus will do things right. If you live in Colorado, Georgia, Maryland, Massachusetts, New Jersey or Vermont, you can get a free copy of your credit report each year from each of the three reporting agencies. Otherwise, they cost up to $8 apiece. One should be sufficient unless you find major errors; in that case, check all three: Equifax, Experian and TransUnion. Each has a free 800 phone number.

Explain lapses. If there's a mistake on your report that the bureau refuses to remove or if you have a good reason (like illness) for your lapses, you can write a 100-word explanation that becomes part of your report. Insurers who get the full report—like Allstate—are likely to take it into account. After all, they're trying to write as many policies as possible.

SEARCHING FOR LIFE INSURANCE ONLINE

To hear the purveyors of life insurance in cyberspace tell it, their Websites are the insurance equivalent of utopia, a wonderland devoid of pushy sales agents where a few clicks of the mouse can instantly hook you up with the ideal policy at the lowest price.

And these sites are an excellent place to begin your search for life insurance, since you get quick access to scads of premium quotes. For example, surf over to QuickQuote (www.quickquote.com), and you can sift through a database of more than a thousand policies offered by 18 insurers. InsureMarket (www.insuremarket.com), the site run by personal-finance giant Intuit, limits itself to the policies of only a handful of major insurance firms. But the site also features worthwhile planning materials, including an insurance calculator that can help you figure out how much insurance you need.

But regardless of the number of quotes and other information these sites offer, the overriding fact is that choosing a life insurance policy doesn't lend itself to a quick session of Net surfing like, say, buying a music CD. Even the bare-bones term policies to which online sites mostly restrict themselves carry plenty of complications. If you buy without also doing a bit of research offline, you could pay more than you should or even end up with the wrong type of policy.

Probably the biggest surprise in store for online shoppers is that the premium quote you see on the screen may not be the one you get when you sign a contract. For example, a while ago we went to the Quotesmith (www.quotesmith.com) site in search of $500,000 worth of term coverage for a nonsmoking 39-year-old male resident of Illinois. We specifically asked for policies that would guarantee not to increase premiums for at least 10 years. Within seconds, we homed in on a policy from Old Republic Life with an annual cost of $305, or $150 less than one listed from First Colony Life. But you would get Old Republic's rock-bottom rate only if you were in perfect health and didn't have a dangerous occupation or hobbies and if your family had no history of heart problem or other chronic illnesses. You can find out about these qualifications for Old Republic's policy, as well as those for other policies offered through the site. But to do so, you must click open the policy and read the "Plan Acceptance Guidelines."

What we *couldn't* do at Quotesmith was factor health and family history into the screening process. So if we'd wanted a quote that reflected, say, a family history of heart disease, we would have had to click our way through the guidelines of dozens, if not hundreds, of policies, a process that could have taken hours. And even then, we wouldn't have known the exact premium until the company sent a medical technician to administer a physical, draw blood and take a medical history.

QuickQuote, InsureMarket and InsWeb (www.insweb.com) try to give more accurate quotes by asking questions about your health and background. InsureMarket, for example, allows you to select your cholesterol level and blood pressure from pulldown menus. But plug in numbers that are even slightly off, and you may not find the policy with the lowest premium. When we asked for a $350,000 10-year policy for a 35-year-old woman from California with blood pressure of 136 to 140 over 81 to 85, for instance, Lincoln Benefit Life had the lowest premium of $239.50 a year. Take her blood pressure up a notch to 141 to 150 over 86 to 90, and Transamerica Occidental Life offered the lowest premium ($255.50) while Lincoln Benefit's quote jumped 41% to $337.50.

Another, albeit smaller, shortcoming to online shopping is that you're pretty much limited to term insurance, and a specific type of term policy at that: level-premium term, which charges the same annual premium typically for five, 10, 15 or 20 years. Most insurance shoppers won't find these two restrictions a problem. Term should be the policy of choice for most people since it gives you the highest immediate amount of coverage for whatever premium you can afford. And a level-premium policy lets you lock in your annual insurance costs, as opposed to annual renewable term (ART), whose premiums start small but increase dramatically as you get older.

But in some cases ART is the better choice. "A smoker who's serious about quitting would be better off buying an annual renewal term policy until he's quit smoking for 12 consecutive months," says Dick Weber, an insurance consultant in Safety Harbor, Fla. "Then he can reapply as a non-smoker for level term at lower rates." If the smoker shopped only online, he might never consider this option.

Finally, despite the online sites' vaunted databases, we found you can sometimes do better by picking up the phone. For example, when we called Zurich Direct to verify a quote we'd pulled off the InsureMarket site, a phone representative offered to write the same coverage for $405 a year instead of the online price of $465.

So what's the best way to use the Web to buy insurance? You can begin by thinking of the Internet as a research tool and not a one-stop electronic mall for insurance. First, get current medical information from your doctor, including recent cholesterol and blood-pressure readings. Next, visit the sites we've mentioned and come up with a handful of five or six policies that appear to offer the best rate. Then, get on the phone and call an independent insurance agent who carries policies from a wide assortment of insurers to see if the agent can beat the quotes you've gathered online. Granted, we're talking more work than screening and clicking. But the extra hours you spend now will pay off in lower premiums for years to come.

GET BETTER HEALTH PROTECTION

For Americans in need of individual health insurance, recent years have brought good news, bad news and lots of confusing news. Among other protections, the Health Insurance Portability and Accountability Act of 1996 aimed to make life easier for anyone who either quit or lost a job with group health benefits and needed to find individual coverage. In essence, it required states to force carriers who sell individual policies to do business with such applicants, regardless of health status or age. As an alternative, states could furnish their own means of insuring these individuals—say, through catchall "risk pools."

But the law—fully effective in most states since January 1998—has hardly been a magic wand. Insurers must offer policies only to those who have had at least 18 months of coverage, most recently through a group policy, have exhausted all COBRA coverage (the 18 months of medical insurance your old employer has to offer you under the federal Consolidated Omnibus Budget Reconciliation Act of 1986), and are not insurable under any other group plan. And since the law is silent on price, in some states insurers can set premiums at 140% to 600% of standard rates. For a booklet on the law, call the Department of Labor (800-998-7542). Meanwhile, here's how to find a policy you can feel good about.

Call your state department of insurance. They'll give you a list of carriers selling individual policies in your state. Some states provide additional information about pending premium hikes, complaints and quality ratings, so be sure to ask. (The insurance department can also tell you if your state is one of those offering "risk pools," a last resort that often charges up to 125% to 150% of a basic private-policy premium.) In some cases, an insurance agent can help, so ask friends or colleagues for recommendations, or call the National Association of Health Underwriters (202-223-5533) for referrals.

Tap professional or alumni connections. Several trade organizations offer group policies to their members. For instance, a free-lance writer who belongs to the Washington Independent Writers Association in D.C. can join an HMO or a point-of-service plan with no exclusions for pre-existing conditions. Some college alumni associations also offer coverage to grads. Call your alma mater, or call the Alumni Insurance Agency and Administrators (800-726-2422).

Check out the carriers. Several states and many large employers require managed-care plans to be accredited, generally by the National Committee for Quality Assurance (NCQA), a nonprofit evaluating body. As a result, consumers can check NCQA reports on the Web (www.ncqa.org) or via phone (800-839-6487) to see how most large plans stack up on quality of staff, equipment, care and patient satisfaction. Incidentally, you also may be able to check out doctors and hospitals. State agencies in Florida,

Maryland, Massachusetts, New York and Rhode Island will tell consumers if a doctor has been disciplined for poor patient care or, sometimes, criminal conduct, and the Pacific Business Group on Health (www.healthscope.org) rates group practices in California, Oregon and Washington State on patient satisfaction, preventive services and care of the chronically ill. In New York, New Jersey and Pennsylvania, you can get reports comparing how well individual hospitals care for patients, measured by mortality rates and other indicators adjusted to reflect risk factors such as a patient's age.

Seek solace in the IRS. Generally, if you're self-employed you can now deduct 45% of the cost of health insurance premiums you pay for yourself, your spouse and any dependents. That deduction will slowly rise to 100% by 2007.

FIGHT DENIALS OF MEDICAL CLAIMS

Once you have health insurance, your troubles aren't over. You know what we mean. For example, ever wished you could hand off troublesome health insurance claims to some third party who would simply take care of them for you? Lately, a little-known class of pros has popped up that would be glad to oblige: Claims assistance professionals, or CAPs, will pay medical bills, file claims on a regular basis and fight those exasperating claim denials—all, of course, for a fee.

But before you pay someone else to fight your battles, follow the steps they might take. You can easily handle some of them yourself.

If you have filed a claim and received less money back than you expected, start by scrutinizing your Explanation of Benefits. This rundown of what your insurer covers and why a claim was denied can offer clues to a mistake. For instance, a denial for an "inappropriate service" could mean that the doctor used a wrong code. A quick call to your insurer may be enough to clear up the misunderstanding. Another common spot for mistakes is the claim form you filled out to begin the process: One missing or incorrect digit in your birth date, Social Security number, health insurance plan identification or group plan number will trigger a denial.

A claim may also be denied because your insurer needs more details, such as a letter from the doctor stating why the treatment was medically necessary. "It's easy to get more payment if you simply submit more information," says Lori Donnelly, a CAP in Bethlehem, Pa.

Whatever you do, "don't pay a cent until you're sure the insurer has covered what it's supposed to," warns Mary Rzeszut, owner of the claims assistance company SMV Billing Solutions in Mineola, N.Y. If you a pay a doctor's bill that the insurer eventually covers, you could wait months for a refund. If you can't resolve a claims problem with a few phone calls, turn to free helpers: your employer's benefits administrator or your plan's formal appeals process.

Only then, if you're still not satisfied and your bills amount to $1,000 or more, should you consider hiring a CAP. Otherwise, you could end up spending more to settle your claim than you would to pay off the bill. After a free consultation, most CAPs charge $20 to $60 an hour. For a one-time appeal, many CAPs ask for 15% of the settlement, which can save you money over hourly billing in a complicated case.

And before hiring a CAP (listed in the Yellow Pages under "Insurance Claims Processing Services" or "Health Organizations"), keep in mind that they aren't licensed or regulated in most states. "Some CAPs have simply attended a two-day training session in Reno," says Mike Donio of the non-profit consumer group People's Medical Society in Allentown, Pa. So look for someone who has worked in the insurance business or medical profession. One starting point: the Alliance of Claims Assistance Professionals in Wheaton, Ill. (630-588-1260) will make a referral.

TAKE CHARGE OF YOUR CREDIT CARDS

Your main considerations in getting the most out of your credit cards should be securing the lowest fees and interest rates, managing to extract maximum benefits from rewards such as free air travel miles and not paying for perks you don't need. Toward that end, we offer this advice.

How to earn a free plane ticket fast. Once you pay an annual fee for a rewards card, you may find yourself itching to rack up points. You're in luck. Nowadays you can charge everything from a nine-piece bucket of Kentucky Fried Chicken to heart surgery. Here's a sampling of novel places that accept plastic—and a tally of how far extreme charging can take you.

♦ **College bursars:** One-third of U.S. universities now let you charge tuition. Two semesters at Harvard: 30,000 frequent-flier miles.

- **Hospitals:** Almost 95% of hospitals take credit cards. A three-day head-to-toe physical at the Mayo Clinic: 1,900 miles.

- **Charities:** Chances are your favorite charity takes plastic. At a recent Christmas, the Salvation Army outfitted sidewalk bell ringers in Pittsburgh and Akron with credit-card terminals. One generous impulse: 100 miles.

- **Realtors:** In 1997, a Manhattan real estate broker began letting clients put commissions on Amex. Clayman Realty's sales commission on a two-bedroom apartment: 24,000 miles.

- **Auction houses:** Sotheby's in New York City lets you charge any bid up to $25,000. The Duke and Duchess of Windsor's throw pillow: 13,800 miles.

- **City halls:** Paying taxes and other government fees by credit card is around the corner. Drivers in Boston can put their registration and traffic tickets on plastic. Parking ticket on Newbury Street: 20 miles.

- **Fast-food joints:** Parking garages and fast-food restaurants are starting to take plastic. Domino's Pizza has armed delivery folks with portable card swipers. One large pizza: 12 miles.

- **Grand total:** 69,832 miles, or two domestic round-trip tickets.

Don't be a victim of false fears.

Don't be a victim of false fears. An official-looking piece of mail came to our attention recently, urging its recipient to phone a "credit monitoring hotline" for important credit report information. That hotline turned out to be a recorded warning that "right now, someone, somewhere, could be making unauthorized charges to your credit card..."

Sounds ominous—enough, perhaps, to make you want to pay for some protection, right? That's just the idea. In fact, an entire industry has developed to prey on heightened credit fears, some stemming from the growth of online buying and the perception that credit-card information sent over the Web is easily stolen. You'll be forced to cover a thief's tab, so the thinking goes, and the process of clearing your name will be tortuous, if not impossible.

But few of these services are worth the cost. For starters, experts say that Internet-related fears are largely hype. "I haven't heard of a single instance of private information stolen while in transit over the Web," David Medine said last June. Medine is the associate director for credit practices at the Federal Trade Commission. "The risks are way overblown," he said.

Even if you are the victim of credit theft, the consequences aren't nearly as dire as some would have you believe. The issuers of the Yahoo credit card and the AT&T Universal card promise to indemnify you against Internet transactions improperly made with your card. And under federal law, as long as you report an unauthorized charge within 60 days of the date of your bill, you can't be held liable for more than $50. In practice, credit-card issuers rarely ask victims to pay a dime.

Some pitches hype credit dangers even more than the one we heard. In September 1997, for example, the FTC filed a lawsuit against one company, alleging deceptive telemarketing. The firm sold $189 insurance policies that covered up to $10,000 in unauthorized credit-card charges. The pitch, says the FTC, was that by the time you saw such charges on your bill, it would be too late to have them removed. An attorney for the company says the firm did nothing wrong, but agreed to put a stop to the practice. The FTC's Medine says other firms have been under inquiry for similar pitches.

BE AGGRESSIVE WITH YOUR BANK

Want the ugly truth about the banking industry? The big banks charge higher fees than the small banks. And banks that operate in several states charge higher fees than those that do business in just one.

In the midst of bank merger mania, that's not exactly comforting. Add to that the fact that mergers can be a hassle—as accounts, tellers and branches are eliminated—and you can understand why some consumers are up in arms over the deal frenzy.

But here's our view: The fears are overblown. The banks involved in big transactions—Citicorp, BankAmerica, NationsBank and others—were already large institutions operating across state lines and charging high fees. They can't go much higher. Plus, there wasn't much geographic duplication in the B of A/NationsBank deal, which means the chances are good that your favorite teller still has a job.

Whether or not your bank has been invited to the party, mergers have presented you with an opportunity. You may be able to trim your banking costs as competitors offer free checking or cut-rate CDs or even free cell phones to lure you away—and the big banks ante up to keep you. As you weigh all those offers, however, don't lose sight of one crucial question: Are you getting what you really need from your bank? That may sound like a no-brainer, but a lot of people are in accounts that just don't fit—around 20%, according to Seamus McMahon of First Manhattan Consulting Group. Say you're still paying $8 a month for checking, even though you now maintain enough of a minimum balance to avoid it. Switch accounts, and you pocket nearly $100 a year.

The key is that you have to take the initiative and manage your bank. If the bank has a program that meets your needs, it should be easy to switch accounts. If not, find yourself a new bank—or a nonbank, for that matter. Credit unions and brokerage firms each have advantages worth considering. Here are some guidelines to help you figure out what sort of institution is best for you:

If you keep $500 in your checking account, says Gary Cohn of the consulting firm Datatron, there's no need to pay for checking in most markets.

If you have no desire ever to see another teller, look for an "ATM-only" or an "express" account, which typically is free if you also direct-deposit your paycheck.

If you're determined to earn money-market rates on all your savings, you may be better off in a cash management account at a brokerage or at one of the large banks where deposits are swept daily—but you generally need a combined balance of $5,000-plus to qualify.

If you're a heavy ATM user, you belong at a bank that has a lot of machines. According to a survey by Star System, the country's largest regional ATM network, we now use our cards an average of 15 times a month. Paying a $1.50 surcharge even half the time would cost you $135 a year. That more than offsets any savings you might reap on checking at a smaller bank.

If your biggest concern is convenience, you should look for the new financial supermarkets—the sort of one-stop shops that Citigroup wants to be. You may pay a modest premium for being able to get auto insurance and an auto loan at the same place, but if you're the type who won't cross the street to avoid an ATM surcharge, you probably won't mind.

If you really detest paying bank fees, try a credit union. (If you're not offered one at work, look for one that's based on location.) Because of the tax advantages they enjoy, credit unions can undercut the fees at most banks. And although they tend to sport fewer ATMs, some credit unions have begun rebating the surcharges tacked on by other banks.

Here's one last thought: We'd all be better off treating our banks the way we should be treating our long-distance telephone services—check in with them at least once a year to make sure we're in the right programs.

Bank hopping may be a hassle right now, but it's getting easier. According to First Manhattan's McMahon, banks have already figured out a way to allow customers to switch with no more than one signature on one piece of paper. Within two years, he predicts, this will be commonplace.

SHOP FOR COLLEGE FINANCIAL AID

At 16, Katherine Haynie put together a car stereo and fell in love with audio engineering. So when she applied to college, she set her sights on the prestigious Massachusetts Institute of Technology. A National Merit Scholarship finalist with combined SAT scores of 1,520, the Davie, Fla. student was an ideal candidate for admission but not for financial aid. MIT bases aid strictly on economic need. The university admitted her but, since her mother and stepfather earned more than $100,000 the previous year, offered only a $2,625 loan. Katherine's mother, who was paying off hefty debts, could not afford MIT's $34,100-a-year tab.

Enter the University of Miami, which had just created a major in audio engineering. Eager to attract top students, UM showered Katherine with cash, awarding her a whopping $22,700 in grants and loans. Her out-of-pocket cost: just $5,000 a year. For Katherine, the choice was simple. "The University of Miami is too great a deal to pass up," she says, adding, "Maybe I'll think about MIT for graduate school."

Let's face it: Financial aid has become a free-for-all. Shrinking government funding, soaring tuition prices and shifting aid-eligibility formulas have eroded what just 10 years ago was a relatively straightforward process. Today, fewer and fewer colleges grant financial aid purely on the basis of need—and those that do have made the standards too stringent for most middle-class students to qualify.

Meanwhile, colleges with strong endowments are handing out aid based on academic merit or special talents, regardless of need. Indeed, Washington College, a small liberal arts school in Chestertown, Md., knocks $10,000 a year off the tuition of any member of the National Honor Society it admits.

The result, as Katherine Haynie found out, is that you may get little or no aid at one college, while another will let you in for virtually nothing. "The experience was very stressful," says Katherine's mother, Mary Griesemer. "And some colleges were cold and unhelpful."

What brought on this upheaval in the financial aid office? Look first to Washington. Since the early 1980s, federal funding, which accounts for 75%

of all financial aid, has not kept pace with rising enrollments or inflation. For instance, the Pell Grant for low-income students is worth 25% less today, in inflation-adjusted dollars, than it was in 1978. What's more, back then Pell Grants, which don't have to be repaid, made up 76% of all federal funding for student aid. Today, loans account for 77% of federal aid.

Private colleges have tried to make up the difference by awarding aid from their own coffers. In effect, though, students who pay full tuition subsidize the rest: The doubling of so-called institutional aid in the past 10 years has helped push up college tuition costs an average 7% a year since 1980. That rate is beginning to slow, but last year's 5% price hike is still far ahead of inflation and real wage growth.

But there's good news too. Yes, the big aid squeeze has worsened the pressure on families who aren't rich enough to afford college easily but aren't poor, either: Most families earning $50,000 to $100,000 are deemed too well-off to qualify for much in the way of federal grants or need-based aid. On the other hand, merit aid can help—if you know how to target a school that appreciates what your child has to offer. So your prospects will depend mainly on how well you can play the aid game. Says Brad Barnes, a college aid counselor at College Quest in Denver: "To get your fair share of aid, you will have to fight for as much as you can."

To help you in that fight, we've come up with 10 key questions you should ask yourself—and strategies for making the most of the answers. But first, consider these three developments in the financial aid arena.

New flexibility at top schools. A few prestigious schools that still base financial aid on need alone are making it easier for cash-strapped middle-class and upper-middle-class families to qualify. Princeton announced last year that it would no longer count home equity as an asset for most families earning up to $90,000 a year—a move that could increase aid packages to those families by an average $3,000 to $4,000. Princeton will also award grants, rather than loans, to families with incomes below $40,000.

Yale and Stanford have followed with similar home-equity breaks. Harvard hedged its bets, telling students admitted to its freshman class that it would consider matching rival offers. "Princeton's move ups the ante for all top colleges and universities," says Philip Wick, financial aid director at Williams College in Williamstown, Mass. "All of us may have to move in a more realistic direction and award more aid."

Spurred by Princeton's announcement, the College Scholarship Service— the College Board unit that collects data used to determine financial need—

is proposing changes to its formula that would cut some families' expected contributions. "There's a growing feeling that our methodology assesses families earning between $50,000 and $100,000 too harshly," says Edwin Below, a former financial aid officer at Wesleyan University in Middletown, Conn. who heads the CSS standards committee. The new rules are likely to be approved for the 2000–2001 academic year.

Fatter discounts from second-tier schools.
"Once you look past the 45 or so highly selective colleges, it's much more of a buyer's market," says Michael McPherson, president of Macalester College in St. Paul and co-author of *The Student Aid Game.* A 1997 survey of 340 institutions by the National Association of College and University Business Officers found that the average private college or university is giving back 36.7% of its published price as aid to freshmen, an increase of nearly 40% since 1990.

You might think that colleges would lower their sticker prices rather than discount so heavily. But as Arlington, Va. education consultant Arthur Hauptman notes, discounting "enables schools to tailor their financial aid packages to attract the students they want [and] also maximize their net revenue." What that means in plain English is that colleges want to give away as little as possible—and only those who ask for a discount will get it.

Some 65% of private colleges and 27% of public colleges use this kind of targeted aid, according to USA Group Noel-Levitz, a Littleton, Colo. enrollment-management company. In fact, a growing number of colleges (including Baylor University and Ohio State) actually hire firms like USA Group Noel-Levitz to help them decide how to get the biggest bang from their financial aid dollars. Using software that analyzes such factors as students' demographic background, academic record and intended major, these firms calculate the precise amount of aid to offer each applicant—a process college administrators call financial aid leveraging. "The goal is to take advantage of the family's willingness to pay," says Thomas Williams, president of USA Group Noel-Levitz. "It doesn't make sense to offer $1,500 to meet an average student's full need when you can offer $500 to three students you really want and get them all to come."

New help from the tax man.
The 1997 tax bill gave a few modest goodies to parents paying for their children's higher education. Keep in mind that you may take only one of these tax breaks for each student in your family in any given year.

If your kids are entering college now, look into the Hope (Helping Outstanding Pupils Educationally) Scholarship, a tax credit of up to $1,500 a year per student for parents of freshmen or sophomores. For juniors or seniors in college, there's the lifetime learning credit, a tax credit of as much as $1,000 a year. There's another option, too: If your kids are already in college, you may be able to deduct interest on the first 60 payments of their education loans. (If your own income is too high to be eligible for that tax break, your kids can probably deduct the interest.)

With that groundwork laid, let's get into the nitty-gritty of strategy. Here are our 10 questions.

1. Have I done all I can to fit into financial aid formulas? If you're truly canny, you'll begin planning for financial aid eligibility before your child learns to drive. Here's why: Many private colleges ask, as part of the aid application, to see your tax return for the year beginning Jan. 1 of your child's junior year of high school. If you can minimize your income or draw down assets before that point by shifting the timing of moves you'd been planning, you can maximize your aid eligibility. Three savvy and legitimate steps: remortgaging your house to fund renovations, which will reduce your home equity and therefore your net worth (this affects eligibility only at private schools); drawing down savings to pay off credit-card balances, which reduces your assets (colleges don't count credit-card debt as a liability); or leaving a job to start your own business.

Some experts suggest that you try to collect a year-end bonus early or take a loss on an investment (to offset gains on other holdings), but it's probably not worth the bother for aid alone. Those tactics reduce your income for only one year, and you're facing four years of financial aid applications.

Income shifting is more problematic if you're seeking aid from highly selective universities like Cornell and Harvard, which may also ask to see your tax return for the year beginning Jan. 1 of your kid's sophomore year. "That way, colleges can spot discrepancies in income and assets from one year to the next," says Monique Thomas of Collegiate Financial Aid Services in Darien, Conn.

2. How much will I be expected to pay? It's essential to get at least a rough idea how your aid application will be rated by colleges. So each year your child is in high school, get both the federal and institutional financial aid formulas (from financial aid guidebooks, college guidance counselors or

Internet sites such as www.finaid.org) and calculate your expected family contribution—the amount colleges figure you could afford to pay.

If you stick to public schools, which use so-called federal aid methodology, these estimates should be quite reliable. Private colleges, though, tweak numbers based on their own formulas, which can change from year to year and aren't disclosed. "There are many gray areas, so colleges can interpret the data favorably or unfavorably, depending on how much they want you," says financial aid consultant Kalman A. Chany, the author of *Paying for College Without Going Broke*. That means one student might get a fatter aid package because the college needs more cellists or kids from the South, while another student might get less because there's an oversupply of pre-meds.

Even highly selective institutions may engage in bidding wars. "Although Ivy League schools give mainly need-based aid, they still offer preferential packaging," notes David Vonasek of College Planners, financial aid specialists in Belmont, Calif. "They can vary the grant portion for the students they really want."

3. Has my child chosen a financial "safety school"? When college advisers at high schools talk about safety schools, they mean schools that will definitely admit your child. We mean something entirely different: a school your child would be willing to attend, where you're likely to have negotiating leverage. The seven to nine colleges your youngster applies to should include one or two financial safety schools.

How do you identify financial safety schools? First, advises Carol Loewith, an educational consultant in Fairfield, Conn., consider both public and private schools of different sizes in different locations. Second, look for schools where your child's grades and/or SAT or ACT scores will rank "in the top 10% to 25% of the freshman applicant pool," says Michele Hernandez, a former Dartmouth admissions officer and author of *A Is for Admission*. Then identify the ones with strong endowments and generous per-student aid packages. You can find this information in college guidebooks or the literature provided by the schools.

That strategy worked for Brian Smith of Houston. A student council president and varsity basketball player, he had a 4.16 grade average and combined SAT scores of 1,330. Those numbers were good enough to get the Catholic prep school salutatorian into Princeton, Harvard and Yale, which offered him $3,500 to $8,500 in aid. But he had also applied to the University of Virginia in Charlottesville (average SATs: about 1,300), which rolled out the red carpet with a Jefferson Scholar Award, providing full tuition, room and board, plus an annual $2,500 stipend and a summer study trip to Europe. So long, Ivy League. "UVA has an outstanding program with really exceptional students," says Brian, adding, "I'd like to go to law school at Harvard or Yale, with no debt."

4. Will B's get my child enough aid to go to a private school? They can. Consider Erica Fine Singer of Easton, Conn. With a B average and combined SAT scores of 980, she thought Ithaca College, a competitive but fairly low-profile private school in Ithaca, N.Y., would be a long shot, despite her extensive extracurricular activities and strong teacher recommendations. But Ithaca, which has a relatively generous reputation in financial aid circles, awarded her an aid package worth $12,725, nearly half the total cost. What's more, owing to a reciprocal agreement between Ithaca College and nearby Cornell University, Erica will be able to take classes at Cornell for no extra charge.

5. Should my child apply early decision? Not if you really need aid. Yes, the chances of admission are better, since many elite schools now select a third to more than half their freshmen via early decision. But as Morton Schapiro, professor of economics at the University of Southern California and co-author of *The Student Aid Game*, points out, "These colleges don't want you to apply to lots of other schools, where you might get merit aid offers. And once they have you, they have little incentive to offer the best possible deal on financial aid."

Take the experience of Kenna McKenzie-Young. The Tucumcari, N.M. student, who had a 4.2 grade average and combined SAT scores of 1,380, was accepted early to Swarthmore College, near Philadelphia (total cost: $32,130). Kenna expected to get about $20,000 in aid, since her divorced mother, Marjorie McKenzie, earns less than $50,000 and supports three children. But Swarthmore offered only $4,649 in aid. "We were really disillusioned," says Marjorie.

The problem was Marjorie's interest in a family cattle ranch and farm, which Swarthmore viewed as an asset that she could borrow against. Marjorie argued that the farm belonged to her entire family, including siblings, nieces and nephews, and she wasn't willing to stake it on one child's education. But Swarthmore refused to increase its offer. (When asked about the decision, Swarthmore replied by fax that "schools may differ in their evaluations of a particular family's financial circumstances. We cannot emphasize enough how diligently we work to make the valuation process fair and generous to all our students.")

"Because Kenna applied early decision, she lost any potential negotiating power," contends Alan Posich of Educational Consulting & Tutoring Service in Albuquerque, who helped the McKenzies appeal. After Swarthmore allowed Kenna to apply elsewhere, she was accepted by Grinnell College, near Des Moines, which gave her $15,820 in aid, including $7,600 in grants and scholarships. Says Kenna: "It worked out for the best."

6. Am I explaining my finances clearly? The McKenzies' experience illustrates a common pitfall: If your finances are complicated, you risk losing aid. Financial aid officers sift through hundreds of applications in a few weeks. Your child's folder may get just 20 minutes of the administrator's attention, which may not be enough to get a handle on unexpected medical bills, support of an older relative or income that varies from year to year.

To prevent misunderstandings, write a brief letter to the college financial aid officer, giving the pertinent facts and attaching documentation if necessary. "Keep it short," urges College Board's Edwin Below, "and explain exactly how the problem affects your ability to pay."

7. Should I hire help? If you think a lot of money could be at stake, you may want to consult an independent financial aid counselor; the cost ranges, on average, from $100 to $500. (Admissions counselors, who advise on where to apply as well as on aid, charge $1,000 to $2,000.) That's what Mitchell and Shelley Cohen of Holliston, Mass. did when their daughter Heather was accepted to George Washington University in Washington, D.C. in 1997. The Cohens, both schoolteachers, wanted to do the best possible job before committing to spend more than $120,000. "I hire someone to do my taxes," Mitchell says. "I wouldn't try to fill out aid forms myself."

Stuart Farmelant of Student Aid Advisors in nearby Newton, Mass. submitted Heather's aid forms and then appealed when GWU offered only a $2,625 loan. The university assumed that the Cohens could borrow on their home, but it had lost value since they bought it at the height of the '80s real estate boom, making a home-equity loan impossible. After the Cohens backed up their claim with an independent appraisal, the school awarded Heather a $4,000 grant.

This year, the Cohens' net worth went up, and GWU cut Heather's grant to $800, while raising her loan to $3,500. Farmelant wrote an appeal, explaining that Mitchell and Shelley Cohen had covered some of his parents' medical expenses, installed his mother in a nursing home and his father in an assisted-living community and traveled to Florida once a month to care for them. GWU raised Heather's grant to $3,000.

8. Do I face special problems as a divorced parent? In the past, public schools and many private ones asked for financial information only from custodial parents. Lately, both public and private colleges have become much stricter about requiring noncustodial parents to complete a form stating how much they're able to pay for college. Students with absent or uncooperative parents must be prepared to supply plenty of documentation, including notarized statements, past tax returns or copies of divorce agreements, to substantiate a lack of support. "Most colleges are pretty understanding," says Jayme Stewart, a college counselor at York Prep in New York City. "But in the cases of deadbeat parents, or where the situation is tough to prove, the aid you get may depend on how much the college wants you."

9. Is the aid offer clear and complete? Once you've been notified of an award, get out your calculator. "Aid letters can be vague and misleading," says Macalester president Michael McPherson. "The letter may tell you that the school is giving a certain amount but leave it up to you to calculate how much more you must actually pay. Or you may not be told whether the aid offer is renewable and under what circumstances." Ask questions and try to get written guarantees so you're not caught short later.

That's what happened to Matt Bahar at Loyola University in Chicago. His parents, Gerry and Sue Bahar of Antigo, Wis., expected their out-of-pocket cost of $4,000 a year to drop to $2,000 for Matt's sophomore year since they'd also be paying college bills for their daughter Becky, now a freshman at St. Scholastica in Duluth, Minn. So they were startled when the cost for Matt's second year remained $4,000, because Loyola had raised its tuition and housing fees. When the Bahars appealed, the university offered a $2,000 low-interest loan. "It was disappointing and confusing," Sue says, though she was pleased with Loyola's responsiveness.

10. How can I get a school to raise its aid offer? As the Bahars' example shows, there's no harm in asking for more aid. Financial aid officers, who generally earn less than $40,000 a year, will not be impressed by the burden of mortgage payments on your vacation home in Southampton or Vail, but a sensible, well-crafted appeal that explains why your circumstances require more aid—especially if bolstered by an offer from another school—may boost your package. At Williams College, for instance, 20% of the 600 aid applicants last year appealed the initial offers, according to financial aid director Wick; scholarships and loans were increased in about two-thirds of those cases an average of 20%, or $3,000. Less prestigious schools may be willing to up the ante even more.

Your best strategy is to be clear, courteous and ready to send any necessary documents by fax or overnight mail. Remember too that you aren't playing Powerball. Most colleges are far from wealthy. And any money you get will mean that much less for another bright, deserving student. "It's not a God-given right that your child should go to a costly college," notes Jayme Stewart of York Prep. Still, with the right planning, there's no reason why your child's education should bankrupt you.

CUT THE PRICE OF A NEW CAR

If you want to get the best possible price when it comes to buying a car but you don't have the time, patience or nerve to haggle, you may want to hire a car-buying service. Because professional buyers work with the fleet departments of dealerships and bypass the overhead of expensive showrooms and regular salespeople, these services often can save you money—even after you pay the fee, typically $165 to $395.

At the high end of the fees, national full-service buyers like AutoAdvisor (800-327-1976) and CarSource (800-517-2277) will find you a specific car or truck at a nearby dealer, handle the negotiations and—after you approve the price—tell you where to pick it up. For a lower fee, CarBargains (800-475-7283) will send you printouts of bids from at least five dealers in your area. You have to check with those dealers to pick colors and optional equipment and to finalize the contracts.

These days, some 10% of those who buy or lease a new car or truck get a referral from some kind of service. With the emergence of Internet shopping, that number could well rise. Web operations like Auto-by-Tel (autobytel.com), AutoVantage (autovantage.com) and Microsoft's CarPoint (carpoint.com)—three of the biggest—are free to you. But they refer you to only one dealer in your area for each inquiry. They are paid by the dealer, and they do not give you competitive bids. The dealerships in such services promise a discount below sticker price—but you don't know how far below until you get the quote.

To assess the services, MONEY correspondents in five cities (Boston, New Orleans, San Diego, Seattle and Portland, Maine) comparison shopped three Internet buyers vs. CarBargains. Each correspondent sought prices on the Toyota Camry and the Ford Explorer.

The result: In nine of the 10 comparisons, the lowest CarBargains bid beat the lowest Internet bid, even after adding on the $165 service fee. In some cases, our correspondents had to make repeated and insistent phone calls to local dealers provided by the Internet services to get a price quote. Comparing the Internet buyers only, none of the three had a clear advantage.

The CarBargains' price advantage wasn't always that large, but in one comparison, the difference was dramatic: Rowe Ford Sales in Westbrook, Maine, just outside of Portland, bid $210 under invoice for a Ford Explorer XLT four-door, four-wheel drive. The lowest Internet bid from a dealer in the region was $800 higher.

Of course, even the highest-priced full-service buyers cannot always match a nearby dealer with the model, color and options you want. If you have your heart set on something and can afford to wait up to three months, consider an advance factory order through a buying service.

Generally, no-haggle dealers will probably give you the fewest hassles, but not the lowest prices. Internet buying services are likely to lead you to a price similar to the no-haggle dealer's. Our conclusion: The traditional fee-for-shopping services are still likely to give you the best combination of price and convenience.

ARE YOU BEING CRAMMED?

What's the biggest phone gripe these days? It's not slamming (finding your long-distance service switched without permission). It's "cramming," a rapidly growing phenomenon in which charges for unwanted services, such as call waiting or paging, show up on your bill—at up to $40 a pop. The 2,000-plus cramming complaints lodged in the first half of 1998 outnumbered those for slamming by two to one.

Either your local phone company or an outside firm may charge you for services you didn't order—or get. Last July, at the urging of the Federal Communications Commission, phone companies adopted anti-cramming guidelines. They include verifying requests for new services and naming on your bill the firms that are charging for them. Plus, the Federal Trade

Commission (FTC) vowed to crack down on the firms that sell or collect fees for bogus services.

How do you spot cramming? "Many billers give legitimate-sounding names to these charges," warns Teresa Schwartz, deputy director of the FTC's Bureau of Consumer Protection. Items such as "Miscellaneous Charges and Credits," "Minimum Usage Fees," "Activation," "Call Manager," "Basic Access," "Special Plan" or "Enhanced Services" could be real charges—or evidence of cramming.

If you think you've been crammed, call the 800 number on your bill and ask that the suspicious charges be verified or removed. You should still pay the other items on your bill. Follow up with a certified letter, and get in touch with the FTC (202-326-3134).

PAY LESS ON LONG-DISTANCE CALLS

If the growing competition for your long-distance business leaves you feeling more beleaguered than excited, that's understandable. In 1995, Robert Self, publisher of *Long Distance for Less*, conservatively estimated that the astounding variety of companies, business and residential calling plans, and phone cards meant that a person could make a single call in some 20,000 different ways. Then things became even more confusing. With between 400 and 900 companies out there vying for your long-distance dollar, Self said in 1998, there were 50,000 ways to make that call. So right now, if you're like most long-distance consumers, what you need isn't more choices. You need a strategy for evaluating the choices that already exist—and the ones that are around the corner.

The good news is that it's not as complicated as it sounds. Despite all the options out there, the fact remains that most people are overpaying for their long-distance service, some by as much as 60%. With a pinch of telecommunications knowledge and a dash of strategy, you can make sure you are not one of them.

Get a plan. So how do you evaluate whether the long-distance service you have is best for you? First, figure out what percentage of calls you make during the three main time periods that the phone companies base their rates on. Peak time, when rates are highest, is generally 7 a.m. to 7 p.m. weekdays. Off-peak means 7 p.m. to 7 a.m. weekdays, or weekends (7 p.m. Friday to 7 a.m. Monday); most carriers treat the two off-peak categories the same, some don't. We're not suggesting, of course, that you need to sit down with a calculator and your last 12 months worth of bills. Just eyeball the ones from the past few months; that should be enough to help you determine a basic calling pattern.

Once you've figured it out, call your provider and ask if you're on the best plan available, recommends Boyd Peterson, telecommunications analyst at the Yankee Group, a Boston research and consulting firm. The Washington, D.C.-based Telecommunications Research and Action Center (TRAC) estimates that 60% of callers are not on any discount plan at all. The vast majority of the unenlightened—or unmoved—are with AT&T, which still has the largest share of the overall market. If this is you, wise up. "Get off standard rates," advises TRAC's Geoff Mordock. "It's like paying list for a used car."

And even if you've signed up for a good calling plan in the past, don't assume that it's still the best deal out there or that your carrier will steer you toward a cheaper alternative as the particulars of the company's offerings change. Keeping up with better offers (even from your carrier) is largely up to you. The upshot: Lots of long-distance consumers are unknowingly sticking with plans that don't stack up against the competition. "People signed for them a couple of years ago," says Stuart Zimmerman, head of Fone Saver, a Stamford, Conn.-based company that will analyze your phone bill. "They could get a better deal; they just don't know any better."

Next, use the lowest rate you hear to call the companies back and play one against the other. Even if you don't want to experiment with smaller long-distance outfits, you can often improve on what you're now paying—sometimes without switching carriers at all. "Most of the time, the Big Three [AT&T, MCI and Sprint] will match one another," says Self. That works to your advantage, particularly if you receive a titillating offer from another company.

The rate of change in the long-distance industry is about as difficult to keep up with as a teenager's telephone usage. So TRAC's Mordock recommends checking your service every six months (three if you have time) to make the best deal. "The more you spend, the more frequently you should be looking at it," Peterson adds. Bottom line: When it comes to long distance, it pays to shop around.

FIND THE BEST CELL-PHONE DEAL

For years, Detroit's Vic Doucette resisted the lure of the cell phone. "It's just another bill," he would tell his wife. "We don't need it. It's an extravagance."

But after an accident last year, when the couple broke down in a bad part of town late at night, he had a change of heart. And Doucette, like anyone else considering cellular service these days, was in for an education.

"It's getting extremely confusing," acknowledges Jeff Battcher of BellSouth Mobility, who notes that competition has been accompanied by a myriad of price plans, providers, technological standards, restrictions and on and on. Thus the list of questions you need to ask yourself is getting longer and longer. Analog, digital or PCS? Should you sign a contract? Which services will you need? Voice mail? E-mail? Caller ID? What are "roaming rates"? Do you really need cellular service at all?

The only question you don't have to worry about: Is now a better time to get a cell phone than, say, a year ago? That's because the competition that's making your choices seem so confusing is also the making the answer so simple: yes. Until 1996, each major market in America was legally held to two wireless providers; now there are usually at least three or four (and in some cases more) competitors per marketplace. And as the newest wireless technology, PCS, has picked up speed, cellular prices have steadily headed south, with the average monthly service falling from $69 in 1992 to $44 five years later.

The key is knowing how to weed through the choices and find the deal that's right for you. Vic Doucette researched, asked friends, visited seven or eight cellular-phone stores and got a deal he's happy with: He signed a two-year contract with AirTouch Cellular for $9.99 a month through 1998 and $14.99 a month after that. AirTouch threw in a free analog Motorola phone and five free minutes a month. Not bad.

Then again, if he really wants to use his cell phone only in dire emergencies, we found a way he can do it without paying for a service at all. We'll tell you about that soon.

First things first. Stop drooling over that $700 Motorola StarTac 8000 in the window. The most important decision in going cellular isn't picking a phone; it's picking a service. Unlike cable or online providers, not all cell services work with all hardware. And while the phone is a one-time expense (or perhaps no expense at all, since many services toss in a phone for free), it's your service that will determine what you pay for months or years to come. It also determines sound quality and where your phone will work.

To decide what kind of service you need, start with the basics. The three options for the technology that underlies wireless service are analog, digital and PCS. You'll hear a lot about this when you start shopping around; much of it will be static about technical details.

Here's all you really need to know. Analog cellular is the plain-vanilla choice; digital and PCS are newer technologies that offer certain advantages to heavier users. The latter two are very similar; PCS is less widely available, but if it's offered in your area you may be able to get a great deal as PCS carriers scramble for market share. Another key difference: Analog services often throw in a free or dirt-cheap phone, but you have to sign a contract and lock yourself in for a year or more. Digital and PCS providers rarely make you sign a contract, but you'll have to spend $100 to $200 more for a phone.

The truth is, you shouldn't make a decision about which technology you want until you've figured out how you're going to use your cell phone—which we'll get to next. Meanwhile, while the salesman gives you the hard sell on digital, keep two things in mind. First, the carriers want customers on digital plans because digital is a more efficient product for the providers; they can service many more customers on a digital frequency than on an analog one. Second, despite what digital boosters will tell you, analog is not about to go the way of the Betamax. As Tim Ayers of the Cellular Telecommunications Industry Association (CTIA) told us, "It has a long life ahead of it."

Know your needs. What you really plan to do with your cell phone can determine what kind of specific service plan to sign up for, and what kind of special promos to utilize. Here are five typical user categories:

♦ **Emergencies Only (Really).** You figure a cell phone could save your life. Focus on cheap per-month charges—somewhere between $10 and $20. Yes, that will probably cover few, if any, calls a month. But the high charges on extra minutes don't matter because you're hardly ever going to use your phone. You'll probably want to go analog; why shell out extra for a digital phone?

Here's something else you should know. As of last year, the FCC has required wireless carriers to "transmit all wireless 911 calls (from both subscribers and nonsubscribers)." Translation: You can call 911 without having any cellular service at all.

♦ **Emergencies Only (Not Really).** You bought the phone because it was a logical decision. You could break down in the middle of nowhere. You could be accosted in a dark alleyway. Or you could be running late to a fabulous party and not have time to stop and call. Oops. See how easily your definition of emergency can expand.

If you're likely to expand that definition of emergency, focus on a cheap base rate, with an eye on what you'll be charged per minute when you spill over your initial allotment. Make a realistic estimate of the number of minutes per month you'll use the service and do the math.

Also, you may have a clear idea of what qualifies as an emergency, but the people you give your number to may not. So check whether your provider gives you the first minute free on incoming calls.

♦ **Middle of the Road.** You plan to use the phone between 20 and 200 minutes a month, mostly in your hometown. Again, you'll have to do some calculating based on the estimated number of minutes you'll be on the phone. Providers offer all sorts of plans that include a set number of minutes for the base monthly price. Depending on that fee, the cost of additional minutes can range from, say, 45 cents to 85 cents. So if you lowball to get a better monthly rate, keep an eye on what you'll be paying if you go into overtime.

The good news is, you have a lot of options. Callers in this range end up paying roughly the same for analog, digital and PCS services (once you factor in the expense of a digital or PCS phone). So, little things can make a difference. If you'd like to be able to leave the phone on all day so you can receive calls, go for digital: It offers longer battery life. If you don't want to shell out the up-front cash, go for analog: The phone won't be as expensive, and the service may give you one.

Finally, if you'll literally be using your phone from the road, digital and PCS service offer an advantage over analog. You're less likely to run into wireless traffic jams that prevent you from making calls in high-density areas at peak times.

♦ **The Roamer.** You will use your cell phone constantly while traveling. Focus on "roaming charges"—for minutes you spend on the phone outside your home calling area. They're billed at a separate rate—sometimes as high as $1 a minute—and generally aren't included in your monthly allotment. If this is important to you, shop around for a per-minute rate closer to 50 cents.

In this category, analog offers the advantage of their near-universal coverage. Geographically speaking, digital service is still more limited than analog, and PCS is more limited still.

Nevertheless, providers have been giving a strong price incentive for roamers to go digital. The favorable digital rates mean that, for roamers, the phone itself can be an important consideration. A "dual mode" phone handles analog and digital cellular frequencies, so if you're using digital service and wander out of your coverage boundary, the phone will automatically switch you to an analog network. Most carriers have usage agreements with the other carriers, so you won't end up with an outrageous cellular bill from some company you've never heard of.

But remember that you're paying long-distance rates on top of these charges. It's up to you to see to it that those charges are handled through your long-distance carrier of choice.

♦ **The Power User.** You don't expect to leave your house without your cell phone, and you'll burn up between 250 and 1,000 minutes of air time per month. We have one word for you: digital. According to Shea Silidker of the Strategis Group, if you're using the phone between 300 and 1,000 minutes a month, your bill could be far cheaper in the long run with digital cellular and PCS than it would be with analog. Also, if you're using the phone this much, you'll probably want the multiple services that digital offers— caller ID, call forwarding and voice mail—and the longer battery life.

Last call. When you find the service you want, don't sign a contract until you read the fine print and see if it includes such details as termination fees, contract requirements and other such deal breakers. But should you even sign a contract at all? If you must, go for the shortest one possible, says Bob Rosenberg, president of Insight Research Group, who thinks contracts are usually a bad idea. "If the prices keep dropping," he says, "do you want to be locked in?"

THE BEST INTERNET SERVICE FOR YOU

More than 100 national Internet service providers (ISPs) would like to be your gateway to cyberspace (with another 4,900 or so regional players at the fringes), and what separates one from the other is what you pay every month and the ease of making a connection. Once you're on the Internet, your favorite Websites look the same no matter how you got there.

Before you pick an ISP, ask yourself: Do you primarily go online to read and send e-mail, or do you want to track your portfolio all day? Are you a frequent traveler who needs an ISP available anywhere, or do you always surf from home?

Another consideration is whether the ISP has a nearby local access number. If not, you could add phone charges of 10 cents a minute or so to your online tab. If you call your ISP's toll-free number to cut your phone bill, you could pay a surcharge of up to $5.95 an hour.

Finally, you may want to think twice before you sign up for a temporary deal or pick an up-and-comer that's likely to become a takeover target. Hopping ISPs isn't as simple as changing your long-distance service. Just ask anyone who's had to change an e-mail address or reconfigure a computer to support new ISP software. With that in mind, here are top choices for four types of Net users.

All you use is mail. If your main online activity is exchanging e-mail with your kids, you hardly need a $19.95-a-month unlimited Internet access plan. America Online (800-540-9449, www.aol.com), whose fee for unlimited time online is among the priciest out there, has a good but less publicized deal for anyone who checks e-mail only once or twice a week: For $9.95 a month, you recently could get five hours of online time. However, each additional hour cost a hefty $2.95, so if you spent, say, 10 hours online, you would have owed $24.70.

You're a casual surfer. What if you do more than send e-mail but you're still only an occasional Web visitor? Again, you don't have to pay $19.95 a month. Provider MindSpring (888-677-7464; www.mindspring.com), which gets an above-average connection rating from Inverse Network Technologies' monthly call-failure survey, recently charged $14.95 a month for 20 hours (and $1 for each additional hour). There was a $25 start-up fee, however, so it took about six months to beat a $19.95 unlimited plan.

You're online more than five hours a week. A typical Internet user spends 9 1/2 hours a week online, according to Forrester Research, a Cambridge, Mass. Internet and technology research firm. Most major national ISPs, including AT&T WorldNet, Earthlink, Microsoft Network and Prodigy Internet, charge $19.95 a month for unlimited Internet access, as do the big regionals. Some ISPs, however, will cut a deal if you prepay. Prodigy (800-213-0992; www.prodigy.com) was recently charging $189 for a year's worth of unlimited service, which works out to $15.75 a month. And Erol's (888-463-7657; www.erols.com), which serves the Northeast, had a deal for $191.40 for the year, or $15.95 a month.

In addition, small regional ISPs often undercut the big national players. If you live in the Chicago area, for example, you can go online all you want for $14.95 a month with ChicagoNet. For a low-cost provider near you, go to www.thelist.com, which lets you search a list of 5,000 or so ISPs by area code. But remember, if you go online when you travel, you'll want to stick with a national ISP with access numbers throughout the country.

You need fast access. Heavy Internet users know price isn't everything. A reliable connection is. A recent poll by the San Jose-based Internet research firm World Research found that users' biggest complaint was "slow log-in." Unfortunately, your ISP may not help here. "Most people blame the ISP, when it's really the Internet," says Nathan Garcia, co-host of the syndicated radio show *On Computers.*

You *can* do something about the second most common complaint: "too many busy signals." What you want is a low user-to-modem ratio: 12 to 1 or less. Regional providers tend to have better ratios. Since you may have a hard time getting that number from the ISP itself, check out Inverse Network Technologies' call-failure ratings at www.inversenet.com. One national ISP that has snagged an A+ rating from Inverse for all hours in two straight recent surveys is Concentric Network (800-939-4262; www.concentric.net), which charges $19.95 for unlimited service.

Finally, another good way to test an Internet service, says Jack Rickard, editor of *Boardwatch,* a monthly trade publication for providers, is to get an ISP's local access number and call during high-traffic times (early morning, late afternoon and Sundays). If you get lots of busy signals, you may have the same problem when you try to log on—and no price deal is worth that hassle.

SOFTWARE TO HELP MANAGE MONEY

When the new upgraded versions of the top two personal-finance programs—Microsoft's *Money* and Intuit's *Quicken*—hit the store shelves, we set out to determine whether either one had pulled ahead in the ongoing battle for software supremacy. After test-driving the deluxe versions of both programs, we concluded that neither has outpaced the other enough on any front to justify switching loyalties. But if you're buying your first piece of personal-finance software, *Money 99* is a better choice for computer or money-management neophytes; *Quicken 99* is the way to go for more sophisticated computer users or personal-finance hounds.

Consumers have been the clear winners in the three-year face-off: These programs have been transformed from modest checkbook and credit-card registers into powerful and comparably matched money-management command centers. Even before this year's upgrades, both came standard with tax, budget and financial planning information; electronic bill paying, banking and online brokerage access; and convenient links to the Web for investment tools and research.

And for the most part, the new versions raise the bar to about the same height. Both programs have added an improved array of alerts (which tell you, for example, when an account balance slips below a specified amount), more advanced online banking and bill payment functions, and highly customizable viewing options. Both now use Website-style designs with arrow navigation, scrolling pages and layouts you can modify.

There are, however, subtle differences that can make one or the other program the better choice for certain new users. *Money 99* (Windows only; $34.95 Basic; $64.95 Financial Suite; upgrade rebates of $10 or $25, respectively), which comes pre-installed on more computers than *Quicken* does and is given away free by many financial institutions, tends to have better help sections and account-setup guides, and seems more specifically designed for newcomers to computerized money management. Load it up, and the program kicks things off with a getting-to-know-you interview ("Are you married?" "Are you self-employed?") and then recommends which sections you should explore.

On the other hand, *Quicken 99* (Windows and Mac; $29.95 Basic; $59.95 Deluxe; upgrade rebates of $10 or $20, respectively) has several nifty extras that a more seasoned computer user will appreciate. The new "QuickEntry" feature allows you to log transactions into a ledger on your PC's desktop so you don't have to boot up the program for every entry. Likewise, its "WebEntry" form lets you record transactions, like credit-card purchases, from any computer with Internet access—at work, for instance—and download them into *Quicken* later.

Quicken also pays greater attention to year-round tax planning—offering, for example, a capital-gains estimate to help you determine when to sell securities, as well as free tax filing via *TurboTax Online*. And it has easy links to Quicken.com, which is nearly as good as the $9.95-a-month *Microsoft Investor* for investing tools and analysis—and it's free.

One question remains for those who already own one of the programs. Are the upgrades worth the price ($39.95 for the deluxe version of either after rebates)? Probably not, if you're perfectly satisfied with a relatively recent version of either or if you rarely go online. If, however, you want smoother Internet connections and electronic transactions, or if you're itching for the latest enhancements (which will be most noticeable if you're using a version older than last year's), then yes, get with the program.

GRAB SOME ONLINE AUCTION BARGAINS

It's 3:30 p.m., half an hour after the closing of a one-day online auction that we bid in a few hours ago. We click over to Onsale (www.onsale.com), the largest online auction site on the Web, and check to see whether our $54 bid for 14 Omaha Steaks (retail price: $120) was the winner. Drat! Someone swooped in with a $59 bid 10 minutes before closing and will soon be enjoying bargain prime filet mignons and sirloins while we chew on sour grapes. We decide to steal his strategy when we try again tomorrow.

Welcome to the world of "going, going, gone" for the computer age. Thousands of cybersurfers are turning to Web auction sites for the fun, convenience and outstanding bargains (sometimes as much as 80% off retail) available through this specialized kind of shopping. About 100 such sites offering everything from boats to Beanie Babies now exist, up from just a handful two years ago, according to John Jackley, president of the Internet Auction List (www. internetauctionlist.com), a directory of 1,500 links to traditional auction houses and resources. Onsale alone boasts more than 400,000 registered bidders and generates more than $2.5 million in weekly revenues. David E. Gilmore, a real estate auctioneer in Kenner, La. and chairman of the technology committee of the National Auctioneers Association (NAA), isn't surprised that the sites are taking off: "You can experience much of the excitement and competition of a traditional auction but from the comfort of your own home."

Most Web auctions follow the familiar "Yankee auction" rules: open bidding with the prize going to the highest bidder. Upon visiting the site, you'll see a listing of goods with a picture of each, its description, shipping method and charges and often the suggested retail price. Beside each item is the number for sale, the minimum opening price, the date of the auction and the time it ends.

Auctions typically last anywhere from a few hours to two weeks. After registering (which usually requires submitting a credit-card number), simply type how much you're willing to spend for an item onto an electronic bid form found on the Web page, then click on send. As each auction progresses, the site lists the current highest bids; you can post a follow-up bid if you've been trumped. If you win, the site will notify you via e-mail, charge your credit card and send the product to you.

The best stuff to buy at online auctions are things you'd usually buy in a department store or at the mall—that is, items with well-known brand names whose features are easy to compare. Not surprisingly, many sites feature great deals on computers. For example, Onsale, WebAuction (www. webauction.com) and ZAuction (www.zauction.com) commonly sell both new and refurbished computers at deep discounts. All three also offer bargains on stereos, TVs and home-office machines. You can find housewares, linens, collectibles and clothing at FirstAuction (www.firstauction.com), a site run by the Home Shopping Network. For jewelry, try a specialty site like Fine Jewelry Direct (www.finejewelrydirect.com); for wine, Winebid (www.winebid.com); and for sports equipment such as snowboards, in-line skates and sunglasses, SportingAuction (www.sportingauction.com).

For unique goods such as art, antiques and real estate, you're probably best off with traditional non-Web auctions. "Even experts can't adequately evaluate things like houses or horses by seeing just a picture and a list of specifications on a screen," says auctioneer Gilmore.

Here are some key rules to help you become an online auction champ and never the chump.

Read the terms carefully. Policies about your power to cancel bids, your obligation to buy if you win and your ability to return purchases vary widely in cyberspace. At many sites, for example, all sales are final; you can't return something if you decide you don't like it. So carefully read the rules of each site you consider patronizing. If its policies aren't posted prominently, keep moving.

Bid low and early. The item you want may not generate much attention, so you might get lucky. Check back about 15 minutes before the auction closes. If the action is heating up but prices remain under your limit, stay out of the fray and place your bid in the last minute.

Encrypt your plastic. Be sure to submit your credit-card number via an encrypted browser such as Microsoft Explorer 3.0, Netscape Navigator 3.0 or a later model to reduce the chances that a hacker might steal your number.

Beware shipping fees. Charges range from a few dollars to more than $100 for large items. Be sure to factor those fees into your final bid. And, as with all auctions, whether in cyberspace or at the county fair, know the value of what you're bidding on.

Stick to your price. Auctioneers rely on competition between bidders to push their profits up. Don't get caught in a frenzied bidding war. If you win with a price higher than you'd pay elsewhere, you've actually lost. Be patient; a similar item will almost certainly come on the block again soon.

ARE NEW EURO CHECKS WORTH IT?

Euros—the new multicountry European currency—won't be available in hard form until 2002. But companies like American Express, Thomas Cook and Visa International are already beginning to offer euro-denominated traveler's checks.

Is there any reason to get them? That depends. The obvious drawback is that they can be used only to purchase items priced in euros in the 11 participating countries (Austria, Belgium, Finland, France, Germany, Ireland, Italy, Luxembourg, the Netherlands, Portugal and Spain). While most of the euro nations' major cities are starting a dual-pricing process, most merchants outside the big cities probably won't take the checks. (You can, of course, convert them to local currency at most exchanges.)

Still, if you're planning to spend time in more than one euro-friendly nation, the checks do offer a certain convenience. Using them where possible could also save you a bit by avoiding an exchange transaction—which typically carries a fee of 2% to 5%—since you'll get your change in local currency. You should be able to find specific euro exchange rates in the same places you can now find other currency information.

INFORMATION CAN BE EXPENSIVE

It used to be that calling directory assistance was easy and cheap. Nowadays, it can cost from 12.5 cents to as much as 85 cents a call, according to a study by the Telecommunications Research and Action Center (TRAC) in Washington, D.C. And it's been made more complicated by an explosion in the number of area codes—the U.S. now has more than 200, up from 150 two years ago.

The latest wrinkle: AT&T and MCI are offering consumers new directory assistance services. Instead of dialing 411 for local information or 1-(area code)-555-1212 for out-of-town numbers, you'd dial 00 through AT&T, or 10-10 9000 through MCI. The good news: You don't need to know the area code to get your number. The bad news: AT&T's service costs 95 cents a pop, and MCI's is nearly a buck. Bottom line, says TRAC's Sam Simon: "It almost never makes sense to use these numbers for local directory assistance." And if you have access to the Web, TRAC offers a smarter call. The nonprofit consumer group's Website (www.trac.org) offers links to eight phone directory sites, where you can get numbers all over the U.S. for nothing.

◆ INDEX